O'BRIEN

First edition 2024.

Kinsella Publishing.

Wesley Walker quote on front cover from Greg Prato, *Sack Exchange: The Definitive Oral History of the 1980s New York Jets* (Toronto: ECW Press, 2011), p. 312, Kindle edition.

DAVID M. SMITH

O'BRIEN

A LIFE UNDER CENTER

David Smith is a freelance writer and historian, having studied at the Universities of Hull, Iowa, Liverpool, and Chester. He has lived and worked in places as diverse as Oxford, London, Los Angeles, Berlin, Cannes and Monaco and has written on topics including sport, history, the movie industry, and home entertainment technology. Sport was his first love, and he first heard of the New York Jets in 1983, shortly after Ken O'Brien had been drafted. David now lives near Chester, in the northwest of England, and remains (against all common sense) a dedicated Jets fan.

Contents

Many people helped with the creation of this book and I owe them all thanks:

To Bob Dunning, who saw every game Ken O'Brien played in college. His personal perspective on Kenny's college career added an element to this story that was missing until he generously offered his time and insight.

To Peggy Shonka and Thomas E. Hepler of Ourlads Scouting Services. Thomas, the founder of Ourlads, dug through his archives to find the assessment of O'Brien from the very first draft preview presented by them, back in 1983 (a lot of things started in 1983, it seems).

To Greg Prato and Michael Holmes at ECW Press, for permission to use some of the excellent quotes gathered by Greg for *Sack Exchange: The Definitive Oral History of the 1980s New York Jets*. Anybody looking for more insight into the Jets teams of this period could do no better than get hold of a copy of Greg's book.

To Mike Manico, who generously allowed me to use quotes from a series of excellent interviews he conducted with Ken O'Brien, Al Toon, Wesley Walker and Jo-Jo Townsell for NYJetsNews.com.

To Brian Geiger, at the UC Riverside Center for Bibliographical Studies and Research, for his guidance on using quotes from the superb California Digital Newspaper Collection, a treasure trove of information on many things, including O'Brien's college career.

To Eric Nebeker and Kevin Miller at the Archives and Special Collections of the UC Davis Library, for their help with securing permission to reproduce images of O'Brien's college career originally published in *The California Aggie*.

To Robert Shupp, who provided the image of Ken in action against the Rams in 1986, which occupies the back cover of this book.

Introduction

This is the story of one player in a team sport. There will inevitably be times when I have to step away from Ken O'Brien to assess what was going on around him, but for the most part I have attempted to tell his story. O'Brien would be the first person to raise issue with this, and would insist that any of his accomplishments were part of an overall team effort, but this is not a history of the New York Jets of the 1980s and early '90s. It is the story of one player.

So much has changed in the 40-plus years since the Jets drafted a tall, big-armed quarterback out of a university many people had never heard of, at least in a footballing context. I started to follow the Jets in the same season O'Brien was drafted, 1983, and I understood little of what was going on over his first couple of seasons, but by 1985 I had a decent enough grasp of the game (for a Brit, at any rate), and it was clear that the Jets had found themselves a special player. I make the argument in this book that for a limited period of time – midway through the 1985 season to the latter part of 1986 – O'Brien was the most feared attacking force in the game. It was a good time to be a Jets fan and, naive as I was, I thought it would last forever.

Things had started to turn by the time I attended the University of Iowa on a student exchange program in 1988, and O'Brien had been benched by the time I saw my only live Jets game in the United States (I've watched them play three times in London in more recent years). Out of university, my first job (in 1990) was as a staff writer on a weekly American football newspaper, *First Down*, under the guidance of a great editor, Steve Anglesey. Steve was also a Jets fan, and although the Jets and O'Brien were going through some lean years, writing about the NFL for a living was pretty much a dream job.

Since then I have carefully built up a collection of game tapes and currently have more than a hundred full broadcasts of Jets games (and one Eagles game) in which O'Brien played. Watching these, and researching events from various newspapers, has given me a far greater understanding of the sport and my favourite player than I was able to get first time around.

But I return to my initial point... quarterback may be the most influential position in any sport, but football is still a team game and surgically removing one player from the mass of others around him is not an easy task. I hope I have succeeded without belittling the contributions of his teammates. I hope I have succeeded in bringing a neglected career to life, because through watching these old games, it has become clear to me that O'Brien was a far better player than he is generally given credit for.

Other Jets have found special places in my heart: Freeman McNeil, Wesley Walker, Jim Sweeney, Al Toon, Lance Mehl, Aaron Glenn, Marvin Jones, Curtis Martin, Wayne Chrebet, Jericho Cotchery, Nick Mangold... the list goes on and now includes new names like Garrett Wilson and Breece Hall. But there can only ever be one favourite, and that will always be No. 7.

And by the way – if you're reading this, Woody Johnson, put that number in the Ring of Honor.

November 2024

For long-suffering Jets fans everywhere

April 26, 1983...

The NFL was a different place in 1983, and nowhere was that more evident than on the day of the annual college draft. Today, the draft is a three-day spectacle on primetime television, an event watched live by millions. In 1983, it was a one-day marathon (and they squeezed 12 rounds into that one day, rather than the seven rounds of the modern draft).

There was no 'green room' where the top prospects wait to hear their name called by the NFL commissioner (and wait… and wait… in some agonising cases), so it was no surprise that Ken O'Brien was not at the New York Sheraton on the morning of April 26, 1983 – none of the college players about to find out where their NFL careers would start were there.

There was an audience, however – a few fans getting up early to hear NFL Commissioner Pete Rozelle announce that the Baltimore Colts were on the clock with the first pick of the first round. It was 5 a.m. on the West Coast, and O'Brien was still asleep in California, unaware that he was about to become the second-most controversial draft selection that day. The top place in that category went to Stanford quarterback John Elway, who had made it clear he wanted no part of the dysfunctional Colts and would not sign for them if they used their overall No. 1 pick on him. The Colts duly selected the Stanford signal caller anyway, and the draft had its first major storyline.

While O'Brien slept, the selections kept coming, one future Pro Bowler after another – Eric Dickerson to the Rams, Curt Warner to the Seahawks, Chris Hinton to the Broncos (although he would soon be traded to the Colts in part-exchange for Elway), Billy Ray Smith to the Chargers, Jim Covert to the Bears…

Everything is hopes and dreams on draft day, so nobody knew that the first off-note had been played by the Chiefs when they made Penn State's Todd Blackledge the second quarterback selected, with the seventh pick of the first round. Two more quarterbacks were taken with the 14th and 15th picks – Miami's Jim Kelly going to the Bills and Illinois' Tony Eason to the Patriots. There would be two more quarterbacks taken before the first round ended, and with Pittsburgh's highly talented Dan Marino still on the board, the NFL teams picking later in the round began to get excited. When the 21st pick rolled around, the Steelers were widely expected to nab their hometown hero as a future replacement for the great Terry Bradshaw, but rumors were swirling that Marino was headstrong, hard to teach. He had thrown 22 interceptions in his senior year… and the Steelers blinked, drafting defensive tackle Gabe Rivera instead. The Chargers and Cowboys made their picks, and still Marino was available as Rozelle made his way to the microphone to announce the 24th selection, which had just been made by the New York Jets.

Rozelle was far from an empty corporate suit. The commissioner knew the game, and he knew a storyline when he saw one, even if it was written on something as small as the piece of card in his hands. He glanced at the name on the card, appeared to do a double-take, and then smiled mischievously. Holding a hand up to the waiting fans, as if to say 'wait a minute, you're going to love this,' his smile became broader.

'Oooooh,' he said, with relish, as if aware that the draft was getting to the really good bit. 'New York Jets. The Jets take, as their first-round selection… quarterback…' (there were some growls of approval from the gathered fans, but Rozelle was just teasing them) '… Ken O'Brien of California, Davis.'

Rozelle sat down with a big grin on his face as the fans in the New York Sheraton, and those watching live on ESPN, digested the news.

It was now around 7 a.m. in California, and O'Brien had a Spanish test scheduled that morning. A phone call from the Jets woke him with the life-changing news, but despite the fact that he would soon be signing a contract worth hundreds of thousands of dollars, he decided to go in to take his Spanish test anyway. He was just that kind of guy.

O'Brien with running back Shawn Rogers (Alan Sakamoto, California Aggie, *Dec. 8, 1982)*

Chapter One
The Road to the Draft

On the face of it, O'Brien was the archetypal California boy – laid back, unflappable, he was often described by journalists as having 'surfer's eyes' – but he was actually a native New Yorker, having been born in Brooklyn. He had moved out west with his family at the age of three and Sacramento became his new hometown, where his father, also Ken, worked as an orthopedic surgeon. Being the oldest of six children would teach Ken something about responsibility, but he was never a demonstrative type. Teammates would later comment on his cool demeanor in the pocket, but that didn't mean there was no fire in his veins. The young O'Brien was a fierce competitor, and adept at just about any sport that involved a ball.

'I would think I was like any other kid,' he recalled in an interview with Mike Manico. 'Every day you'd get home from school, you'd study and then you'd go out and play, and you'd change with the seasons. I remember going to bed every night and dreaming about playing football... I was a sports fanatic, I loved it all. Once I got to high school, I knew I could throw a little bit. I had some very good and very nice people as coaches, who spent a lot of time with me when they didn't have to, and really worked on my confidence.'[1]

At St Ignatius High School and then Jesuit High, he played basketball, baseball and football and had a decision to make when it came time to choose a college.

'Coming out of high school, I had only played a little bit of quarterback,' he told Greg Prato for his book, *Sack Exchange: The Definitive Oral History of the 1980s New York Jets*. 'I was just growing into my body – I was tall and skinny, and just growing as I got older, as opposed to being pretty mature when I went in.'[2]

UC Davis was tempting due to its progressive head coach, Jim Sochor. Sochor was different to the standard 1970s football coach. Where bombast and bullying were the traditional ways to tackle the job, Sochor favored a more thoughtful, measured approach. He was a diminutive man, standing just five-feet-eight inches tall and weighing 150 pounds, but his soft-spoken manner was a good fit for O'Brien. Sochor had already turned UC Davis into a regional powerhouse, and his success had caught the eye of John Madden, who once tried to get Sochor to join the Oakland Raiders as an assistant coach. A former quarterback himself (he led San Francisco State to three Far Western Conference championships in his playing days) progression to a coaching career was a natural step for Sochor.

He joined the Aggies in 1967 and was named head coach in 1970. At that time, the team hadn't enjoyed a winning season for 22 years, but Sochor put that right immediately, going 6-4 in his first campaign and then following with 18 consecutive conference championships before retiring after the 1988 season.

With iron discipline the standard in college football, Sochor again distanced himself from the pack by having few team rules. One, however, was insisted upon. Just as a Spartan was never allowed to drop his shield on the ground, so a UC Davis football player was never allowed to drop his helmet. Sochor preached respect for the item that was both a symbol of the team itself and a vital life-saving piece of equipment.

Sochor and O'Brien were a good match... but their partnership almost never got started. During a recruiting visit to UC Davis, O'Brien was disappointed to find that only an assistant coach was on hand to show him around the campus and facilities. Sochor was busy elsewhere and O'Brien found this insulting – so insulting that he chose to attend a different university. Sacramento State would therefore be the first stop on O'Brien's college career, in 1978, but it was a bad fit. Coach Bob Mattos operated the run-oriented veer offense, and the Hornets were a poor team, winning just one game all season (which included a 39-0 shutout at the hands of UC Davis). That loss was especially painful for O'Brien, as it was his fumble, after a blindside hit on a passing attempt, that opened the door for the first Aggies score of the day.

After being redshirted the following season, a transfer was the obvious route, and in 1980 O'Brien would finally suit up for Sochor. The Aggies preferred a balanced offense, but quarterback Matt Weinrich had struggled in the previous year, completing just 39 passes in 10 games and amassing 629 yards. Sochor, who had alternated between three quarterbacks in 1979, wanted the stability that an undisputed starter would bring. O'Brien was the most physically imposing of the candidates (listed at 6'4" and 205 by this point), but was just one of four players vying for the quarterback job as the season approached.

There were very nearly five players. Tony Eason, the player destined to be picked ahead of O'Brien in the first round of the 1983 draft, was also looking for a change from a run-oriented offense and had put out feelers to the Aggies. Sochor had checked his grades and found them wanting, and also felt that he had enough options already.

'It would probably have been a real tragedy had they both come at the same time,'[3] Sochor would later comment.

'It was an absolutely perfect situation,' O'Brien remembered. '[UC Davis] had great coaching, ran a pro-style offense, and had a coach there that spent nothing but hours and hours with me off the field teaching me all about football, defenses and pass protection. Part of the benefit of going to a Division II school was, at that time, there were no rules on

O'Brien in action against Santa Clara in 1980 (Don DeBear, California Aggie, *May 28 1981)*

how much time you [could] spend with coaches and players – so it was unlimited. We became best friends.'[4]

Sochor never had reason to second-guess his decision to bring in O'Brien.

'Once you saw him on the practice field, and the way he threw the ball deep, with so much air under it, you knew he was an extraordinary talent,'[5] said the coach.

At *The Davis Enterprise*, the town's local newspaper, one reporter shared Sochor's first impressions of the Aggies' new quarterback. Bob Dunning had already been writing for the paper for 10 years, and would go on to watch every game O'Brien played in college.

'My first impressions were that he was big, strong, confident, very friendly and accommodating, didn't act like a big shot,' Dunning remembers. 'He looked like he should have been playing at a higher level. It was obvious. I covered, live and in person, home and on the road, every game Ken played at UC Davis. I'd watch other college games on TV and sometimes the NFL and you'd see a receiver streaking all alone 50 yards down the sideline and the quarterback would overthrow him.

And I would marvel and say, "Ken O'Brien never overthrew anyone". He could perfectly lead the receiver, even from long range. Especially at long range, in fact. It's like he had radar on the football.

'He wasn't especially mobile, but he was strong enough and tall enough to stay in the pocket. Now, he was great, sure, but I can't say I knew he'd be drafted in the first round, especially with so many truly great quarterbacks in the draft that year. But he was a prototype of an NFL quarterback in those days. Big and strong and a complete pocket passer.'

Dunning was also impressed with O'Brien's humble nature: 'I interviewed him regularly, and he was very modest. He knew he had talent, but didn't lord it over anyone. Not an ounce of cockiness. I saw him years later at a memorial gathering for his old coach, Jim Sochor, and he was still the same.

'UC Davis was not an especially sports mad campus (I was on the tennis team there as an undergraduate), but the Aggies had so much success in football that their home games were regularly sold out – about 10,000 fans coming to watch.'

Despite O'Brien's promise, running back Ronnie Austin was the team's main offensive threat, averaging more than 100 yards per game in 1979. He did even better in his senior year, eventually piling up 1,100 yards on 224 carries and scoring 13 total touchdowns, and the Aggies leaned on him heavily in their early games as O'Brien struggled to find his feet. A tie against Nevada-Reno in their first match-up was followed by victory over Northridge State and then a loss to Cal Poly San Luis Obispo. O'Brien threw three interceptions in that defeat, completing just 15 of his 33 attempts. To add a little extra sizzle, Sacramento State were next up, and with the Aggies at 1-1-1, the season was on the brink of slipping away. With the stakes high, coach Sochor spoke up.

'We might have to tighten the reins on Ken a little bit,' the Aggie coach announced to the gathered reporters. 'He's really intelligent, but still doesn't have much playing experience. When quarterbacks make mistakes, it's costly. Ken is somewhere in the stage DeBerg was in last year,' he added, referencing the 49ers quarterback, Steve DeBerg. 'He's sometimes brilliant, sometimes he gets sophomoritis.'[6]

On a suffocating day (the thermometer hit 100 degrees) O'Brien started the game against Sacramento State with a hot hand, completing his first seven passes before a relentless Hornets pass rush slowed him down. Ronnie Austin scored the only two touchdowns of the day as the Aggies ground out a 16-6 victory. There were glimpses, however, of the kind of offense Sochor was looking to build, especially on a 60-yard first-quarter drive. A mix of accurate passes from O'Brien and powerful runs from Austin allowed the Aggies to take eight minutes and 20 seconds off the clock on their way to a field goal.

The following week, four field goals from Rod Holmquist, including the 46-yard game-winner with 2:17 left on the clock, saw the Aggies past Humboldt State, and when high-flying Cal State Pomona (coached by former LA Rams quarterback Roman Gabriel) came to town on October 18, Sochor was looking for more from his passing game. O'Brien had amassed 1,057 yards in five games, but Pomona's Fred Collins was matching him yard for yard.

'We'd like to throw for a little more yardage than we have,' said Sochor. 'Even though we've thrown for over 200 [yards] a game, I'd like to see a little more.'[7]

The game turned out to be a thriller, and O'Brien answered his coach's call with easily his best game of the season so far. He piled up 344 yards through the air, passing for three touchdowns, while adding a further touchdown and a two-point conversion with his legs. One play in particular stood out, and it was exactly the kind of play for which O'Brien would become famous in New York. A simple drop back, a mammoth heave downfield into the arms of a speedy receiver (in this case Jon Delfatti, although it would one day be Wesley Walker, Al Toon or Rob Moore with the Jets), and within seconds the Aggies had struck for the 76-yard score that gave them a lead they would not relinquish. The 35-21 victory, overturning a 14-21 halftime deficit, was very much a coming-out party for O'Brien.

'The bomb is a big weapon,' said coach Sochor, while looking ahead to the remaining four games on the schedule and a potential playoff push. 'It's a play that has been available to us all year, but against Pomona was the first time Ken had been able to hit it. We'd like to have gone deep even more than we did. We knew before the season started that the key to O'Brien's success would be what kind of touch he had on the ball and how well he could throw deep. Ken's throwing the ball really well now.' [8]

With O'Brien finding his form, the Aggies had climbed to No. 16 in the Division II national rankings. Four more victories would almost certainly see them make it into the postseason, and Sochor's alma mater, San Francisco State, was up next. With the Gators boasting their own prolific quarterback, Russ Jensen, the game was always likely to be a shootout, and it was tied at 24-24 going into the final period. Five turnovers from their defense, along with a 24-point fourth quarter, saw Cal-Davis lift its record to 5-1-1 with a 48-32 victory.

Santa Clara, sitting at 5-2, were the next hurdle, and a defeat would eliminate UC Davis from postseason contention. A packed Toomey Field saw 9,800 fans in attendance as the Aggies battled down to the wire before falling, 27-34. They had a chance to take a late lead when Holmquist lined up for a 32-yard field goal attempt with the scores tied at 27-27 and only 3:46 left in the fourth quarter. His kick was blocked, however, and the Broncos drove the field to score the winning touchdown. A late Aggies drive looked promising, reaching the Broncos' 17-yard line, but O'Brien lost the ball after a blindside hit and the game was over.

It was a heart-breaking defeat, although O'Brien had thrown three touchdown passes. They would be his last of the year, as he finished with an impressive 2,180 yards and 13 scores in his first season at UC Davis. A pair of seniors, Don Barber and Jeff Zimmerman, were his favourite targets, catching 28 and 27 passes, respectively. The Aggies had averaged 380 yards of offense per game on their way to a 7-2-1 overall record and a 5-0 conference mark, which was good enough for their 11th consecutive conference title... but not good enough to make the playoffs.

O'Brien was named as quarterback in the All-Far West Conference

Sochor (left) with o-line coach Nick Alexander (Tom McNeil, California Aggie, *Nov. 16, 1981)*

team, along with tailback Austin (who was also the conference's player of the year), flanker Mike Kane and a trio of offensive linemen – center Frank Scalercio, guard Mike Irwin and tackle Bill Beckman. Outside linebacker Neal Fromson and cornerback Mel Byrd were first-team All-FWC picks, while defensive end Rich Mohr was the conference's defensive player of the year. Sochor was named coach of the year. It added up to a star-studded team, but as is always the case in college football, it was set to change.

O'Brien could look back with satisfaction on a record-setting campaign after leading the Aggies to wins in their final two games, but his innate modesty prevented him from claiming all the glory for himself.

'We had the best receivers in the league,' he said. 'They deserve a lot of the credit. They made a lot of great catches that would have been incompletions anywhere else.'[9]

O'Brien also shouldered the responsibility for some of the mistakes that had cost the Aggies in their two defeats. 'Hopefully I won't repeat the mistakes I made this year, next season,' he said. 'In the two games that we lost, we just made crucial mistakes. I feel that we were the better team both times which makes it a real disappointment that we didn't reach the playoffs. I feel the worst for the seniors, though. I have another shot at a playoff season. They don't.'

Sochor had no doubt that he had something special in his young quarterback, already seeing potential for him to take his game to the next level.

'He could play for anyone in the country,' said the Aggies coach. 'At USC, he could start next season. Because of his physical stature, he can see things from the pocket that other quarterbacks have trouble with. He also has an exceptionally strong arm. He had an exceptional year for a sophomore. We knew he could throw the ball with a lot on it. We didn't know if he had the touch and finesse it takes to be a great quarterback. This season he demonstrated that he does.'

O'Brien teamed that natural physical ability with a strong work ethic that matched any Sochor had seen before.

'He has an insatiable appetite for learning,' said the coach. 'He thrives on gaining more knowledge of defenses and coverages. That's why he's learned more than anyone we've ever had. He's come a long way in only one season. He'll be a highly looked at prospect for the pros. Some teams have already expressed interest.'

O'Brien himself had dreams of playing in the NFL, but was determined to keep his feet on the ground after just one successful season of college ball.

'I'm going to play as well as I can and continue football as long as possible,' he said. 'If that leads to the pros, great. If I discover that I'm not good enough, though, I can fall back on my education. It won't ruin my life.'

In football, progress seldom happens on a smooth curve. There are ups and downs, and O'Brien's junior season was most definitely a down. It wasn't as if there was complacency heading into the new season. O'Brien worked out in the gym, adding a little extra heft to his slender frame, and he had twice-weekly meetings with Sochor to discuss game situations.

'Ken and I are working closely together,' said Sochor in May 1981. 'We're talking about all aspects of the game.' [10]

A new factor was the attention O'Brien had drawn during his sophomore campaign. With that came expectations, and the press could be an enemy as wily as any on-field opponent if not handled well, but Sochor had little doubt his young signal-caller could deal with the increased attention. 'Ken is down to earth,' he said. 'He's not awed by the press and all the attention he's been getting. He handles it well. He knows that the team comes first.'

In terms of his play, O'Brien knew he needed better footwork. He would never be renowned for his running ability, but back in the 1980s that was not as big of a deal as it would be for a quarterback today, where mobility is placed at a premium. Even so, there was work to do in this area.

'I don't have to run the 40-yard dash,' he commented. 'I just have to work on getting back [to set-up] quicker.'

He was chosen by his teammates as one of the captains for the 1981 season, and looked forward to more success as he became more familiar with, and comfortable in, Sochor's system.

'Last year, I didn't have time [before the season] to throw with my receivers and get to know them until the beginning of the season,' he said. 'But I did get to know the system better with each game.'

Going into the new campaign, O'Brien revealed he would be given more latitude by his coach, and would be able to call audibles if he saw something that he liked in a defense's set-up.

'We do audible, but not a majority of the time,' he revealed. 'When we see something we can take advantage of, we might audible into something different. I like to throw the long ball. I hope we throw a lot of bombs. I'm confident in my arm that I can get the ball there and that a receiver will be open.'

O'Brien's growing maturity and comfort in the offense promised big things for 1981, but he did admit to one element in his personal make-up that required monitoring. It was something that would surprise anyone who witnessed his coolness under pressure and overall relaxed demeanor.

'People tell me I have a temper,' he said. 'I've tried to overcome it, but I'm a real competitive type. I have a hard time losing and it bothers me at times. It takes control.'

'Ken has a little temper, but he keeps it under control,' his coach agreed. 'He gets mad at himself when he makes a mistake. But he's a leader by his presence. Mo [Mike Moroski, former Aggies quarterback and by then a member of the Atlanta Falcons] was like that. Ken is low-key and keeps a low profile on the field.'

Although optimism was justifiably high, the team would miss the services of their top running back.

'We don't have Ronnie Austin,' O'Brien said of the schools' record-setting tailback, who had recently graduated. 'With good receivers and good runners, we should be a little more wide open. We have had an extra year together. Next year, I hope we have a few new twists.'

'The key is preparation,' said Sochor. 'We're spending a lot of time preparing him for the defensive things he'll see next year. People have been trying all kinds of things [defensively] against us. Some teams drop everyone off, some stunt a lot of people. We're going to add a few more things offensively because Ken can do more things… Last year was his first in the program. He's progressed well.'

As the season approached, O'Brien engaged in informal workouts with teammates even before official preseason training began. On three or four evenings a week, a group of up to 10 Aggies would meet and practice pass patterns. O'Brien was still trying to improve as a runner ('I've been trying to run two or three miles a day, but it's not my favorite thing in the world to do,'[11] he admitted), but one thing that did not seem to require any work was the pure process of passing.

'I go out and throw just to keep my arm in shape,' he said. 'It seems like I can throw whenever. It's like having a gift, I can throw whenever I want – it's not like I have to work on it a whole lot. It's just a matter of getting the timing down and getting to know the offense. I'm a lot more comfortable this year with everything that's going on.'

Preparation included visits to the San Francisco 49ers training camp with Sochor, where O'Brien watched how the pros did it... and didn't see too much difference from things at UC Davis.

'We tried to learn whatever we could,' he revealed. 'It's not that much different from here. I'd say the coaching is even because our coaches are pretty educated and they know everything that's going on [in the NFL]. I was mainly looking at the quarterbacks, just little techniques that they have mastered that can help.'

Given the level of optimism around the Aggies, the 1981 season turned out to be bitterly disappointing – it was essentially over after just two games, losses to Puget Sound and California State University, Northridge. There had been ominous signs leading up to the first game, as the line in front of O'Brien was ravaged by multiple issues. The team's strongest lineman, guard Ron Smith, was ruled ineligible for academic reasons, while fellow guard Nick Spinelli injured his knee in preseason and faced the possibility of missing the entire year. On top of that, tackle Bob Taylor decided he'd had enough of football and retired. Such disruption was always going to have consequences, and although the center, senior Frank Scalercio, was on hand to offer experience and ability at the pivot position, O'Brien was harried all day against the Loggers of Puget Sound – a disbelieving crowd of 7,500 at Toomey Field saw their quarterback go down under 12 sacks.

Still, there should have been enough production to eke out a win. O'Brien passed for 219 yards (Dave Snow caught six passes for 111 yards) and Darryl Goss, replacing the departed Austin, managed 62 yards on his 14 carries. It ought to have been enough to build on, especially as the

Aggies defense was in rare form, limiting the Loggers to just 91 yards of total offense. The football gods, however, were in a capricious mood. A botched punt gave the Loggers the ball at the Aggies' 15-yard line in the second period and they managed to navigate their way to the end zone for the game's only score. O'Brien led his team to the one-yard line in the fourth quarter, but a third-and-one pass was broken up and a fourth-and-one run was stuffed for a loss. Later, the 12th sack of O'Brien, on a desperation fourth-and-17 play, ended the contest.

Sochor spoke of his frustration after the game: 'Not taking anything away from Jim Simonson [Puget Sound's head coach] who did an excellent job of preparing his team, but we've got a lot of work to do on our offensive line,' he said. 'We've got to establish a better ground game and give Ken more time to throw. We weren't picking up anybody tonight.'[12]

As preparations got underway for the team's next game, Sochor also touched on a problem that was to recur during O'Brien's career: 'He held onto the ball longer than he should have. That just put more pressure on the offensive line and himself. He has been working on that this week.'[13]

The Aggies would be without one of their defenders for the game against CSU Northridge – defensive tackle Jim Travnick punched a locker in frustration after the loss to Puget Sound, and injured his hand. It was that kind of season, and the second game only underlined this fact. Sochor was dejected after his team once more failed to turn statistical dominance into a win.

'I guess you can say that we played just well enough to not quite win,'[14] he said.

The Aggies still hadn't scored a touchdown in 1981 when they entered the fourth quarter of their second game, trailing 14-3. A fortuitous completion to Allen Fleming (it looked at first like an interception, but the officials ruled it a simultaneous catch) set the stage for the Aggies' first six-pointer of the young season, a nine-yard pass from O'Brien to the speedy Delfatti. A failed two-point conversion followed, but Mike Shaw quickly followed up with a 26-yard scoring run on a draw play.

This time, O'Brien found Delfatti for the two-point conversion and the Aggies had their first lead of the season, at 14-17. Two late Matador field goals then snatched victory away, leaving the season in tatters. A disappointed O'Brien took the blame on his shoulders.

'What hurts me,' he said, 'is that we didn't have enough points on the board. Mistakes don't matter if you do well enough to win.' [15]

O'Brien had actually performed acceptably. Although completing less than half his passes, he managed 214 yards through the air and also scrambled for 93. Protection was a big issue again, however, as he handed back 50 of those rushing yards on sacks. Even so, the cumulative statistics from the first two games looked more like those for a 2-0 team, rather than a shellshocked 0-2 outfit. The Aggies had amassed 41 first downs, as opposed to just 20 by their two opponents. They had 381 rushing yards compared to 186, and 440 passing yards compared to just 220.

'We can't seem to win at home,' said Sochor following the game. 'Maybe we can win on the road. We're anxious to get out of town after two straight losses. Maybe it will be good for everybody.' [16]

Sochor's words turned out to be prophetic, as the Aggies' luck changed dramatically on their road trip to face Cal Poly Pomona. If they should have won their first two games, given the disparity in statistical output, they should certainly have lost their third, where they were outgained 242 yards to 165. O'Brien was sacked six times in the first half alone and UC Davis trailed 7-3 deep into the third period. He then took matters into his own hands, ignoring his coach's call to take a timeout when facing a fourth-and-one at the Broncos' 15-yard line. Instead, O'Brien kept the ball on a QB sneak and picked up the first down, before Daryl Goss ran for the go-ahead score at the start of the final quarter. With the offense struggling, the Aggies defense saved the day, linebacker Steve Enos running wild and also blocking a punt, which he returned for a touchdown. It was a scrappy 19-7 win, but it got the Aggies season back on track.

It didn't stay there for long. In their first conference game of the year, they snatched victory in daring fashion… only to hand it back in the final seconds of the game. Humboldt returned the opening kick-off 101 yards for a touchdown, and the Aggies lost their excellent kicker, Holmquist, to a knee injury when he was hit during a 28-yard field goal attempt (which was missed). A penalty on the play allowed the Aggies to continue their drive and score the touchdown that tied the game at 7-7, but they had fallen into a 10-17 deficit as the clock wound down in the fourth quarter.

With heroics called for, O'Brien delivered, hitting Allen Fleming with a 68-yard bomb to set up an eight-yard scoring strike to Jeff Ramsey. Sochor then gambled, going for the win rather than the tie, and O'Brien delivered again, hitting tight end Scott Forbes for the two-point conversion that made the score 18-17 with only 24 seconds left. Incredibly, that was enough time for Humboldt (who connected on a 21-yard pass, with a 15-yard penalty on top) to set up a field goal to grab the win. It was the first conference defeat for the Aggies since 1973, snapping a 38-game streak.

Amid the despondency, it was clear that O'Brien was not having the kind of season expected of him. After four games he had a respectable 761 yards to his credit, but had hit on only two scoring throws, as well as completing barely half of his passes. The stats meant nothing to him – it was only the results that mattered.

'I'm far from the level of play that I would like to be at now,' he admitted. 'In fact I'm about three wins away. If we were 4-o, it would be a great season no matter how I was doing, but we're 1-3 and searching for answers. All I want to see us do is win. If we win and I'm 0 for 40, that's fine.'[17]

Sochor wondered if the pressure on O'Brien was getting to him, saying, 'Everyone has high expectations for Ken. He's a possible pro prospect. At quarterback, he's always in the focal point and because of it he's felt some extra pressure. The expectations aren't as high now, with our slow start. If he relaxes, I think he can turn everything around and have an outstanding second half of the season.'

O'Brien agreed that he felt pressure, but mostly from himself.

'I push myself pretty hard, because I like to do the best job I can,' he said. 'There's no more pressure on me than I put on myself. Last year the team was great. We had a lot of guys who had been in the system for a while and they know how it operates. This season we're younger, but after four games, we've already learned a lot. There are still seven games left [actually six]. I'm hopeful that we can turn it around.'

The mild-mannered Sochor then went further than he usually did. He did not quite issue a Joe Namath-style guarantee, but he sounded bullish as he looked ahead to the next game, against Cal Poly San Luis Obispo: 'We're going to let it all hang out and play like hell and come back with a victory,' he said.

The Aggies did play like hell, but not in the way Sochor had meant. The UC Davis offense did not muster a single point, and the usually stout defense collapsed to allow 428 yards, 316 of them on the ground. O'Brien was again harried all game, but Sochor saw positives in his quarterback's performance.

'He was more assertive in calling audibles and he looked more comfortable,' said the coach. 'He was constantly under duress and harassed by the defensive line. We kept breaking down at the tackle position.'[18]

The Aggies stood at 1-4, out of contention for postseason play and staring down the barrel of the first losing season of Sochor's time as head coach. They were still in the hunt for another conference title – only one of their losses had been to a conference opponent. It was time to circle the wagons, but one player who would not be taking part in this new beginning was Jon Delfatti. Having lost his starting job following some lackluster performances, he had quit the team.

For an offense, and a quarterback, that was already struggling, the loss of a deep threat like Delfatti was a blow. How much of an impact it had on the team's next outing is debateable, but O'Brien attempted just 13 passes, completing seven for 91 yards in one of the worst statistical performances of his college career. The Aggies leaned heavily on Goss, giving the tailback 34 carries, which he turned into 116 yards. Still, it was O'Brien who provided the spark on the game-winning drive late in the fourth quarter. Having been held in check all game, he cut loose with a 20-yard completion to tight end Scott Forbes, followed by a 17-yarder to receiver Dave Snow. The drive chewed up both yardage and time, until freshman kicker Ray Sullivan (replacing the injured Holmquist) booted the 26-yard field goal that gave the Aggies a precious conference victory by the underwhelming score of 6-3.

O'Brien would probably have liked to start the season all over again. His disappointing output, often running for his life behind a makeshift line which saw four different starting combinations in the first four weeks, had seen him complete only 48.7 percent of his throws, and he still had just two touchdowns on the year.

'He has been sporadic at times,' coach Sochor admitted. 'He'll have to get rid of the ball sooner.'[19]

That problem remained an issue in the next game, against Santa Clara. Despite one of his best performances of the year, O'Brien still completed just over half of his passes thanks to a number of costly drops, and he lost 62 yards on sacks despite improved protection from his line. A strong first-half showing (O'Brien passed 22 yards to Ramsey to open the scoring, and fullback Mel Yarbor added a second score on a 33-yard run) melted away and the Aggies trailed 14-17 with less than two minutes to play and only one timeout remaining. With the Broncos in possession, they could have kneeled down three times to run out the clock, but instead they attempted a sweep and fumbled, with Aggies defensive tackle Troy Fringer recovering.

O'Brien then led a quick scoring drive, finishing the job with his second touchdown of the game, an eight-yarder to Snow, to give the Aggies a nail-biting 21-17 win. Results elsewhere meant the Aggies were once more in control of their destiny – win all three of their remaining conference games and they would retain their FWC crown.

The Chico State Wildcats were the perfect opposition to build a little more confidence. For some reason, the Aggies had their number, and a 38-9 victory delighted 6,500 fans at Toomey Field. O'Brien looked something like his old self, passing for 199 yards and two touchdowns (his second straight game with two scoring passes) on 12 completions.

'He played with a lot of confidence tonight,' Sochor said of his quarterback. 'He executed well. He made some good audibles, he handled the team very well, he kept everyone in control. He still could have better nights.'[20]

Key to O'Brien's solid showing was a fine display from the maligned offensive line.

'I'd like to praise our offensive line,' said Sochor. 'They've taken a lot of heat and abuse this year, it's been very tough for them. We have three sophomores in there now and they all played well. I thought they protected O'Brien. We told them that the game would be decided, from an offensive standpoint, if our offensive line could control Chico's defensive line. Our line rose to the occasion and I thought we really outplayed them.'

The win set up a critical game with conference-leading Hayward, who boasted a 3-0 conference record. Sochor did not go as far as to say it was a winner-take-all scenario, but he did declare it would be for 'a lot of the marbles'.

Two big plays saw the Aggies home, despite another quiet performance from O'Brien. A meagre 61 yards through the air was compensated for by a 41-yard interception return by Steve 'Big Play' Enos and a 53-yard scoring gallop from Goss as UC Davis earned a 23-14 victory that vaulted them to the top of the FWC standings and lifted them above .500 for the first time that season, at 5-4.

The final game of the year pitted the Aggies' No. 1 rated defense against the No.1 rated offense of Sacramento State. In a mud-bath, the Aggies won thanks to an offensive explosion in the second quarter, and a powerful performance from Goss in his final game as an Aggie. Goss carried the ball 30 times for 154 yards, scooping up the FWC rushing title in the process. He also added a 22-yard scoring reception from O'Brien, who handled the treacherous conditions well.

'Ken played really well tonight,' said Sochor. 'He didn't fumble the ball and that's tough in this kind of mud and slop. Kenny handled the ball on every play and made sure of the handoffs and called some good audibles. He played very smart football.'[21]

O'Brien was quietly pleased with the offense's success, as he passed for another two touchdowns to pad his 1981 stats, but also gave credit to the team's dominating defense.

'We peaked in the first half, we really did well,' he said. 'The defense played really well. They've been doing it for us all year. We were a little conservative in the second half, didn't do what we were planning on doing, but we had a lead so there was nothing wrong with that.'

O'Brien also displayed a little of the fire that always burned beneath the surface, having listened to a lot of talk from the Sacramento team in the build-up to the game: 'They were just talking a lot,' he said after the win. 'Somebody had to shut them up. Maybe next year they won't be so loud.'[22]

The win gave UC Davis their 11th straight FWC title (technically the title was shared with Hayward, but having won the head-to-head encounter, UC Davis could rightfully claim bragging rights) and ended their season with a 6-4 record, quite an accomplishment following the 1-4 start. For O'Brien, however, there was work to do if he was to resurrect his chances of making it to the professional ranks. He was named the top quarterback in the FWC for the second consecutive year, but his numbers were significantly down on the previous campaign. Completing less than half of his passes and throwing just eight touchdowns was unlikely to catch the eyes of pro scouts.

In August 1982, UC Davis' football players gathered for the start of preseason training. Around 120 players showed up, some experienced, some fresh-faced hopefuls chasing the dream of representing their college on the gridiron.

Change was in the air. The Far West Conference was now the Northern California Athletic Conference, although the member teams remained the same. More substantial changes had transformed the

Aggies roster – player turnover from the previous season was immense, with just five starters returning. On offense, O'Brien would be joined by receiver Allen Fleming and two offensive linemen – tackle Andy Craig and guard John Johnson. Only one starter, Pat Doherty, was returning from 1981's stellar defense.

O'Brien would rely on Fleming as his most experienced receiver, while the ground game would have a new focal point for the third straight season, as junior tailback Shawn Rogers stepped into the role. Rogers' versatility made him perfect for Sochor's plans for the season. The Aggies coach had taken his entire coaching staff to the San Francisco 49ers training camp during the offseason, soaking up wisdom from offensive backfield coach Bill Matthews. There would be an increased emphasis on screen passes and Rogers' safe hands were perfect for this. After two weeks of training, Sochor's cautious optimism had ramped up a level, and he was clearly upbeat when interviewed just before the start of the season.

'We have a group of players that have a great attitude,' he enthused. 'They are eager to win and with the talent we have, we'll be contenders again. This is a lot like the '77 team,' he added, comparing his new squad to his 11-0 1977 outfit. 'We have a good blend of players. We have had the best freshman recruiting year since I've been here. We have veterans that are willing to teach the younger players and some fine junior college transfers.' [23]

The coach was also bullish on O'Brien, who was looking to bounce back from his disappointing junior campaign.

'Keep your eye on O'Brien,' Sochor said. 'He's throwing the ball very well. He has a great attitude and is in great shape.'

Sochor's team would be tested in their first game of the season, as they were pitted against Division I opponents in the form of the University of the Pacific. A level above the Aggies, the Tigers were also in a different weight division, outweighing them across the board. In the build-up to the game, UOP coach Bob Toledo complained to anyone who would listen that his team had been given a no-win situation – blow

UC Davis away and people would say that was expected. Get caught up in a close game and they would be ridiculed for not winning more easily.

Toledo did not seem to have contemplated the possibility of actually losing, but from the start it was clear the Aggies had a point to prove. Although significantly outweighed by their opponents, the UC Davis defense kept a lid on the Tigers' offense. Safety Bo Eason (who would go on to play four seasons with the Houston Oilers) opened the scoring with a 40-yard punt return, and special teams would be kind to the Aggies all day. The Tigers fumbled a return of their own to set up another score, but the Aggies still found themselves trailing 22-17 in the final period.

A second Tigers fumble on a punt return set O'Brien and the Aggies offense up at the UOP 40-yard line, and from there he drove them to the game-winning touchdown, a nine-yard pass to Fleming. UC Davis had defeated a Division I opponent, and even though Pacific would go on to have a miserable campaign, finishing 2–9, it was a major scalp, giving Sochor a 'feeling of euphoria'.[24] O'Brien had passed for just 132 yards, but he was not picked off.

In contrast to the first game of the season, the Aggies' second outing was a romp. Against Cal Poly-Pomona, they clicked in all phases of the game, and the scoreboard reflected their dominance. Outgaining their opponent by 438 yards to just 95 translated into a 37-7 victory, and O'Brien was in majestic form, completing 19 of 29 passes for 253 yards and a touchdown, a 15-yarder to Rob Cuenin. He found nine different receivers on the day.

The team was attracting attention, but Sochor's balanced offense, in which Shawn Rogers, Mel Yarbor and Dan Hawkins demanded touches, made it difficult for O'Brien to stack up the kind of gaudy numbers that would really catch the attention of the media. Even so, Sochor had no doubt his quarterback was primed for his best season.

'This may not totally show up in Ken's stats this season,' said Sochor, 'but his leadership and maturation will allow for him to do many things this team needs.'

Against Northridge, in the Aggies' home opener, O'Brien proved his coach's misgivings were unfounded. He exploded for his best game as an Aggie, completing 30 of 44 passes for 413 yards and two touchdowns. He had come within six yards of Jim Speck's single-game passing record for the Aggies, set in 1973.

'I think Ken would have broken the record had it not been for a few dropped passes,' Sochor said after the 30-20 victory. 'He was on target all night; he threw deep well and scrambled well. He's matured a lot.' [25]

Northridge had scored first, but O'Brien opened the Aggies' account with a 44-yard bomb to Mike Barber late in the first half, and he added 16- and 33-yard completions as the clock ran down to set up a Ray Sullivan field goal for a 10-7 lead at the half. Two rushing touchdowns gave Davis a healthy cushion, but Northridge cut it to just four points early in the final period, triggering some uncomfortable flashbacks to the previous year's game, when the Broncos had come from behind to sneak a win. Rogers then showcased his versatility, taking a swing pass from O'Brien, breaking three tackles and racing 59 yards for the insurance score, on a play described by Sochor as 'one of the best single efforts I've ever seen an Aggie player make.'

Sochor returned to his marbles metaphor when looking ahead to the next opponent. Whereas last year's game against Hayward had been for 'a lot of the marbles', the stakes had apparently been raised as the Aggies prepared to face San Luis Obispo.

'This game is for many, many marbles,' said the coach. 'It will definitely have a large effect on who is strongly considered for the National Division II playoffs at the end of the season.' [26]

An extra 2,000 seats were temporarily installed in the north end zone of Toomey Field, in anticipation of a big crowd, with Aggies fans eager for revenge after the physical drubbing dished out by the Mustangs the previous year. That had been UC Davis' last defeat, but an eight-game winning streak had not been enough to get them into the national rankings. SLO, on the other hand, had received an 'honorable mention' in the rankings despite their 2-2 record – both of their defeats had come against Division I opponents. Perhaps feeling slighted, the Aggies destroyed SLO by a score of 24-0 in front of 9,750 home fans.

The physically bigger SLO team had tried to overwhelm UC Davis as they had done the year before (when they piled up over 300 rushing yards) but the Aggies defense held firm and limited the Mustangs to just 157 yards of total offense. O'Brien had a mixed day, throwing two touchdowns, but also two interceptions, while amassing just 137 yards through the air. Most of his success came in the second quarter, when he engineered a short drive, capping it with a seven-yard touchdown to Fleming, and quickly followed up with another scoring pass, this time to Randy Williams.

The Aggies quarterback had success with his legs too, especially on the final scoring drive of the day, when he carried the ball three times for 31 yards in setting up a one-yard scoring dive from Rogers. UC Davis could not be ignored any more. At 4-0, they found themselves ranked No. 9 in Division II football. It was the first time they had cracked the Division II Top Ten since week eight of the 1978 season.

Their next game would be against third-ranked Santa Clara – nobody could accuse the Aggies of benefiting from a soft schedule – and with the NFL embroiled in a players' strike, and the nation hungry for more football, there were even rumours that the game might be televised nationally. The rumour came to nothing, denying the Aggies a huge amount of exposure, but the extra seating at Toomey Field was crammed to creaking point as 10,000 fans gathered for what Sochor promised would be a barnstormer.

In the early going it appeared that he was right. O'Brien led the Aggies on a quick-fire drive to start the game, hitting tight end Bill Woehler on a 34-yard pass to set up a nine-yard scoring toss to Fleming. The Mustangs hit back immediately with a 73-yard bomb to their star receiver, the six-foot-five Davis Drummond. O'Brien then put together another drive, scrambling for 12 yards and then connecting with Randy Williams for a 23-yard score. Following a Mel Yarbor touchdown run, UC Davis had the ball at the Santa Clara 49-yard line with time running out in the half. Looking only to get into field goal range, O'Brien lofted a bomb to Fleming, which he took to the one-yard line, from where O'Brien powered over for a 28-7 lead at halftime.

It had been a great half for O'Brien, as he had piled up 202 yards and two touchdowns on just 12 completions, as well as doing damage with his legs. It was a major surprise, therefore, that he failed to add to his stats in the second half – he did not complete a single pass as the Aggies were content to bleed the clock with runs while the Mustangs were swamped under a fierce pass rush (John Giagiari was sacked seven times). As a result of the win, the Aggies vaulted to No. 4 in the Division II rankings, and with their conference schedule just about to start, the second half of their season looked much easier than the opening five games. Although this made an unbeaten record a tantalising possibility, it also meant it would be difficult to climb higher in the rankings – the quality of their remaining opponents just wasn't high enough.

'It all depends on the margin of the scores in our remaining games,' Sochor explained, 'and what the teams ahead of us do.'[27]

The playoff system made it likely that UC Davis would be rewarded with a home game in the postseason, if they continued their winning ways. The top eight teams in the rankings were eligible for the playoffs, and the top-ranked team from each of the four regions would usually play host for their first playoff game.

Before thinking about that, the Aggies had to be on their guard to avoid a let-down against Chico, who came into the game with an impressive 4-1 record. In their fourth straight home game, the Aggies found themselves locked at 7-7 after the first half of play, and down 13-7 in the third quarter. From there, O'Brien took command of the game to write his way into the UC Davis record books as well as elevating his team to 6-0.

Another huge crowd was on hand, but the 9,500 fans would have been nervous as the Aggies stumbled their way through the opening exchanges, before changing tactics to pull away.

'The second half we started taking advantage of what they were giving us – the deep pass,' said Sochor. 'We should have taken advantage of that in the first half.' [28]

With O'Brien cutting loose, the Aggies went 80 yards in nine plays, Randy Williams catching a 24-yard scoring pass to put the Aggies on top by a point. O'Brien then found Fleming on a 64-yard touchdown – the pass was underthrown, but Fleming had beaten his defender so convincingly he was able to come back for the ball – and the pair connected again from 75 yards to complete the scoring. O'Brien's final figures – 18 of 31, for 346 yards, three touchdowns and no interceptions – saw him pass Jim Speck for both completions and career yardage as an Aggie. With Jacksonville State losing, the win pushed UC Davis up to No. 3 in the Division II rankings.

After the early tension against Chico, the Aggies appeared determined to take no chances against their final four opponents, beating them by a combined score of 165-26. Against San Francisco State (a 42-6 win), Sochor unleashed a perfectly balanced attack that saw his team run for 195 yards and add 195 through the air. O'Brien threw two more touchdowns to Fleming, both in the third quarter, and the Aggies were so far out of sight, they turned to their back-ups in the final period.

Against Hayward (technically atop Davis in the conference standings at 3-0), Sochor's boys did not let up, building a 28-0 halftime lead and cruising to a 41-6 triumph. O'Brien only threw one touchdown, a 17-yarder to Woehler, with the team relying on Rogers (129 yards and three touchdowns on 15 carries) and a defense that piled up 12 sacks.

'Aggie fever' was gripping the town by now, and yet more seating was set up for the team's final home game of the year. This allowed 12,700 fans to witness a 51-6 dismantling of Sacramento State. It is possible that too many fans were squeezed in, because a temporary stand nearly collapsed during the first quarter, but in the end the worst thing the fans had to contend with were the chilly temperatures and a fog bank that enveloped the field in the third quarter.

O'Brien made another entry into the UC Davis record book by throwing three touchdowns, lifting his career total to 38, which beat the

O'Brien throws a touchdown to Dan Hawkins (Gavin Payne, California Aggie, *Nov. 30, 1982)*

previous mark held by Mike Moroski. O'Brien finished with 308 yards on 20 of 28 passing, with Fleming once more his top target, grabbing nine passes for 198 yards and two scores. The rout was so emphatic it put the Aggies on the front page of their campus newspaper, and O'Brien was drawing serious attention.

'S.F. State coach Vic Rowen called him, perhaps the finest quarterback to ever play in the conference,' [29] said Sochor, with satisfaction. O'Brien had also been selected to play in that season's Japan Bowl, a showcase for the best graduating players, regardless of division.

The victory over Sacramento State was enough to confirm the Aggies' playoff berth, despite there still being one game left on the regular season schedule. The NCAA confirmed that the Aggies would play host to an opponent to be determined, with the game being played at 1:30 p.m. on November 27. Attendance would be capped at 11,600 after the scare in the Sacramento game.

With the playoff date secured, it would have been easy to overlook the final game of the regular season, against Humboldt, but Sochor knew how important it was to maintain momentum. Having just won the 100th game of his UC Davis career, Sochor was eager to keep the victories coming.

'If we beat Humboldt,' he said, 'I'll be willing to go on record and say this is the best team we've ever had. It is very important to the team that we remain undefeated. They have a strong desire to go down as the best team in Aggie history.'[30]

The Lumberjacks limited Davis to a field goal for the first 29 minutes and 59 seconds of the game. Putting that one remaining tick to good use, O'Brien eluded the Humboldt pass-rush and fired a 35-yard strike to Fleming. Three touchdowns followed in the second half – two passes from O'Brien and a quarterback sneak.

'The game was kind of ragged because of the conditions,' said Sochor, 'and it was tough for the quarterbacks to set up and throw. I thought Ken did an excellent job the way it was.'[31]

O'Brien passed for 254 yards and three touchdowns, bringing his season totals to 2,415 yards and 20 scores, with just five interceptions. He had completed over 61 percent of his passes and the stellar performance resulted in him being named the Offensive Player of the Year in the Northern California Athletic Conference.

A snapshot of how much the game has changed, even at the college level, can be seen when considering the offensive line in front of O'Brien. UC Davis had put together a dominant offense, but the men protecting the most important player on the field were tiny compared to today's behemoths. Greg Young, a starting tackle and agricultural managerial economics major, was just six-foot-two and 215 pounds. The biggest man on the line was the six-two, 245-pound right guard, John Johnson, while fellow guard Keith Bachman (six-three, 225 pounds) was singled out by Sochor for special praise after the regular season was wrapped up.

'Keith has been a tremendous addition to our team,' said the coach. 'O'Brien gets more time to throw because Keith is in there.'[32]

Northern Michigan had been confirmed as the opponent for the first round of the playoffs. The Wildcats came into the game with their own hotshot passer, Tom Bertoldi, who had matched O'Brien's yardage output with 2,437 yards, but had thrown just 11 touchdowns, while his 17 interceptions were enough to get the Aggies defensive backs salivating. Running back George Works (129.2 yards per game over the season and an incredible 23 touchdowns) would also be a major threat.

In the biggest game of his career so far, O'Brien came out firing, hitting a 67-yard touchdown to tight end Woehler on just the third play of the game, and following up later in the first quarter with a 91-yard touchdown to Fleming. He threw his third touchdown of the game (a 10-yarder) to Hawkins, adding the two-point conversion on a pass to Woehler. It was part of another stunning day for the Aggies signal-caller, as O'Brien completed 14 of 20 passes for 308 yards, while scrambling effectively and also scoring on a one-yard sneak. His play helped Davis open up a 42-7 lead in the final period, before the Wildcats scored two late consolation touchdowns to make the scoreline more respectable.

Sochor's defense had intercepted five passes and although they gave up more than 400 yards of offense, Works was held to just 44 rushing yards. The Aggies would be at home again for the semifinal game, against North Dakota State, and O'Brien appeared to be in unstoppable form. The record-setting quarterback was the focal point for all journalists looking ahead to the semifinal, but he shrugged off the scrutiny and refused to accept the credit that his play was attracting.

'Personal records don't mean that much to me,' he insisted as the spotlight grew brighter. 'The only record I'm really concerned with is the win-loss record. As the coaches always say, "No personal achievement means anything unless your team wins the ballgame."' [33]

O'Brien's modesty no doubt went down well with his teammates, and it was true that the suffocating defense had played its part in the 16-game winning streak that had already brought the Aggies a pair of conference titles and now had them on the brink of playing for a national championship. As the clock ticked own on his college career, he knew he had a chance to leave on the ultimate high.

'I've been really impressed and satisfied with our performance this season,' he said. 'This is the kind of situation I dreamed about during the off-season. It would be a perfect ending to my career here in Davis if we could win the national championship. If we don't, I'll feel like I missed something.'

Uncharacteristically, he allowed himself to look ahead, to what a victory in the national championship game would mean: 'A victory in that game would prove that we are the best team in Division II football,' he said, allowing himself to dream. 'We all believe we can do it.'

O'Brien's coach was not the kind of man to elevate one player above the rest of the team, but he could not prevent himself from praising his quarterback as the semifinal approached.

'He's a real team leader,' said Sochor. 'He was elected team captain by his teammates for the third time in a row this season. No other player has been elected team captain that many times. Everybody we've played has been very high on his abilities.'

When reminded of his role as a team leader, O'Brien stayed firmly in modesty mode.

'This is the most important honor I received,' he said, referring to being named a team captain. 'This shows that I have the respect and confidence of my teammates. I don't like to get too verbal, so I try to lead through my performances. I'm most confident doing it this way. That's the way I best express myself.

'If I thought we needed a cheerleader, I might change my style [but] I gained the confidence of my teammates through my performance. On this team, all 70 guys have confidence in each other. Then all it takes is to get the ball to the right person and let the rest of the team do the work. We're very fortunate here in Davis in that we have a lot of quality athletes.'

A third All-Conference selection, a visit to Tokyo looming for the Japan Bowl and being named quarterback of the Kodak All-American

O'Brien scores against North Dakota State (Tom McNeil, California Aggie, *December 8, 1982)*

team were major accomplishments, but in O'Brien's opinion, they were all the result of a team effort.

'All of these awards are byproducts of how well the team played,' he insisted. 'Without the offensive line, great receivers, a fine set of running backs, and our defense, I wouldn't have won these honors.'

Just about the only things O'Brien would claim sole credit for were his physical attributes: 'Because I'm 6'4", I can see over the offensive line,' he said. 'And my arm is strong enough to do anything asked of it.'

Sochor had thoughts on what made his quarterback so successful.

'He reads defenses well and for this reason he rarely throws an interception,' he said. 'He has had only six passes picked off in 11 games, which is incredible. He also has a great field of vision and he utilizes all of his personnel. On each play he knows where the second, third and fourth receivers will be.'

O'Brien's ability to go through his progressions, however, opened up the one real vulnerability in his game, a tendency to hold the ball too long, waiting for something to develop downfield. He believed the work he had done on increasing his mobility had paid off.

'I've worked hard at developing my running ability and it's coming along slowly,' he said. 'I wouldn't say my forte is running, but I'm able to take advantage of a situation if the defense is going to give it to me. I think that this has had an impact on the team's performance this season.'

Allowing himself to look even further ahead, past the semifinal, past the potential championship game, past the Japan Bowl, O'Brien was clearly relishing the prospect of playing professionally.

'It's always been a goal of mine to play in the NFL,' he added. 'I've never thought of anything else. I know I have to be ready for the unforeseen [and] I feel I have other options. First, though, I'd like to give football a shot.'

He had even given some thought to the best situation he could land in with an NFL team, and it was clear he had no plans to sit on the bench once he reached the pros: 'The ideal situation would be to go with the team that wins the Super Bowl and whose quarterback is retiring and so is the back-up,' he said, a little playfully, allowing himself to dream of the perfect scenario. 'I'm ready to give 100 percent to whoever wants me, though. Hopefully somebody will.'

Sochor had no doubts on that score.

'Most professional teams have had a scout out to watch him,' Sochor said. 'His stock has gone up considerably this year. It will really help him if we win the national championship.'

The semifinal was the Aggies' chance to go one step closer to their dream, but North Dakota State would offer a new challenge. The Bison were a formidable running team, ranking in the top 10 nationally. They ran the veer offense, the same system O'Brien had operated at Sacramento State. The veer was a ball-control, run-based attack, and UC Davis had not faced it for three years – it was the sort of power-based offense that could overwhelm a smaller, speed-based defense like that of the Aggies. Bison Quarterback Mark Nellermoe had more than a thousand yards rushing, albeit at a grind-it-out average of

O'Brien is helped from the field after suffering a serious injury against North Dakota State (Tom McNeil, California Aggie, December 8, 1982)

just 3.9 yards. As a team, they had piled up more than 3,000 rushing yards in their 12 games.

'This team won't be forced into an early deficit,' Sochor said of this opponents. 'They generally play close games so they don't need to pass as much. They usually don't score too many points. They run the ball and force you to get frustrated. They try to force you to do things you shouldn't do. They lull you to sleep and then they throw against you.'

North Dakota State also had a big edge when it came to playoff experience, having gone all the way to the national championship game the season before – they knew how to win in the postseason.

On the day before the game, one UC Davis student had clearly seen all she needed to see of the Aggies' handsome young quarterback. In the personals section of the classified ads column of the student newspaper, *The California Aggie*, a female student laid her cards on the table: 'No 15 Ken O'Brien How would you like to complete a pass with me? Call Melissa 758-1731 soon'.[34]

Completing passes did not prove to be a problem in the semifinal, with O'Brien hitting on 25 of 38 attempts, for 253 yards. Perhaps taking a leaf out of the Bison playbook, O'Brien stayed on the ground to do the real damage in the game, scoring on three short touchdown runs, the third of which gave the Aggies a 19-7 lead in the third period.

Then, disaster struck. After a 14-yard completion, O'Brien fell to the ground and, while everyone expected him to bounce back up, he stayed down. He had severely twisted his left ankle and sprained his left knee as well as suffering a hairline fracture in his left fibula. O'Brien's game was over, and the Bison closed to within five points before mounting a nail-biting drive to try to snatch the game. The drive took North Dakota State to the UC Davis eight-yard line, from where they ran four plays in search of the touchdown that would have crushed the Aggies' dreams. As they had all season, however, the defensive unit held up its side of the bargain, turning the Bison away four times and preserving the victory.

'I was thinking all along, that if we're good enough, we'll make it to Texas [for the championship game],' said a relieved Sochor after the game. 'And during that last drive by North Dakota, I was thinking the same thing; if we're good enough, we'll hold them. And we did.'[35]

As anticipated, the Bison had unleashed their passing game at key moments. Nellermoe heaved a 69-yard pass for their first score, and set up their second with a 35-yard completion. On their last play of the game, he went to the air again, but the pass fell incomplete in the Aggies end zone amid claims of pass interference.

There was no doubt, though, about the biggest storyline. O'Brien was a major question mark for the championship game, to be played in just a week's time. The broken fibula was not the issue – as it was not a weight-bearing bone he would have been cleared to play even with the fracture. The problem was the badly sprained ankle, and he was now in a race to regain fitness.

By the Thursday before the championship game, O'Brien was showing signs of improvement but was officially listed as doubtful. Whether or not there was any realistic chance of him playing, or if Sochor simply wanted to keep Southwest Texas State guessing, is not known, but in the event, O'Brien was unable to suit up and despite taking an early lead on a 44-yard field goal by the diminutive Ray Sullivan, the Aggies were overwhelmed by a powerful Bobcats rushing attack and fell to a 34-9 defeat.

Sochor was philosophical after the game, citing 'too many turnovers and too much Southwest Texas'[36] as the key contributing factors to the disappointing end to the season. 'We turned the ball over more today than we ever have,' he said. 'I think we've had only 15 turnovers for the season and we turned it over seven times today. That's something we're not used to.'[37]

It was a tough debut for sophomore quarterback Scott Barry, who had only one week's notice that he would be starting in the championship game. Barry, however, showed flashes of genuine ability.

'Scott showed he is going to have an excellent career for us,'[38] said Sochor, who was proved correct as Barry would go on to enjoy two brilliant seasons for the Aggies in 1983 and 1984. As for what might have happened had O'Brien been fit to play, Southwest Texas State coach Jim Wacker had no doubts.

'Your team revolves around a lot of people, and if you had O'Brien in the game it might have been closer,' he said. 'But we would have still won.'

O'Brien's college career was not quite over. By the middle of January he had recovered enough to fly out to Tokyo for the Japan Bowl, although how effective he would be was open to question.

'He's still not 100 percent,' said Sochor. 'Not only will he not start, but I don't even expect him to see much action. His ankle is still bothering him. He still has some tender ligaments. Don't look for him to make a great spectacle… I told him to just go and enjoy the trip without any high expectations. The best thing he could do is see the sights and above all, come home healthy.'[39]

Sochor believed the injury, which prevented O'Brien from getting exposure on a bigger stage, may have hurt his draft prospects.

'A lot of teams would like to have seen him play,' said the coach. 'Nonetheless, the indication we've received from the pro scouts is that he'll be drafted somewhere in the first five rounds. The west coast teams are most interested because they've seen him play and they know him better.'

On the flight to Tokyo, O'Brien had been accompanied by his childhood friend, Tony Eason, older brother of O'Brien's teammate, Bo. Tony had recently played in the East-West Shrine Game and might have played against O'Brien had fate not intervened. O'Brien had been selected for the West squad, but had been replaced by Steve Clarkson, the quarterback for West coach Jack Elway at San Jose State. Now Eason and O'Brien would face off in the Japan Bowl, and their paths would cross many times in the future.

The Japan Bowl was a mixed experience for the two friends. In a wild aerial shootout, featuring five touchdowns and seven interceptions, Eason threw a six-yard touchdown pass to Mike Martin but then suffered a separated shoulder. A gimpy O'Brien completed seven of 11 passes, including a 44-yard bomb to Wes Howell. It was a nice little cameo performance in a 30-21 victory for the West All-Stars, but the curtain was coming down on an eventful college career. O'Brien picked up one more accolade, making the inaugural NCAC Academic Honor Roll, thanks to his 3.2 grade-point average in political science. All thoughts, however, were turning to professional football, and as well as intrigue over which round he would be selected in during the upcoming college draft, a new wrinkle had been added.

By the time the 1983 Annual Player Selection Meeting rolled around, O'Brien had already been drafted, by a brand new football league.

Chapter Two

The Class of '83

On January 4, 1983, the newly formed United States Football League held its inaugural draft and O'Brien was selected, in the sixth round, by the Oakland Invaders. The Invaders were an interesting option for O'Brien, who had hopes of staying on the West Coast for his pro career. The USFL, in an attempt to build regional identities for its franchises, allowed teams to select local players as 'territorial picks', before the main draft, where they would be able to make a play for talent anywhere in the country.

Being drafted in the sixth round was not necessarily a fair reflection of the Invaders' enthusiasm for O'Brien. USFL teams had to weigh up the possibility of their draftees preferring to play in the more established NFL, and nobody wanted to blow an early pick on a player who might never suit up for them – for this reason, Jim Kelly wasn't selected until the 14th round, by the Chicago Blitz. Dan Marino was a first-round pick, selected by the Los Angeles Express, but even they hedged their bets, also taking UCLA QB Tom Ramsey in the fifth round.

The Invaders also held the territorial rights to Stanford's John Elway, and made a serious push to sign him before the NFL draft, reportedly offering a $6.4 million contract, more than any NFL team would offer. The Invaders would play at the old Oakland Coliseum (vacated when the NFL's Oakland Raiders had become the Los Angeles Raiders in 1982) and they were building a strong identity, inevitably piggy-backing a little on the image of the NFL's bad boys who had moved down the coast to sunnier climes. How well O'Brien would fit into such an environment was uncertain, and he was also unimpressed when the team spent most of its energies pursuing Elway.

As a spring-and-summer league, the USFL would get started in March, before the NFL draft had even taken place, so a hard push to sign O'Brien may have borne fruit, given his preference to stay local, but by this point he was more or less set on trying his luck in the NFL draft.

'It has always been my goal to play in the NFL,' he said. 'The best possibilities exist there because it's the best league. I have to consider all my options, but I'm really geared up to play in the NFL. If I get that opportunity, I'll take it.'[1]

The USFL would therefore remain a fallback option, although it would tempt many other big names from college football during its tumultuous, three-year existence. Another fallback, perhaps less enticing but nevertheless offering the chance to be paid to play, was the Canadian Football League. British Columbia owned O'Brien's rights in that league, but were interested neither in signing him, nor in allowing other teams to approach him. It was not quite 'NFL or bust', then, but all the signs pointed to him heading to the major league.

'Ken wants to play in the NFL and he's getting a lot of attention,' said Sochor, who claimed that scouts from every single NFL team had been out to visit. Intriguingly, the Jets were mentioned in a list of teams who had shown particular enthusiasm for the Aggies star.

'The Jets flew Ken back to New York two weeks ago,' Sochor revealed just a couple of days before the draft, 'which leads me to believe that they're very interested. I won't speculate on which team will draft him. All the teams know about him. He'll get an opportunity to play in the NFL. The NFL is the prime league. That's where the big money is, where they play the Super Bowl and where there is the most stability.'

O'Brien had pulled back from his early comments regarding what sort of team he would like to land with in the league. Starting immediately was no longer the primary goal.

'My chances of starting right away [in the NFL] are smaller,' he admitted, 'but this will give me an opportunity to really learn a new system. Most players who are immediately thrown into a starting role don't succeed. Of course, I don't want to sit on the bench too long.'[2]

Sochor was performing his last role in the development of the best player to ever suit up for him, helping O'Brien navigate the potentially treacherous waters to the ranks of professional football.

'Coach Sochor has always been there for me,' said O'Brien. 'He talks to the scouts and really helps a lot.'

'We've had many discussions about his play and his future,' said Sochor, 'but I'm not trying to lead him in any one direction. I advise him with new and added information. Ken is making his own decisions about his future and I'm just trying to help him in any way I can.'

The disappointing end to O'Brien's college career may have temporarily dented his prospects, but as the days wound down to the selection meeting it was clear he was a player on the rise.

'As the draft drew nearer the indications were that he might be gone by the second round,' said Sochor. 'Both the Los Angeles Rams and the Cincinnati Bengals expressed a lot of interest in him. I was sure one of those two teams would take him in the second if he was still around.'[3]

'Two days before the draft I got a call from [Rams coach] John Robinson. He said, "Do you think O'Brien could play right now if anything happened to our first guy?" And I said yes, I do.'[4]

Interestingly, Ourlads (the scouting service, producing its first draft preview that year) mocked O'Brien to the Rams, but he had received tantalising information from the team that eventually drafted him.

'The Jets had come to talk to me and they said if I went in a high round, don't be surprised,' he revealed after the draft.

ESPN was broadcasting the event live, with George Grande acting as host, and the major talking point as things got underway was whether the Baltimore Colts would be pig-headed enough to draft Elway. Multiple teams were maneuvering in an attempt to gather enough draft capital to pry the overall No. 1 pick out of Baltimore's hands, but nothing had yet been concluded. New England had the best offer on the table – first- and second-round picks in both 1983 and 1984, but the Raiders were trying to trade for extra draft picks with the Chicago Bears, and that would allow them to put together a competing bid. The Chargers were rumoured to be considering a move and as the minutes ticked down to Baltimore's pick, the Broncos were mentioned as a late possibility.

Elway himself had been unequivocal. He would rather play professional baseball that suit up for the Colts, but when the draft opened, the Colts immediately took the star quarterback from Stanford, using just seconds of their allotted 15 minutes for the pick.

'I think somebody panicked in that organisation,' said *Sports Illustrated* writer Paul Zimmerman, in his role as draft expert. 'I think what they intended to do was to go right down to the wire, to the last second, and try and make their best possible trade, and I think somebody said, "let's do it now". I don't know why they didn't wait to the very end of the 15-minute period, unless everybody backed out.'

The first round rolled on with speculation over whether or not Baltimore would pull off a trade for Elway dominating the conversation. As the picks rolled by, talk turned to the Jets, who were picking 24th. Grande raised the possibility of them going for a quarterback. With Elway, Todd Blackledge, Tony Eason and Jim Kelly already off the board, this was generally assumed to mean Dan Marino.

'We talked before the draft about the possibility of the Jets possibly going for a quarterback,' Grande said. 'That is not out of the question, even though they have a good one in Todd and yes [Pat] Ryan did not play that much last year but he's not exactly an unknown quantity, so there is a question that that may be the direction they could go in, they can draft for [a] back-up.'

Zimmerman then weighed in (tongue-in-cheek) on what he was hearing about the Jets' thinking.

'My intelligence agents in the field reported that the Jets were interested in Blackledge very much,' he said, '[they have] a question mark on Marino, they liked defensive tackle Mike Charles of Syracuse very much and they also liked George Achica, defensive tackle of USC. You can't get that kind of information from Mike Hickey,' he went on, referring to the Jets' director of player personnel, 'because he likes to set you up with misinformation.'

Howard Balzer, a writer with *The Sporting News*, agreed with Dr. Z, adding that the Jets' youth and depth would play into the final decision: 'They don't really have any glaring needs,' he said, 'so they really can't go wrong whatever they do. It's going to be a player who's going to step in, he might not start right away, but he's going to give them depth and they keep building on this and they're in a good position really.'

Dr. Z spoke up once more: 'I think they really feel that the strength of their team has got to be the pass rush,' he said, surmising that Achica would be a solid selection to maintain the team's greatest strength.

After Dallas selected defensive end Jim Jeffcoat, the Jets turned in their selection card immediately. ESPN's experts pontificated a little more about the strong position the Jets were in as Rozelle walked up to the podium with a wry smile on his face. A suddenly rowdy audience quieted down as he made the announcement that shocked the football world.

'Now there's the guy that everybody knew they'd pick,' quipped Grande after O'Brien's name had been read out and the assembled draftniks had reacted raucously. ESPN cut to Leandra Riley (who was conducting an interview with Giants punter Dave Jennings, who would later punt for the Jets), while Dr. Z and Balzer looked thorough draft publications, clearly wanting a little more information before making a comment on the most surprising pick of the first round so far.

'There's a riot going on here,' Dr. Z said, just before they cut to Riley.

'It almost reminds me of the Giants back in '79,' Jennings commented, 'when they took Phil Simms and a lot of people said "Phil who?", and so we might have the same type of situation here.'

ESPN's Sal Marchiano was soon talking to the draftniks gathered at the Sheraton, saying that some were yelling 'who is Ken Davis?' After hearing a comment in his earpiece, he corrected himself to 'Bill Brian' and finally 'Ken O'Brien'. He got there in the end.

'The talk was the Jets were going to go for a quarterback,' said Mike Eisenberg, one of the many fans gathered at the Sheraton attempting to win Super Bowl tickets by predicting first-round picks, 'but everybody said if Marino was going to be around at that time they'd take Marino. Obviously the Jets know something that the people up here don't. Ken O'Brien was a surprise pick to the fans, but the Jets' draft over the past few years has been impressive, so we shall see in a couple of years how good the pick was.'

Marchiano wrapped up the brief interview with perhaps the most incisive quote yet on the matter: 'I wonder if Richard Todd is asking "who's Ken O'Brien?"'

ESPN's coverage of the draft was still in its infancy. The first time the draft had been televised live was 1980, after the fledgling league had approached Pete Rozelle with the seemingly crazy idea of broadcasting from a hotel room for multiple hours. The NFL's owners had hated the idea, but Rozelle had recognised the potential. The coverage was still unpolished by modern standards, and the network had clearly been caught on the hop by the Jets' selection. Whereas ESPN had a video montage ready to roll for almost every player drafted before him, there was nothing on hand for O'Brien. Still, experts like Chris Berman were able to think on their feet.

'You thought they [the Jets] would go with the best athlete available,' Berman commented. 'However, a lot had been written that they wanted a back-up quarterback, Richard Todd [is] 30, so we're looking down the line two or three years, that they wanted somebody other than perhaps

Pat Ryan to step into the breach. They obviously didn't like Marino, I got that feeling this past week and in O'Brien, a couple of people that I have talked to both liked him very much as a sleeper.

'You can talk about the knocks a little bit, Bob, but he has a definite pro arm and what they like about him is his ability to read defenses and you see what the Jets can do, that maybe Kansas City and New England couldn't do in choosing a Blackledge or an Eason, is they can have him sit three or four years and just learn everything, like [Gary] Hogeboom has done with Dallas. It's not like, okay we better educate him and get him in the line-up in our first or second year. They've got plenty of time with him behind Richard Todd.'

It was a measured appraisal and one that would prove to have some merit. Although it turned out Hogeboom was not quite ready to step in for the Cowboys (he wouldn't get his chance until 1984), the Jets were indeed intending to bring O'Brien along slowly. It was the sort of luxury pick that did not have to pay off immediately.

But could the Jets have gone elsewhere in the first round and still swooped for O'Brien in the second? That had seemed like a very possible scenario until O'Brien's stock had started to climb in the weeks before the draft. An added element was that one of O'Brien's teammates at UC Davis had been Craig Walsh, son of San Francisco 49ers coach Bill Walsh. Walsh knew a thing or two about quarterbacks and each time he had travelled over to watch his son play, he had apparently been impressed by the Aggies' quarterback.

'Each time he would come back,' revealed Zimmerman while ESPN was still digesting the pick, 'he would rave about the quarterback, O'Brien, and I think they [the 49ers] were looking at him in a lower round. Maybe the Jets knew that and figured that [picking him in the first] was the only way they could get him.'

The 49ers would make their first pick of the draft two spots above the Jets in the second round – waiting may have been too much of a gamble for the Jets' front office. It is also important to consider that most experts had serious reservations about Marino. His poor senior season

(17 touchdowns and 23 interceptions) led many to conclude he lacked the mental discipline necessary for the NFL. Berman suggested that with some good coaching, he could replace Don Strock as the Dolphins back-up, but there was doubt that Miami had a coach good enough to act as a quarterback-whisperer for such a wayward talent. These assessments proved to be way off the mark – Marino led the AFC in passer rating as a rookie and took Miami to the Super Bowl in his second season – but the Jets' preference for O'Brien was not unfounded.

Even so, going as high as he did was a shock even to O'Brien.

'It surprised me that I went in the first round,'[5] he admitted, but he realised he was walking into a good situation, with no pressure to come in and contribute immediately. 'Initially, it will be in my best interests to play behind Todd,' he said. 'This will give me a chance to study the Jets' offense and prepare myself to someday step in as a starter.'

Sochor was understandably delighted to see his quarterback drafted.

'I'm ecstatic,' said the coach. 'I think it's marvelous. It's justified. He's going to be a fine NFL player. The Jets are lucky to have him. Basically it's a guarantee you're going to make the football team. The Jets wouldn't have taken him unless they planned to make him an integral part of their program. This pretty much assures Ken's future in the NFL.'

Sochor believed that O'Brien would gain confidence from the selection, and that New York was a great landing spot.

'This is going to be a great boost to his confidence,' he said. 'And the best thing is there won't be any added pressure. The Jets have a good quarterback in Richard Todd so there's an opportunity for Ken to learn the New York system while he backs up the No. 1 quarterback.'

O'Brien and his coach were not the only ones delighted with how the draft had played out. O'Brien's father, Ken Sr., pointed out the family connections in the area.

'Ken has aunts, uncles and cousins who live in New York and are Jets fans,' Ken Sr. said. 'I'm sure Ken is thrilled with this situation. It couldn't be a better opportunity.'

'I want to graduate this quarter, but we'll have to see now,'[6] The

Jets' new quarterback said. He had a healthy 3.2 grade point average, but graduation had suddenly taken a back seat. 'I've liked Joe Namath since I was a little kid,' he added. 'He's always been my hero. Hopefully, I can follow in his footsteps.'

In the days before social media, fans had to wait to see O'Brien in Jets colors. Today, he would walk onto the stage to hug the NFL commissioner seconds after being selected. In 1983, it was not until the following day that the local college newspaper printed a photo of him pulling on a Jets cap. 'Ken O'Brien tries on a New York Jets hat for size,'[7] read the caption.

O'Brien hadn't shown up on the Jets' radar until the previous November, when director of player personnel Mike Hickey first started to hear talk of the lanky quarterback on the West Coast who was tearing up the Northern California Athletic Conference. It was easy for a quarterback in California to be overshadowed by Elway – Stanford is just over a hundred miles from Davis after all. One weekend in November, 1982, the bulk of the NFL's scouts headed out to watch Elway play against Arizona. Hickey was in a bunch of just three scouts (the Raiders and Vikings were also represented) who chose to watch O'Brien play against Hayward State instead.

Although he only threw one touchdown, the game showcased O'Brien's strong arm and game awareness. The Jets belonged to a scouting service, the United Scouting Combine, which did not view him as a strong prospect, but Hickey had his own ideas, and he had an ally in offensive coordinator Joe Walton, who ran a sophisticated offense that required a quarterback with smarts as well as an arm. Walton's voice became more important when he took over from Walt Michaels as head coach of the Jets, on February 10, 1983.

The situation was complicated by the presence of Todd, a former first-round draft pick himself, who had played his best football the previous season. The Jets were a force in the American Football Conference, having made the playoffs in consecutive seasons. In 1982, a season that was interrupted by a players' strike, they had compiled a

O'Brien tries on Jets colors for the first time (AP Photo/Walt Zeboski)

6-3 record with Todd at the helm. Two thrilling playoff victories had followed, the Jets' first since their Super Bowl season of 1968, and hopes were high as planning for the 1983 season commenced.

In the modern NFL, no team would draft a quarterback in the first round if they already had a good, relatively young signal-caller under center, but it was a different game in the 1980s. Todd would turn 30 during the 1983 season, and that number loomed much larger back then than it does today. Quarterbacks took a fearful beating, and although rules had already started to be relaxed to help offenses prosper, it would be a long time before quarterbacks were treated like an endangered species on the field. Having an heir-apparent for Todd made sense, especially for a team with no glaring weaknesses elsewhere on the roster.

As the media digested the Jets' decision, there were misconceptions about O'Brien's California lifestyle. His West Coast experience was not out of a Beach Boys album. Northern California was a very different place to the sandy playgrounds of Santa Monica and Newport Beach, but the world was a bigger place back then, and coach Sochor remembered a reporter from the *New York Times* calling up and asking if Davis was a suburb of LA.

'LA doesn't have much rain; night life, like at beaches, can be all year around,'[8] said one UC Davis student who originally hailed from the southern half of the state. Davis felt more relaxed, less pressured than the metropolises of the south, and O'Brien was used to dealing with rain, freezing temperatures and mud. The often-hostile environment of New York winters would not be completely alien to him, and he had the arm strength to drive the ball through the swirling winds at Shea Stadium.

Equally important, perhaps most important, was his football brain. Tied in with that, was the sophisticated offense Sochor ran at UC Davis, which would serve as a solid grounding for a transition to professional football.

'Ken is a winner, leader and student of the game,' commented Hickey, obviously highly satisfied with his top draft pick. 'He has a high I.Q. on and off the field and is a solid person who finds ways to beat you.

Ken has a "live" arm along with good size. He adjusts well to pressure in championship games. As good as Ken is now, he can only get better. He has unlimited potential.'

Hickey's opinion of O'Brien had obviously been instrumental in his high draft status, but the key to his career would be Walton, the offensive mastermind and newly promoted head coach of the Jets. No other relationship would be as important to O'Brien during his professional career. His first seven years, including his best seasons in a Jets uniform, would come on Walton's watch, and O'Brien's development would be largely in his hands. So who was the Jets' new head coach, and how had he risen to his position?

Walton had come to prominence for helping develop Redskins quarterback Joe Theismann. As Washington's offensive coordinator, from 1978 to 1980, he had established a strong bond with his charismatic quarterback.

'Joe Walton is a special kind of guy,' Theismann would say when looking back on their time together. 'We became two bodies in one mind while he was here. In his last three years here I spent more time with Joe than I had with any one member of my own family. I consider the time with him an invaluable experience.'[9]

Walton had played for the Redskins (although they hailed out of Boston in those days) and the New York Giants during a seven-year playing career that saw him catch 178 passes as a tight end, scoring 28 touchdowns and averaging a healthy 14.8 yards per reception. Blessed with an innovative offensive mind, a switch to coaching was the obvious move when injuries cut his playing career short.

As offensive coordinator with the Jets, he had overseen the development of another decent quarterback. Richard Todd's passer rating had been languishing in the 60s before Walton took over the Jets offense, and he instantly vaulted up into the 80s. Key to the improvement was a dramatic reduction in interceptions (from 30 in 1980 to just 13 in

1981). Another key was the fact, scarcely credible now, that the Jets did not employ an offensive coordinator before Walton was hired in 1981. Offensive strategy was previously the result of consultation between players and position coaches in the lead-up to a game, and Todd would call his own plays on the field. Taking that responsibility off his shoulders allowed him to blossom as a player.

'Joe gives you the tools to work with along with the discipline that you need,' Todd said of Walton. 'He commands a great deal of respect, yet he doesn't put himself above you and you feel like you can talk to him about anything. Joe knows, and has shown in the past, how to get the best out of everybody. The guys though should button-up their chin straps because Joe can also be very tough.'[10]

All-Pro center Joe Fields also spoke highly of the man who took over as head coach in 1983.

'Joe Walton brought stability to our offense,' he said. 'He has the knack of patting you when you need it and kicking you in the butt when you need it. He seems to know who to do it to and whom not.'[11]

Immediately following the 1982 season, there were no hints that the Jets would be looking for a new head coach. Under Walt Michaels they had fallen just short of reaching the Super Bowl in the strike-shortened 1982 campaign – but the stress of coaching an NFL team was getting to him. A stern disciplinarian, he displayed increasingly erratic behavior in the last weeks of the 1982 season. A prank phone call at halftime of the playoff game against the Raiders tipped him over the edge into a full-on tantrum, while Miami's failure to protect the Orange Bowl turf during a downpour prior to the AFC Championship Game proved to be the last straw. Michaels complained bitterly, failed to attend the team's end-of-season meeting after the defeat at the hands of the Dolphins, and was instructed to resign by team owner Leon Hess and team president Jim Kensil a few days later. A payout of $400,000 helped to ease the pain of the break-up and Michaels would go on to coach in the USFL for two seasons. Walton, as the architect of the Jets' high-powered offense, was a natural choice as successor.

'I have had two years to observe him very closely,' Kensil commented after the announcement was made, 'and have seen the fine job he's done both on and off the field. I don't have to tell you what you've seen our offense do in games. Joe has an excellent working relationship with the players and will provide continuity. It is extremely important for the franchise to have continuity and I think Joe will provide that. He also understands the organization fully, accepts it, and will fit in perfectly. We have a strong relationship formed already and I expect it will carry us even further in the future.' [12]

An anecdote from defensive tackle Marty Lyons gave hope that Walton would adapt well to control of the full team, rather than just the offense. Lyons recalled how Walton had approached him as the team prepared for the playoffs the previous season: 'Going into the playoffs, Joe came over to Joe Klecko and me and said, "I know you guys are hurt, but you mean a lot to this team. They need you." That's what we needed to go out and play hurt. Joe Walton has a relationship with everyone on the team, defense as well as offense. We couldn't have a finer replacement as head coach.'

Walton relished the opportunity to take the reins of the team, and he said all the right things upon being elevated to the top job.

'This organization has been very well constructed and very well built,' he said. 'We hope to maintain what we have done and try to make improvements. I am in total accord with the policy of the Jets. I believe in the draft. I think they've done a great job, not only with drafting talented players, but also bringing in quality young men who are great to work with. I have a lot of respect for the program and organization that Walt Michaels helped build.' [13]

Walton's enthusiasm for the Jets' recent draft picks included the selection of O'Brien.

'His college handled a sophisticated offense similar to our style of play and we like that,' said Walton. 'Ken is able to avoid the pass rush, buy time and still complete the ball. He is able to throw on the move with accuracy.[14]

'I've been very influenced by the quarterbacks I have coached,' he went on. 'I learned a lot from Fran Tarkenton and particularly Y.A. Tittle. He was probably the most influential man in my ideas about the passing game and total offensive picture. I try to pick up all my experience from different people.' [15]

The Jets offense had become a force under Walton. In an era before the wide-open passing offenses of the modern NFL, the Jets averaged 211.2 yards per game through the air and 146.3 on the ground. The combined total per game was the third highest in the entire league. Still, Walton saw room for improvement.

'I don't think we've touched the surface as to what we can do on offense,' he claimed. 'I've been here only two seasons, and the first season was a learning year, and then came the short season last year.' [16]

The improvement Walton was hoping for, however, would come with Todd as quarterback. It would take time for O'Brien to earn the trust of his new teammates and coaching staff.

O'Brien shows off his No. 16 jersey at the start of his rookie season – his favored No. 15 was taken by punter Chuck Ramsey (AP Photo/G. Paul Burnett)

Chapter Three
First Steps

O'Brien's first chance to show what he could do came at a two-week rookie camp, starting in May, which he attended despite not having yet signed a contract. Shortly after, the Jets held a four-day minicamp for veterans, and Walton was quickly learning that things were different as a head coach. He was required to be available to the media far more regularly, and player holdouts (All-Pro offensive tackle Marvin Powell wanted a new contract) seemed to weigh more heavily on his mind now. During one of his media sessions, Walton admitted that he had never been involved in planning for the draft before. That was a surprising admission considering the Jets had drafted running backs Freeman McNeil and Marion Barber Jr., as well as tackle Reggie McElroy, with high picks while Walton was serving as the team's offensive coordinator. It also implied that he had input on the selection of O'Brien, but he still insisted that the pick had been made for the future – for depth, injury insurance and the eventual need to replace Todd.

Walton's thinking was clear. He agreed with the draft pundits on ESPN – the Jets had no major weakness and would expect to compete for a Super Bowl berth once more. They had drafted for depth rather than for impact players, and when it came to O'Brien, they were talking about deep depth. Pat Ryan was still expected to be the back-up, with O'Brien as the third-stringer. Ryan was an unknown commodity himself. He had enjoyed his most active season with the Jets in 1982, throwing 18 passes. Going into his sixth NFL season he had yet to start a game, but he claimed not to have been disappointed when O'Brien was drafted.

Another complication was the threat posed by the USFL. O'Brien might have been underwhelmed by the interest shown in him by the Oakland Invaders, but several other Jets draftees had chosen the start-up league. Jo-Jo Townsell, a UCLA wide receiver taken in the third round, was the most high-profile loss (he signed with the Los Angeles Express), but Stanford running back Vincent White (a sixth-rounder who signed with the Denver Gold) and Tulsa kicker Stu Crumb (a 12th-round pick who signed with the Oklahoma Outlaws) also showed that the USFL was a viable option for draftees.

The Jets' second rookie minicamp started on July 16, and 62 first-year players showed up. O'Brien was not among them – having failed to agree on a contract he now added the only pressure he could to the negotiations by holding out. A sense of frustration was growing at Jets HQ, and also a feeling that a long holdout might be on the cards. In the days before rookie contracts were firmly outlined in the collective bargaining agreement, high draft picks often held out through the preseason.

Walton would have preferred to have his top draft pick in camp as he introduced his team to a new style of coaching. Walt Michaels had been known for his gruelling practices, with two-a-days a regular feature. Under Walton, the emphasis (in this rookie camp at least) was on teaching and explaining. The stereotypical football coach had a penchant for bellowing at his players over every misstep, but Walton knew that young players had a lot on their plate just transitioning to the rigors of the pro game. He preferred to explain patiently what they were meant to do, rather than scream it into their faces.

Money, of course, was the stumbling block in the contract negotiations. O'Brien and his agent, Leigh Steinberg, felt the Jets were low-balling him because of his humble college background. Steinberg had theatrically flown back to California after receiving what he considered to be an unrealistic offer from the Jets front office. Thankfully for both parties, O'Brien's holdout did not last long. It was over in just five days after the Jets upped their offer to an acceptable level. At $1.8 million over four years (some sources reported it as $1.7 million and the Jets were famously tight-lipped on financial matters), it was by far the richest pro sports contract ever signed by a UC Davis player, although still slightly less than the deals inked by Eason, Blackledge and Marino, who were all at the $2 million level. O'Brien's contract stipulated that $300 would be donated to charity for each game the Jets won, as well as donations to Jesuit High School and the football program at UC Davis.

A reminder that football players are human beings, with feelings, came in the aftermath of O'Brien's signing. Miffed that the rookie's contract came close to his own, Richard Todd grumbled a little and the team swiftly moved to boost his salary to a level considerably above O'Brien's. Todd received a massive hike, moving up from $350,000 for the 1983 season to $550,000, becoming the fourth-highest paid quarterback in the NFL (Dan Fouts, Archie Manning and John Elway were the only players with higher base salaries). Players could talk as much as they wanted about not feeling threatened by draft picks, but pride was still an important factor to weigh in player relations.

Late in the first preseason game that year, against the Giants at Giants Stadium, O'Brien saw his first game time as a pro in a 23-16 defeat. On his third play, he suffered a 12-yard sack, brought down by linebacker Andy Headen at the Jets' five-yard line (Headen, an eighth-round draft pick, had three sacks in the game). It was to be O'Brien's only sack of the day, however, as the rookie completed seven of 10 passes for 80 yards and a touchdown. His second outing was even more promising. With Todd nursing a thigh bruise, Ryan started and O'Brien was elevated to back-up.

The plan was to play Ryan into the second half, but he suffered a rib injury in the second quarter and O'Brien was thrust into action sooner than anticipated. It was cruel twist of fate for Ryan, who had waited until his sixth season before getting his first start, but O'Brien grasped his chance. Foreshadowing a long partnership with Mickey Shuler, he hit the tight end on three straight passes to set up a Pat Leahy field goal. O'Brien was making an impact with his teammates, but Todd felt confident enough in his position as starter to make a little joke at the rookie's expense.

'He's a real nice guy, smart, strong,' he said of the rookie, 'good arm, good looking. But I'd say he needs a little more training, like five, six or seven years.'[1]

O'Brien professed to be in no hurry: 'In my situation, I don't think it's that big a deal to sit back and learn so when it's my chance I'll be prepared,'[2] he said, diplomatically.

Whereas first-round quarterbacks would almost certainly be thrown to the wolves right away in the modern NFL, there was a little more restraint in 1983... although fans would get antsy if a veteran starter struggled. As such, most of the quarterback class of '83 were expected to start their careers on the bench.

'Not many people come right out of college and start, and the track record of those who have is not all that glamorous and not all that good,' said Blackledge. 'I don't think I'm going to mind sitting a few years,' he added, a statement that would amaze and concern a modern-day fanbase, who might interpret it as a lack of confidence.

The one exception was widely expected to be Elway. By now, he had been rescued from Baltimore by Denver, in a trade that looked one-sided to start with and would only look worse as the years passed and Elway became one of the NFL's top talents. He would be starting the first game of the regular season, against the Pittsburgh Steelers, but his head coach was bracing for difficult times.

'Nobody has ever come into this league and had a bed of roses,' said Dan Reeves, 'but he has mental toughness and is able to overcome adversity. John has more talent than anyone I've ever been around.'

'There are going to be growing pains,' Elway himself acknowledged, 'and I know there are going to be more ups and downs for a rookie than for a veteran. But hopefully there will be more peaks than valleys.'

The approaching regular season obviously meant more to some of the rookies than to others. Elway would start 10 games in a mixed season, throwing seven touchdowns passes and 14 interceptions. Blackledge would play in four games but would not start any. His 58.8 percent completion rate (albeit on just 34 attempts) would prove to be the high point of his career by far and his three touchdown passes, compared to no interceptions, would raise hopes sky high for 1984. These hopes was tempered, however, by incumbent Bill Kenney enjoying the best season of his career in 1983, with over 4,000 passing yards. Things would be complicated in Kansas City.

Eason would be eased into things, throwing (and completing) four passes in his first regular season action, in week two, before starting the last four games of the season. He went 2-2 as a starter, but threw just one touchdown and five interceptions.

Only O'Brien and Jim Kelly (who had been unwilling to play in Buffalo and instead opted for the USFL) would not see the field at all in 1983. Kelly tore up the USFL in the spring of 1984, throwing for 5,219 yards and 44 touchdowns, but even that paled in comparison to Dan Marino's rookie campaign. Against NFL opposition, the Dolphins' new quarterback won seven of his nine starts, passing for 2,210 yards and 20 touchdowns to earn a passer rating of 96.0. The last of the six quarterbacks selected led the entire AFC in passing efficiency.

O'Brien had performed well in his preseason outings, completing 18 of 28 passes for 187 yards. It was the kind of slow and steady start to his pro career that had been expected, but something was about to happen that nobody had planned for, and it would not only overshadow his rookie campaign, it would become a serious problem for his second season as well.

In the early hours of Friday, September 30, 1983, O'Brien was in a New York night club, the famed Studio 54, with defensive end Mark Gastineau. Gastineau was a larger-than-life character both on and off the field, just the kind of person to run into trouble in a busy night club. Depending on which version of events you chose to believe, Gastineau and O'Brien either assaulted a group of fellow club-goers, or inadvertently became involved in a fight when they tried to break it up.

'I accept their version,' team president Jim Kensil commented when the news broke. 'Mark said he was breaking up a fight and I believe him.'

Gastineau added more detail, claiming it was friends of O'Brien who had become involved in a scuffle.

'I was an innocent bystander, and that's the God's honest truth,' said Gastineau. 'I had a good time, unfortunately some of Kenny's friends got into a brawl. I just tried to break everything up. Kenny was doing the same thing.'

The upshot of the ruckus was that two men ended up with broken noses, and Gastineau and O'Brien found themselves accused. O'Brien insisted he'd had nothing to do with events.

'I wasn't involved,' he said. 'I'm here to play football.'

The first year after leaving college can be trying for anyone, let alone someone moving from a quiet California town to the mayhem of New York. An accusation of assault did not make things any easier. It was a rough baptism for the quiet young man from UC Davis, and it would drag on for more than a year. The pair were officially charged with third-degree assault and they pled not guilty on November 2.

It was a learning period for O'Brien – not necessarily frustrating, but far from what he was used to. He didn't even hold a clipboard on the sideline during a game. That duty fell to Ryan, as the official back-up to Todd. As the third-stringer, even practices tended to be dull. O'Brien would act as quarterback for some of the opposition's anticipated plays, but as the season progressed, he revealed that most of his progress was due to work in meeting rooms. Teaching and explaining, the cornerstones of Walton's coaching style, were all that O'Brien had to learn from.

On the field, the Jets had looked like playoff contenders, but a worrying trend was developing. Having improved hugely under Walton's tutelage over the previous two seasons, Todd was regressing. Most worrying was his alarming propensity for throwing interceptions, which had been a major concern earlier in his career, before Walton's arrival. In 1980 he had been picked off on an incredible 6.3 percent of his attempts. Under Walton, that rate had fallen to 2.6 and 3.1 percent in 1981 and 1982. Suddenly, in 1983, he was back to his bad old ways.

With a strong running game and a pass-rush led by Gastineau in his prime, the Jets were competitive, but Todd's erratic play kept bringing them back down to earth. He was passing for more yardage than ever before in his career (3,478 yards by season's end) but he was also careless with the ball. In a five-week stretch that saw the Jets lose four games to drop to the edge of playoff elimination, Todd threw 10 interceptions, including a brutal five-pick outing against the Dolphins in which he was replaced by Ryan. The team rallied to win three straight and get back to 7-7, but the season ended with four more interceptions from Todd in two more defeats as they finished the year a disappointing 7-9.

The season had provided a more detailed look at the coaching style of Walton. As a coordinator he was able to fly under the radar to some extent. Now, as the head coach, he was under a spotlight. A more hard-nosed side to the man was highlighted by the cutting of Dwayne Crutchfield in November. It was a shocking move for the fullback, who had been drafted in the third round the year before. Crutchfield was leading the Jets with 571 yards at a healthy 4.2-yard average, adding 19 receptions and scoring three touchdowns, when he was abruptly released. Rumors swirled that Crutchfield had fallen into Walton's bad books, with accusations of lackadaisical practice habits. In return, Crutchfield claimed there was a racist element to the decision to cut him, and several teammates backed him up on that.

'He wasn't progressing in the areas we wanted him to,' Walton stated, simply. 'He doesn't fit into our plans for the future.'[3]

It was perhaps the first glimpse of an uncompromising side to

Walton, one that would create friction as his Jets tenure wound on. The quarterback position was of more immediate concern, and nothing accelerates a young quarterback's career more than disappointing play from the incumbent. After throwing 26 interceptions in 16 games, Todd's time in New York was at an end. On February 18, 1984, he was traded to New Orleans. Remarkably, for a 30-year-old with a 68.6 career passer rating, the Jets got a first-round draft pick in return. The Saints would regret the trade, as Todd played in just 17 games for them, and threw 23 interceptions. He was pragmatic about his time in New York.

'I think anybody who followed Joe [Namath] was going to have a tough time,' he said after being traded. 'Probably the next quarterback who comes in here will be accepted a little more easily, won't have as hard a time as I did.'[4]

Walton was relaxing on a cruise when the Jets' press office released a simple statement from the coach: 'We think it'll be better for the Jets at this point in time and for Richard Todd,' Walton was quoted as saying. 'A change in scenery would help Richard in his career. He has been a fine quarterback for us and did take us to the playoffs twice, but we do think he needs the change of scenery.'

The move was just the most eye-catching of a more general house-cleaning following a 7-9 season. The Jets, a playoff team and Super Bowl front-runner when Walton took over, were in danger of slipping back into the pack. The once-close relationship between Walton and his quarterback had soured, and Todd would claim that he knew the writing was on the wall when the team began to struggle during the 1983 season. At the heart of the matter may have been Todd's apparent inability to beat the top team in the division, the Dolphins. The Jets had lost five straight games to Miami, and Todd had thrown an eye-watering 17 interceptions in those games.

Walton was making moves to stamp his authority on the team. As well as Todd, defensive stalwarts Kenny Neil, Abdul Salaam and Stan Blinka were also traded away, while veteran tight end Jerome Barkum was released (he was asked to return to the team as a coach but declined the offer). Neil and Salaam were both dealt to the 49ers, netting a second-round draft pick. Along with the first-rounder received for Todd, the Jets now owned four of the first 39 picks in the upcoming draft. Shrewd selections could vault the team back into contention.

In all, seven former starters had departed by the time the team was ready to start preparations for the 1984 season, including cornerback Jerry Holmes, who jumped to the USFL. The big question would be which of the team's two remaining quarterbacks would win the job for 1984 – the promising youngster or the established back-up. Todd himself did not think there was much doubt about the answer.

'You don't draft a guy No. 1, pay him a lot of money and expect him to sit around,'[5] he said.

Walton had this to say about his young passer: 'We committed ourselves to Ken O'Brien in the future and this will speed up his process.'

Indeed it would. It looked like O'Brien's future had arrived.

The trade of Todd inevitably made a splash. At the same time, however, another splash was being made in New Jersey, as the brash and abrasive new owner of the USFL's New Jersey Generals prepared his team for the upcoming season by throwing money at multiple NFL veterans. Donald Trump did not like sharing headlines and he liked losing football games even less. Quarterback Brian Sipe (a former NFL MVP) was the marquee addition to a team already featuring the prolific running back Herschel Walker.

'I've never lost anything in my life,' Trump announced. 'I think we'll win and win immediately.'[6]

These were colorful times in the world of professional football. The Generals would be led by former Jets head coach Walt Michaels.

The draft was approaching again, and back at UC Davis there was excitement at the prospect of another player going high. Free safety Bo Eason, brother of Tony, was expected to be selected in the first three rounds, and there were also hopes for running back Shawn

Rogers and receiver Allen Fleming. Rogers and Fleming had been flown to New York by the Jets for physicals, and O'Brien had been vocal about the qualities of one of his favourite targets while with the Aggies.

'He's told many people he feels Fleming is just as good as some of the receivers they [the Jets] have now,'[7] coach Sochor said.

In the event, neither Fleming nor Rogers heard their names called on draft day and neither made it in the NFL. Bo Eason, however, was the 54th pick of the draft, taken by Houston in the second round. He played 38 games for the Oilers, making six interceptions, before injuries ended his career. It just so happened that the Jets and Oilers were scheduled to play each other in the 1984 regular season, in a game that would be O'Brien's first as a starter.

At first glance, the Jets had made good use of their four early picks, although three of them would eventually be considered disappointments. Help was needed on both lines, in the secondary and at tight end, and the Jets were clearly drafting for need when they made their selections. SMU defensive back Russell Carter was taken with the 10th pick, Arkansas defensive end Ron Faurot with the 15th, Pittsburgh center Jim Sweeney with the 37th and Miami (Florida) tight end Glenn Dennison with the 39th. It was an injection of youth and talent right where the team needed it most and early impressions were positive. All four players made an impact in their rookie seasons, although only Sweeney would go on to have a long career with the team.

Minicamps came and went, and O'Brien spent a lot of time huddled with Walton, poring over game film and discussing the intricacies of the position. Still without his own New York residence, O'Brien spent the offseason at the house of star running back Freeman McNeil. It was clear that he was being groomed for the starter's job, but the New York media became antsy at Walton's refusal to name O'Brien the starter. There was no hurry, but the media like things to move along quickly. Dave Anderson, of *The New York Times*, claimed this was the sort of indecisiveness that had plagued Walton's first season as a coach.

Veterans were not reporting to training camp until July 20, but

O'Brien and Ryan were among the 86 players, rookies and free agents, who got a head start a few days earlier. Walton needed to see his two quarterbacks in action, and announced that they would alternate possessions with the first team during drills. The camp was to be a gruelling one. Walton was reinstating the controversial 'nutcracker drill', where a running back would attempt to get past duelling linemen, and he exhorted his position coaches to fire their players up and get them to hit hard. A new training sled, allegedly weighing a ton, would be used. Off the field, harsh fines were put in place for players who flouted team rules, including the parking restrictions at the team's facility.

It was all in an effort to instil discipline in a squad that Walton felt had slipped into lazy ways during the 1983 season. It was ironic, because players had previously chafed under the regime of Walt Michaels... now journalists talked of receiving calls from agents saying their players preferred Michaels' approach to Walton's.

At the same time, players who were in favor were reaping the benefits. The possibility of talent leaving for the USFL was a big spur, but most important in the team's decision-making was Walton's opinion. His opinion of linebacker Lance Mehl was so high that the Jets increased his salary sevenfold, from just $88,000 in 1983 to a staggering $650,000 in 1984. The deal made Mehl the second highest-paid linebacker in the history of the NFL. Joe Klecko also received a healthy boost, a $300,000 hike that saw him match the $700,000 annual salary of Gastineau. Gastineau's salary ($3.71 million over five years) had created a stir and had even become a benchmark, with other top defensive players demanding a 'Gastineau deal' from their teams. The kind of TV revenue the NFL brings in today was a dream in the 1980s – each NFL franchise received just $15 million in 1984 under the terms of the existing contracts, and this impacted how much the players could receive. Average salaries across the league had risen sharply over the previous few seasons, but were still around a modest $170,000 per year.

The media was uncertain about the revamped Jets. With new starters everywhere, there was doubt over how quickly the team would come together, and the coaching staff clearly shared these concerns. A pair of organized scrimmages against the Redskins, a Super Bowl team the season before, would give the Jets a little battle-hardening before the exhibition games even started. One of the scrimmages would feature the rookies and O'Brien, while both quarterbacks would play with the veterans a week later.

O'Brien did well in the first scrimmage, completing 10 of 16 passes for 123 yards and a touchdown, with one interception. The second scrimmage, though a nightmare for the team as they were manhandled in a 45-10 'defeat', allowed the second-year player to show some poise. After fumbling his first snap, O'Brien went on to complete 12 of 20 passes for 144 yards. He also clearly outplayed Ryan, who mustered a meagre 57 yards on 15 attempts, completing just six passes. These performances were enough to prompt Walton to make a bold decision.

'Kenny is our starting quarterback,' said Walton. 'He will start in the pre-season games and he will start the season. I want two guys who are capable of starting. Pat Ryan knows our system and is a good competitor. Kenny needs the work. He has a lot of talent. He needs to work with the first unit. They need to get used to his voice and he and his receivers must develop their timing. He has all the talent.' [8]

'I'm really happy,' O'Brien responded. 'But I'm going to have to keep going as hard as I can go. It's a matter of pushing myself, preparing. I don't want to let anyone down. I just want to keep learning, do the right things.' [9]

Ryan remained pragmatic, and affable: 'Yeah, I wish I had his arm,' the veteran said of O'Brien's superior physical skills. 'I wish I was better looking, too. You just go with what you've got.' [10]

Just days before this announcement, Walton had been openly musing on the possibility of using a two-quarterback approach, going with whichever player had the hot hand. It is an old football maxim that if you have two quarterbacks, you really have no quarterbacks, and Walton swiftly moved on from this idea. Being a first-round draft pick inevitably gave O'Brien a big advantage over his rival. Ryan was a steady veteran, but he had amassed just 572 yards in his six pro seasons, and the anticipation of unleashing a first-round pick was irresistible.

'I see it as the fulfilment of a dream,' O' Brien said. 'I think I have the system down now. It's just a matter of tuning it.'

The first attempt at seriously tuning his play would come in the Jets' opening preseason game, against the Cincinnati Bengals. O'Brien's first start in the pros was a mixed bag. He performed well enough, completing 14 of 27 passes for 166 yards in a loss, but he also lost one of his top receivers, Johnny 'Lam' Jones, to a broken collarbone in the first quarter. The injury was expected to keep Jones out for at least eight weeks (he returned for the week nine match-up with New England). O'Brien also went down under six sacks, including on his very first snap of the game, a worrying continuation of a trend from his college days.

Rules on protecting the quarterback were much looser in 1984 – defenders were allowed to drive a quarterback violently to the ground, for instance. Nor was it a penalty to hit the quarterback in the knee. Passers who took a lot of sacks not only risked serious injury, there were long-term effects as well. A player would be referred to as 'gun-shy' when he finally spent as much time watching the approaching pass-rush as he did his targets downfield.

O'Brien was far from gun-shy. If anything, he was brave to a fault in the pocket, and his apparent indifference to taking sacks would be a recurring theme throughout his NFL career. He acknowledged the need to increase the speed of his dropback, but the barrage of sacks also revealed a lack of preparation elsewhere. Center Joe Fields commented that he and his fellow linemen had been confused by the Bengals' three-man defensive front and the creative blitz packages they ran out of it. The Jets ran a 4-3, and so did their training camp scrimmage partner, the Redskins. If they really had been under-prepared for a three-man front it was a problem they would need to address quickly – the four-man defensive front was out of vogue and only seven teams still ran it.

Adding to O'Brien's list of problems was a lack of viable targets – if the receiver cupboard was not exactly bare, it was very scantily stocked. As well as Jones getting injured during the game, Wesley Walker was holding out in a contract dispute. The Jets had apparently offered to increase his salary from just over $200,000 to $625,000 but the star receiver wanted more. O'Brien was working with rookie Bobby Humphery (whose best days as a Jet would come after he transitioned to play cornerback) and Derrick Gaffney (another disgruntled receiver playing out the last year of his contract). Kurt Sohn, a special teams standout who had suffered a devastating knee injury in an exhibition game against the Bengals the previous year, was attempting a comeback, but he had yet to catch a pass in a regular season game.

In desperation, the team signed former Eagle Harold Carmichael, a future Hall of Famer and a towering figure at 6'8". Carmichael claimed he still had his route-running ability, though speed had never been a part of his game and wasn't about to appear at the age of 34.

The offensive woes continued in the next exhibition game, against the Oilers. O'Brien struggled in the first half, as he was sacked six times. With a dearth of targets, and an offensive line weakened by the ankle injury suffered by left tackle Chris Ward on the Jets' second play of the game, O'Brien was harried into just eight completions for 62 yards and was intercepted once. Ryan, inserted to start the second half, steadied the ship with a 75-yard touchdown drive, but a pinched nerve in his neck sent him back to the sidelines after just 11 plays. O'Brien went back in and showed improvement, throwing a 44-yard touchdown to rookie tight end Glenn Dennison. He also suffered two more sacks to raise his total to 14 in just two games.

The preseason was turning into a nightmare. Freeman McNeil, the heart and soul of the offense, was told to rest for at least a week to ease muscle stiffness in his right leg. Then, against the Giants in the third warm-up game, Joe Klecko (who had just returned to action following an abdominal muscle injury) pulled the hamstring in his right leg and was expected to miss up to six weeks. Defensive tackle Marty Lyons and offensive guard Dan Alexander were two more starters banged up during the Giants game, with each expected to miss at least a week, while third-down back Bruce Harper was lost for up to 10 days with a shoulder injury.

Klecko's injury was the big news from another preseason loss, but O'Brien again gave cause for concern, suffering another four sacks and passing for just 50 yards. For a team desperate for any sort of good luck, the return of Sohn, exactly one year after his knee injury, was a bright spot, although he failed to catch a pass in two series. Ryan again looked sharp in relief, hitting the impressive Dennison for a score. After three games, O'Brien had completed 52 percent of his passes while Ryan had connected on 66 percent. The departed Richard Todd, meanwhile, had been a star in New Orleans, throwing four touchdowns and just one interception.

It was still only the preseason, and Walton insisted he had no reason to change his thinking on making O'Brien the starter, but history was about to catch up with the young quarterback. The case against O'Brien and Gastineau for their part in the fight at Studio 54 was coming to trial just as the Jets were preparing for their final preseason game and looking ahead to the season-opener. Walton was deprived of two more of his starters in an offseason that was starting to get ridiculous. There was hope the legal process would not take too long. It was only a misdemeanor trial, after all, and was expected to last a matter of days. Instead, it lasted three and a half weeks and removed O'Brien from the Jets' starting line-up as effectively as an unblocked defensive end.

Although the judge in the Studio 54 trial was sympathetic to the needs of the two defendants, allowing them to travel to Los Angeles the night before the final preseason game, the practice time that O'Brien needed so badly had been removed. Walton made the decision to install Ryan as the starter for the Raiders game, and hinted at starting him for the season opener, on September 2.

The trial became bogged down in competing testimonies, as some sought to portray the Jets duo as a pair of thugs, while others claimed they were either not involved at all in the violence, or actively trying to stop it. Gastineau's passing of a lie-detector test would not enter into the jurors' decision-making process – they were removed from the courtroom when his attorney presented the evidence, as lie detectors were not considered reliable. With no security camera footage, the case quickly boiled down to which story the jurors believed. Perhaps perversely, they chose to believe both.

Gastineau, famous for his extravagant celebration of the many sacks he piled up as the league's premier pass-rusher, was found guilty, while O'Brien was found innocent. Quite how the jury squared that circle was unclear, but the upshot was that both players were able to rejoin the team. Gastineau would have to weigh up the possible benefits of an appeal against the extra time it would carve out of his season. For O'Brien, there were no such considerations. He firmly attested that he disagreed with the verdict on Gastineau, but was ready to return to work. The only problem for him? By the time he was cleared of all charges, it was September 12, and the Jets had already played two games of the 1984 season.

Walton's hand had been forced. The final preseason game had ended in a 20-14 victory that injected a little optimism into the team, but neither Ryan nor O'Brien played particularly well – O'Brien finished with just 82 yards through the air, having completed six of 12 passes. The Jets' injury list, already long, added Mike Augustyniak, the running back suffering a knee injury that was expected to sideline him for several weeks. It actually ended his career after just three seasons.

The Wednesday before the regular season opener had been a critical day. Wednesdays were the most important day in the week prior to a game – it was the day the offensive gameplan was installed. If O'Brien was not finished with his trial in time to return to the team by Wednesday, August 29, he would be forced to miss the opening contest… and that was how things played out. Better news came with the return of Wesley Walker, who ended his 37-day holdout without a new deal but with an understanding that negotiations would continue. The Jets, traditionally tight-lipped about contracts, promised nothing in a wordy and emotionless statement released by Jim Kensil: 'Wesley Walker and the Jets have agreed through their respective representatives that Wesley shall immediately report to the Jets and resume his active role with the club pursuant to his existing contract while the representatives pursue negotiations in an effort toward reaching a new agreement between Wesley and the Jets.' Harold Carmichael, now surplus to requirements, was quietly let go having never caught a pass with the team (he would catch just one more pass in his career, with the Cowboys).

At the same time, another offensive stalwart was on the way out. Chris Ward, injured in the first preseason game, was surprisingly waived, after anchoring the offensive line ever since being drafted No. 4 overall in 1978. Ward had battled with his weight and often frustrated the team with his laid-back attitude to training, but he was only 28 and theoretically had several productive years left. He would catch on with the Saints for one more season, reuniting with his former quarterback. Second-year pro Reggie McElroy stepped in as the full-time starter at left tackle.

Amid the moves, Walton announced that Ryan would start the season-opener. Business was about to start in earnest and a light touch was added by Bruce Harper, who handed out t-shirts to all of the Jets who made the final roster bearing the slogan 'I survived Camp Walton'.

It felt like it had been a long season already, but it had yet to really begin.

It is common, when dealing with the New York Jets, to sense a changing of the guard. The emphasis in newspaper and magazine articles often seems to be on the 'new', and that was especially true in September 1984. There were new starters at nine positions, including quarterback, a new home following the decision to share Giants Stadium with their crosstown rivals and even a new radio station broadcasting Jets games, WABC taking over from WCBS. The offensive line was a major question mark, with Stan Waldemore coming back from knee surgery at left guard and the unproven McElroy filling Ward's shoes at left tackle.

When gameday finally arrived, it came as a relief. Gastineau unleashed his frustrations on Colts quarterback Mike Pagel, sacking him four times, and the Jets forced five turnovers (four fumbles and an interception) to keep the ball in their offense's hands. It was most effectively used when given to McNeil, who carried a career-high 29 times and piled up 112 yards. Ryan completed just 14 passes in his first professional start, matching two touchdowns with two interceptions. The 23-14 victory blew away some of the doubts surrounding the team, and seemed to instil a little swagger in the normally quiet Ryan.

'In my mind, I'm the No. 1 quarterback,' he said, 'but once you're in the game, there's no difference starting than coming off the bench.'[11]

Walton was also quietly impressed with his new starter: 'I was pleased with the way Pat played,' said the coach. 'He's tougher than nails. He showed good leadership.'

This was not yet Ryan's team, however. It was still McNeil's. Over the first six weeks of the season, the fourth-year running back broke the hundred-yard mark four times, and the Jets won each of those games. It was becoming clear to all that as McNeil went, so went the Jets.

Still, Ryan began to settle into his role. A dismal showing against Pittsburgh in week two was followed by a string of fine performances from a man who was grabbing his starting opportunity with both hands. In a three-week span, from week three to week five, he completed 63 percent of his passes for 796 yards and six touchdowns. After a two-week dip in performance, he put up the best numbers of his career against Kansas City in week eight – 260 yards, three scores and no interceptions.

In the same game, O'Brien made his regular season debut, completing his only attempt for nine yards, but the starting quarterback job appeared to be out of reach. Ryan was on track for nearly 3,300 passing yards and 26 touchdowns. The yardage projection is not impressive by modern standards, but would have seen Ryan threatening to crack the top 10 in 1984. More importantly, the Jets were winning – 6-2 at midseason, they were firmly in the race for the AFC East title and the playoffs.

One of the keys to Ryan's steady play was the emergence of tight end Mickey Shuler. Both players had joined the Jets via the 1978 draft. Both had sat and awaited their chance. Ryan would later cite the time the two spent together on the Jets' scout team as a factor in their effective work in the first half of the 1984 season. Shuler had 83 total catches over his previous six seasons and had never established himself as a consistent performer. In the first seven weeks of 1984 he was a picture of consistency, catching three, three, three, two, four, four and two passes. He began to make a habit of converting on third down and he snagged five touchdowns, easily the best mark of his career to that point. In week eight, as Ryan enjoyed his best game as a pro, so did Shuler, catching seven passes for 58 yards and a touchdown. The two forgotten men of the Jets offense were making their move, but for one of them, the fairy tale was about to end.

By week nine the Jets were attracting attention, and their divisional match-up against the Patriots was a huge game. With Miami leading the division at 8-0, the Jets could not afford to slip up if they wanted to remain in the hunt for the divisional title. The Patriots were just a game back from the Jets and charging hard. They had won four of their last six games and were getting solid production from Tony Eason, who had thrown 10 touchdowns and just one interception on the year. Surprisingly, this run had not been enough to save the Patriot's coach – Ron Meyer had been sacked in the week leading up to the game, having completely lost the locker room. Raymond Berry, a Hall of Fame player who had been out of football for two and a half years, was taking over.

In a hard-hitting first quarter, the teams traded sacks and punishing tackles. Ryan had already taken a beating when he dropped back to pass late in the first period. Patriots linebacker Larry McGrew came through untouched and drilled Ryan just after he had delivered the pass. Color commentator John Brodie knew a thing or two about taking a hit, having played 14 seasons at quarterback for the 49ers, but he understated things a little when he remarked that Ryan 'got an awful good lick back there' – the Jets' quarterback was rolling on the ground in pain after a shuddering helmet-to-jaw impact.

On the sideline, O'Brien was shown warming up. With the game scoreless, he was about to see the first meaningful playing time of his professional career. Facing a third-and-10 from the New England 35, Walton clearly felt it best to ease his young signal-caller in. He called a running play to Johnny Hector, who took the ball inside the 30 to set up a Pat Leahy field goal.

When the Jets got the ball back, O'Brien's second and third plays were also hand-offs, and McNeil took the ball to the Patriots' eight-yard line on a 53-yard gallop, the longest run of his career to that point. A fourth straight running play positioned the ball at the seven, and Walton was finally ready to let O'Brien throw. On second-and-goal, he dropped back, faded to the right and then zipped a hard pass to tight end Rocky Klever, who was three yards deep in the end zone. The score was the first for both players.

'There was no indecision on O'Brien's part,' enthused Brodie. 'When he rolled out, he looked back, he saw Klever, this is the advantage of having an arm like he does. Watch how fast from the time he sees the play, and sees Klever open, to when it's gone… bang… boom… takes no time getting there, six points for the Jets and that's a wonderful way to start if you're a young, second-year man that's had a, thus far, very difficult time.'

O'Brien's second pass was even more impressive than his first. Following a Patriots field goal, he fired an 18-yard bullet to Lam Jones, who was enjoying a brilliant game on his return to action following the collarbone injury. McNeil then took a short dump-off for 28 yards, and O'Brien had yet to throw a regular season incompletion as a pro as he positioned them for a Pat Leahy field goal. After a Russel Carter interception, O'Brien ripped another pass to Jones, this time for 14 yards. He was four of four for 67 yards and a touchdown and making it look very easy. His fifth pass looked like it might go all the way, but as Hector prepared to gather the ball and head upfield behind a wall of blockers, McGrew leaped high to deflect the pass. Turning back to the run, the Jets moved ahead 20-3 on Marion Barber's two-yard touchdown.

Things looked good for the 6-2 Jets, but the next 27 points would all be scored by New England. Tony Franklin's second field goal chipped away at the lead at the end of the half, and then Walton made an eyebrow-raising decision to start the third quarter. With the option to receive the kick-off, he instead chose to kick, giving New England the chance to build a little momentum. The gamble appeared to have paid off as a Gastineau sack forced the Patriots to give the ball back, but an 82-yard punt from Luke Prestridge, which rolled 42 yards after hitting the turf, pinned the Jets back inside their one. O'Brien rifled a completion to Shuler for a first down on third-and-five and worked the ball out to the 27, but after a holding penalty wiped out another strong run from McNeil, he faced a first-and-20. For the first time since entering the game, O'Brien looked indecisive, twice cocking his arm to throw but eventually hanging onto the ball for more than four seconds and taking a sack. After the Patriots took over, Tony Franklin kicked his third field goal to make it 20-9.

The next Jets drive stalled as O'Brien took his second sack and Craig James scored to bring New England within four. What had seemed like a comfortable game for the Jets suddenly looked precarious. A holding penalty on the ensuing kick return put the Jets back to their seven-yard line and a three-and-out gave the Patriots the ball again. As they drove downfield, Pat Ryan could be seen warming up on the sideline just before Stephen Starring caught the go-ahead touchdown from Eason. O'Brien, with a 132.2 passer rating on the day, was being yanked.

The momentum in the game had definitely changed, but Walton's decision seemed premature. O'Brien had started three drives in the second quarter, from the one, the 25 and the seven. New England's defense had turned up the heat, but conservative playcalling due to the field position had played its part too. Ryan, undoubtedly still affected by the first-quarter hit, was unable to rally his team, throwing two fourth-quarter interceptions as the Jets slipped to a deflating 20-30 defeat.

O'Brien could take some satisfaction in his steady play, and the Jets now awaited word on Ryan's status for the following game. The team's medical staff insisted he had none of the usual signs of concussion after the hit from McGrew, claiming he remained aware of the game situation and the playbook, and had no problems with his vision. He did, however, have a headache that worsened even before he returned to the fray. In the modern NFL it is unthinkable that he would have been allowed to retake the field, but in 1984 he was cleared to play again the following week against the still-unbeaten Dolphins.

Ryan was mostly ineffective, completing just 12 of 28 passes and going down under five sacks, but with the Jets hanging tough (they were the first team to lead the Dolphins at halftime all season and were ahead 17-14 in the final period) there was no way Walton was going to pull his starter. O'Brien did not see any action as the Jets fell to 6-4, with any realistic hopes of a division title now dashed. The following week, Ryan suffered a second concussion against the Colts, in a game the Jets lost by the unusual scoreline of 5-9. Although O'Brien was ineffective when he twice came in off the bench (five of 13 for 50 yards, an interception and another three sacks), a change was in the air after two lackluster performances from Ryan. Sure enough, on November 17, newspapers around the country carried the following simple statement in their sports round-ups: 'NEW YORK JETS–With Pat Ryan still suffering the after-effects of a concussion, Ken O'Brien has been named to make his first professional start at quarterback in Sunday's game at Houston.'[12]

The match-up with the Oilers went in similar fashion to the game with the Patriots. The Jets built a solid lead (in this case 13-0 in the second quarter) before their opponents reeled off a string of scores to take control of the game (it was 27 straight points against New England, 31 against the Oilers). The result was a sickening blow for two reasons. First of all, it put the Jets on life-support as far as the playoffs were concerned. Secondly, it was only the second win of the season for a woeful Oilers team. O'Brien's performance was nothing more than okay from a statistical standpoint. He amassed 226 yards but was not able to find the end zone, and he also suffered another three sacks, but Walton spoke in praise of his young passer, pointing out that several well-thrown balls

Under pressure against the Oilers in his first pro start (AP Photo/Richard Carson)

almost went for scores, any of which might have turned the tide back in favor of the Jets. The team made it clear that if Ryan could recover from his post-concussion symptoms, he would step back into the starting role, but the headaches were continuing as the second game against the Dolphins approached. O'Brien and Marino would square off against each other for the first time.

As the two men prepared for their first head-to-head encounter, there was no rivalry to speak off, because they had experienced vastly different starts to their professional careers. While O'Brien had taken baby steps, Marino had been leaping over tall buildings with a single bound. He had thrown 52 touchdown passes (as opposed to one for O'Brien), had passed for more than 300 yards in five games and had broken the 400-yard mark in two others. He was, quite simply, already one of the best quarterbacks in the game and although the Dolphins had suffered their first defeat of the season the week before (against San Diego), they were untouchable at the top of the AFC East with an 11-1 record. A defeat to Miami, under the spotlights of ABC's Monday Night

Football camera crews, would end the Jets' slim chances of reaching the postseason. As ABC's Frank Gifford commented during the game, 'Mathematically of course, the Jets [would be] still alive, but it would take a lot of happenings, perhaps even an earthquake, to get them in.'

Understandably, ABC was not touting the game as an O'Brien-Marino clash. The juicy storylines revolved around Marino closing in on the record for passing touchdowns in a season, Mark Gastineau's league-leading 18.5 sacks, and the fact that McNeil was approaching the team record for rushing yards in a season. Ominously, the Jets were going up against the top passing attack in the game with an injury-riddled secondary, and they were forced to drop their linebackers deep all game to protect against Marino's passes.

Once the game started, it did not take long for the announcers to become intrigued by O'Brien's potential. Gifford, Don Meredith and O.J. Simpson became steadily more enthused about his play as the game went on. O'Brien started well, hitting his first pass on third-and-nine to pick up a first down. His second attempt, on third-and-eight, was even better, a bullet to Lam Jones earning another first down. He then skied his next two passes and missed a wide-open Mickey Shuler on another third-down attempt. On his second drive, he cut through a strong Orange Bowl wind to find Shuler with two passes to move to the Miami 32 and then lofted a perfect pass to McNeil for a touchdown. Marino answered with his 33rd touchdown of the year, but O'Brien showcased his strong arm on the Jets' next drive, drawing gasps of appreciation from the commentators.

'Gosh, what an arm,' Simpson exclaimed as a pass was fired in towards Jones. It fell incomplete but the boys in the booth were impressed. 'If nothing else, Don,' Simpson said, addressing Meredith, 'Ken O'Brien has a rifle himself. You know, you mentioned earlier that they don't know what he can do. His biggest problem has been thus far this year, everyone knows what Dan Marino can do and Dan Marino was drafted after Ken O'Brien, but I agree with you, if they give this kid a chance, I think he's going to show that he rated being a No. 1 draft choice.'

A perfectly thrown pass into the end zone was then dropped by Jones, and two plays later Shuler dropped a pass that hit him right in the hands. The Jets settled for a Leahy field goal to retake the lead, but two more Marino touchdowns had the Dolphins up 21-10 by the time O'Brien took his first snap of the second half.

In a drive that saw McNeil break John Riggins' team record for rushing yards in a season, O'Brien showcased his arm strength, as well as surprising mobility. On a second-and-two from the Miami 46, he was flushed from the pocket, drifted left and then fired a fastball into Rocky Klever (called 'Clever' by Gifford – the new Jets were not yet household names) for 15 yards and a first down. Two plays later, he moved just enough under heavy pressure from A.J. Duhe to buy time to find McNeil on a short dump-off that McNeil took 26 yards to the Miami five. A Tony Paige touchdown brought the Jets as close as they would get, and the Dolphins ran out 28-17 winners on the back of four Marino touchdowns, which tied the single season record at 36.

Walton had been conservative with his young quarterback, leaning heavily on the ground game, and O.J. Simpson expressed surprise that he was still calling for hand-offs to McNeil in the fourth quarter, while trailing by 11. As if hearing the comment, the Dolphins sacked O'Brien on the very next play and Walton finally pulled the training wheels off in the final period.

O'Brien passed 18 times in the last eight minutes of the game, completing 11 for 115 yards, but the Miami pass-rush began to warm up as well, up, sacking him three times in the last quarter. It had been a gutsy performance from a banged-up Jets team, who had hung in there with the class of the AFC, but the Dolphins had been too much to handle.

'I thought we played very hard,' Walton said after the game. 'We just missed a bunch of big plays that would have helped us a lot. Like I've been saying all along, you're not going to stop them completely. You've got to try to outscore them and get a few turnovers, and we didn't get any turnovers and we didn't score enough.' [13] (Walton was forgetting an interception by Davlin Mullen in the fourth quarter.)

O'Brien is corralled by Bucs defensive end Lee Roy Selmon in the Jets' last game of 1984 (AP Photo/Fred Fox)

O'Brien had done well. Miami coach Don Shula said he had been impressed, but whether O'Brien liked it or not (and he insisted it meant nothing to him) his stats would always be lined up with Marino's, especially after head-to-head games. The situation was neatly encapsulated by Gerald Eskenazi in *The New York Times*, when he wrote: 'Until O'Brien goes to a Pro Bowl, and throws more than 30 touchdowns in a season, he will probably continue to be hounded and haunted by a fact of football life: He was drafted ahead of Marino.' [14]

Eskenazi's colleague, Dave Anderson, put it a little more succinctly. He referred to it as 'O'Brien's Bloodhound' [15], and claimed that it would be on his trail until he was able to outplay Marino and make the Jets a better team than the Dolphins.

During the game, though. Meredith had gazed into his crystal ball and seen the future: 'I've got a feeling that he and Marino will have several good games against one another before their careers are ended,' the former Cowboys quarterback commented, and he was right. O'Brien versus Marino would become one of the marquee match-ups in the NFL for the remainder of the decade. As well as the obvious intrigue over the Jets passing on Marino in the draft, the two players seemed to bring the best out in each other. Jets-Dolphins games, which had been one-sided in recent history (Miami had now won seven straight) was about to become the hottest rivalry in the league, with high-scoring shoot-outs the norm.

For now, the Jets were on the verge of a dreaded quarterback controversy, as Ryan was getting close to full health again. He insisted he was ready to practice, but Walton disagreed and named O'Brien the starter for his third straight game, against their cross-town rivals and landlords, the Giants.

O'Brien had seen six of his passes dropped against the Dolphins, and the painful trend continued in the next game, Lam Jones dropping what would have been a 59-yard touchdown on the Jets' first offensive play. Miscues like this, as well as two field goal failures from Leahy and a fumble in Giants territory by Marion Barber, allowed the Giants to pull away to a 17-0 lead. Jones redeemed himself by catching four passes for 103 yards, including a 32-yard score, but it was Shuler who emerged as O'Brien's favourite target, catching a career-high 11 passes for 127 yards in the 20-10 defeat.

O'Brien had shown poise in passing for 351 yards, but he had taken a beating from the Giants defense. Sacked three times, he was also knocked to the ground after delivering many of his 41 passes. The Jets' offense had been forced out of its usual balanced approach as McNeil was suffering from bruised ribs that made every carry an exercise in pain-management. After the game, an x-ray revealed he actually had a broken rib and his season was over.

The Jets were limping to the finish line in more ways than one, having dropped six games in a row following their promising start. Walker, O'Brien's top threat at receiver, had missed the last two games and had faded from view in the second half of the season. The losing streak looked like it would extend further against the woeful Bills the following week.

Buffalo, at 2-12, somehow opened up a 17-7 lead at halftime. With McNeil out, Johnny Hector and former CFL star Cedric Minter split the carries and produced 131 yards between them, but it was a cameo performance from Walker that turned the tide of the game. In the third quarter, he used his pace to get behind the Bills' defense and catch a perfectly thrown ball from O'Brien for a 39-yard touchdown. The critical score showcased Walker's veteran savvy as well as his speed, and made it clear how much the offense has missed him as he battled through the year with an assortment of injuries.

'It was what we call a "go pattern",' O'Brien explained after the game. 'Wesley has the kind of speed where he can go by the defensive back. That tells you something about Wesley's talent.'[16]

Walker had not simply hared down the field at top speed, though. He had slowed momentarily, fooling Bills defensive back Charles Romes into thinking he was cutting off his route.

'I tried to grab him as he went by,' Romes, said, ruefully, 'but I couldn't even do that. He seemed to slow down – and then he was by me. He just fooled me.'

'A play like that turns the momentum,' a satisfied Walker said of his big score. 'It gets it switched.'

It was one of only two catches on the day for the Jets' top receiver, and Shuler was again O'Brien's favourite target, catching six passes (and he also had a 10-yard scoring reception in the fourth quarter called back on an illegal-formation penalty). Fortunately, two plays after that rookie fullback Tony Paige crashed over from three yards out, and the Jets held on to snap their losing streak. O'Brien had his first victory as a starter in two years, dating all the way back to when he led UC Davis to a win against North Dakota State in the Division II semifinal.

The win was a relief, but Jets' fans had already switched off from a disappointing season – more than 31,500 ticket holders had failed to turn up at the Meadowlands. Walton believed his team had switched off as well. In the season's final extended practice, the coach lost his temper after seeing the offense make one mistake after another. Calling an early end to the practice, he reportedly chased his team off the field.

Some of the players were bemused. Others, especially on the defensive side of the ball, thought Walton was right to show how important it was to maintain standards. If he had employed the tactic for effect (he claimed it had been a spur-of-the-moment thing rather than a calculated move) it did not pay off. For the second consecutive week, the Jets came out flat against one of the league's weaker teams. Tampa Bay had won just five games in what would be John McKay's last season as head coach, but they jumped out to a 17-0 lead in the first half and were 34-7 up in the final period.

That was where the game took a bizarre turn. With Buccaneers' running back James Wilder within touching distance of the combined-yardage record for a single season, Tampa Bay did not take their foot off the pedal. After Wilder scored to make it 41-14 to the Bucs, they attempted an onside kick in an effort to give Wilder a chance at the record. When the onside kick failed, the Bucs allowed Johnny Hector to score unopposed (McKay would later be fined for instructing his players to let an opponent score) and then ran Wilder three straight times on their final possession.

Feeling insulted, the Jets held Wilder shy of the record, but were seething after the game. The mild-mannered O'Brien was unusually cutting.

'All I can say is that we play them again next year,' he said, 'and the only problem is that McKay won't be there.'[17]

O'Brien would make good on his veiled threat, but his own coach was even more livid at how Tampa Bay had ended the game.

'The way it ended was a total embarrassment to the NFL,' he said. 'It set it back 20 years.'

Walton's bad mood lasted into the team's final meeting of the season. With everyone eager to get away and put the frustration of a second straight 7-9 finish behind them, Walton instead subjected them to a lengthy catalog of criticism and forced them to watch game film of the humiliating defeat to the Bucs.

There were whispers by now that it was Walton's punishing practices that were leading to so many players getting hurt, and the nagging injuries suffered by Walker, McNeil, Klecko, and just about the enter defensive secondary, had ripped the heart out of the team.

The next season might be a make-or-break year. In *The New York Times*, Dave Anderson predicted years of mediocrity and struggle for the Jets, claiming they needed an injection of new talent. The Jets were already a young team and there was talent dotted throughout all areas, but the NFL was increasingly a passing league. Miami had shown what a good young quarterback could do. Marino had torn up the record books in leading the Dolphins to the Super Bowl in only his second season, and although matching that level of performance (5,084 yards and 48 touchdowns in the regular season, and another 1,001 yards and eight scoring passes in three playoff games) might have been out of reach, the Jets would need more consistent play from under center if they were going to confound the experts and become relevant again.

It was fortunate, then, that against all the expectations and all the expert opinions, O'Brien was about to become, for a few fleeting moments, arguably the best quarterback in the entire NFL.

O'Brien on his way to 367 yards and five touchdowns against Tampa Bay in 1985

Chapter Four

Top of the World

O'Brien's ascent to the summit of the NFL did not happen immediately. There was the little matter of one of the worst performances of his professional career to get out of the way first, but after that, he went on a tear. The complicated passer-rating formula that the NFL uses to measure a quarterback's efficiency is far from a perfect tool, but there is no doubt that as a performance improves, at least from a purely statistical standpoint, the rating goes up. In the 1980s, before the modern era of ultra-efficient passing (due in no small part to frequent tweaks to the game's rules to protect quarterbacks and receivers) a rating in the 80s was considered good for a single game and excellent for a season.

Over a 24-game span of regular season performances, from week two of 1985 to week 10 of 1986, O'Brien's rating was over 100 in 15 games. The Jets won 13 of those 15. The adage that Freeman McNeil was the beating heart of the Jets' offense became obsolete. It was O'Brien that paced the team. The ratings were built on a high completion percentage and low interception rate, but O'Brien was not playing a conservative, short-passing game that limited the chance of turnovers. Among full-time starters in 1985, only Dan Fouts averaged more yards per pass attempt (8.5 yards as opposed to 8.0 for O'Brien) over the course of the year. In 1986, up to and including week 10, he was even more aggressive, averaging a full yard more per attempt.

With O'Brien at the helm, the Jets had one of the most feared offenses in the game. How that came to be, and how the wings fell off in spectacular fashion at the end of the 1986 season, is the story of O'Brien's brief reign at the top of the NFL.

There were no signs that the Jets thought their young quarterback was ready to take such a big step in his first full season as starter. In fact, there was no certainty that he would even be the starter. Walton kept talking about having two quarterbacks, which was puzzling even to Pat Ryan – competitive though he was, he thought he had lost his chance to nail down the quarterback position after the promise O'Brien had shown at the end of 1984.

That is not to say the team did not have faith that their former first-round pick would be able to establish himself as the starter, but there was the feeling that things were moving faster than planned. Back in April 1983, when O'Brien was drafted, most football experts would have expected Richard Todd to still be at the controls of the Jets' offense as the 1985 season approached.

O'Brien was viewed as a project, and the team's lack of certainty over him was highlighted by the cover of the team's 1985 media guide – pictured on the cover, alongside McNeil and Gastineau, was not O'Brien. It wasn't even Ryan. It was Joe Namath, still casting a shadow nine years after he last played for the team.

O'Brien wasn't the only question mark as the Jets looked ahead to 1985. There were holes all over the roster and, in the days before free agency, there were limited options when it came to patching those holes up. There were changes off the field as well, as Walton sought to finally mold the team into the one he had in mind. In February, the Jets unveiled a new coaching staff and new philosophies on both sides of the ball.

Defensive coordinator Joe Gardi resigned his position after falling out with Walton. Positional coaches Ralph Baker (linebackers) and Billy Baird (secondary) were then fired. Zeke Bratokowski was brought in to act as quarterbacks coach (a personal mentor to aid O'Brien's development) and the picture began to settle when offensive line coach Jim Ringo quit, to be replaced by Bill Austin. Dan Radakovich, affectionately known as 'Mad Rad' by his players, was appointed linebackers coach, with a new defensive coordinator, the highly respected Bud Carson, pulling extra duty as secondary coach.

The changes would make the Jets a very different team on the field. The NFL had almost universally switched to the 3-4 defense in recent seasons, but the Jets had stubbornly stuck to the 4-3 alignment made famous by the New York Sack Exchange, the rampaging defensive line of Gastineau, Klecko, Lyons and Abdul Salaam. The Sack Exchange had faded, as players left or lost effectiveness, and for 1985 the Jets would switch to a 3-4 system under Carson. The former Marine had a dazzling resume, including acting as defensive coordinator on nine playoff outfits and three Super Bowl teams. His most enduring legacy was his role in shaping the 'Steel Curtain' defense in Pittsburgh during a six-year stint that culminated in back-to-back Super Bowl wins.

Having moved on to the Rams and then the Chiefs, Carson's career hit a speed-bump in the form of a spat with Chiefs coach John Mackovic. Carson was fired during the 1984 pre-season and didn't have time to connect with another NFL team – so he coached as a volunteer at the University of Kansas. The Jets were his doorway back into the big-time but there was a potential problem. The team did not have an experienced nose tackle, critical on a three-man line. Joe Klecko had some experience of playing the position, but that had been back in 1978 and his career had recently been blighted by injuries.

There was one more wrinkle amid the turmoil. Perhaps most surprising in the list of firings was that of Walton, who demoted himself from offensive coordinator, promoting Rich Kotite (previously in charge of the passing game) to handle that role. Walton would still call the plays on gameday, but the offense would be Kotite's command. Kotite and Walton had a long history – the new offensive coordinator had been coached by Walton during his playing days.

The quarterback situation took another twist when it was revealed that Ryan had played the entire 1984 season with a strained throwing arm. Injured during training camp, the arm had never been allowed to heal fully due to the need to insert Ryan as starter when O'Brien was sidelined by his court case. Ryan had looked solid in his time as starter, but he claimed he only been able to throw freely and with his usual zip a couple of times. A fully healthy Ryan would once more pose a significant challenge.

For O'Brien, the game might have been starting to slow down a little as he processed the experience gained in the second half of 1984. Teammates had talked of his competitive fire, center Joe Fields revealing that a couple of times he had needed a quiet word to calm down a little during the Dolphins game. Fields may have been experiencing déjà vu – his quarterback at Widener University had also been named Ken O'Brien (as well as football, this O'Brien had excelled at baseball and was drafted by the Philadelphia Phillies in 1974). It was easy to forget how far ahead of schedule the Jets' quarterback was, and how unusual his first two seasons in professional football had been. He had not exactly soured on New York, but it was a more aware, perhaps even wary player who was preparing for his third year in the Big Apple. One of the main adversaries he had faced turned out not to be opposing NFL teams, but the New York media.

'I found out that the media can be extremely harsh,' he said just prior to the 1985 college draft. 'They try to destroy the team's camaraderie and a person's belief in himself.' [1] The Studio 54 experience had clearly had a deep impact on O'Brien's psyche: 'I am wary of what I do now. I was taught a real lesson. People will take advantage of you if they are given the opportunity.'

There were, of course, positives as well. O'Brien was about to get married, and he insisted he was ready to move on from the turmoil of his first two seasons, as well as being equipped to handle the pressures of being a high-profile athlete in New York.

'I've gotten things back together and my head is on straight,' he said. 'I am excited and in shape for this season. We will try to really unite and build together. The Jets have a tough schedule, but we have the talent to make the playoffs.' [2] Asked once more about the comparisons with Marino, O'Brien made a good point: 'There were a lot of people drafted before Marino.'

O'Brien spoke cautiously, but one of his statements was perhaps more telling than he realised: *We will try to really unite*. For his first two seasons, there had been a rift at the Jets, between the players and the head coach. How far the team could unite in 1985 would have a lot to do with how far they went.

Walton was in many ways an old-school coach, who expected his players to be committed, hard-working and disciplined. Those are admirable and important qualities, but in the 1980s the world was changing. Athletes were becoming more aware of their importance to their respective sports, and were less likely to simply accept harsh words from a patriarchal figure. Walton, however, was in no mood to change his approach heading into his third season in charge, even though the results up to then had been disappointing.

'My feeling is that last year we established the work habits and the competition factor and I'm not going to go off course,' he insisted as preparations were underway for the new season. 'It's what I believe. I believe in competition and hard work and I believe if you play hard every week, you've got a chance to win and nothing is going to change my mind about that.' [3]

'Joe wants a more physical football team,' said Fields. 'He wants us to play 60 minutes for 16 games – scratch, bite, kick. Whatever we have to do.' [4]

Playing 60 for 16 was the goal of every team, but some players on the Jets believed Walton's approach made that more difficult to achieve. He ran demanding practices, and there had been enough injuries in 1984 to torpedo a once-promising season. The endless debate over whether hard practices set a team up for success during the season, or made players more susceptible to injury, would rumble on, but Walton believed his team was primed to make a jump back to competitiveness.

'It should only be natural that the experience gained by our young players last year should help us improve,' he said. 'But we have to stay healthy and be able to go the full 16-game route.'[5]

The Jets had been grounded by injuries to their receiver corps and their defensive backfield, so these were the two areas expected to receive reinforcement via the draft. Picking tenth overall in the first round, they would likely be able to add an impact player – in the event, they had their choice of all the 'skill position' players, as four defensive linemen, four offensive linemen and a linebacker were selected with picks one through nine. The best receivers and defensive backs were all available.

High on the Jets radar was a lanky receiver from Wisconsin named Al Toon. Toon, a triple-jumper as well as a football player, had grabbed everyone's attention at the end of the 1983 season, when he caught 24 passes for 537 yards in the final three games. He had been named 1st team All-Big 10 after a senior campaign that saw him catch 55 passes for 750 yards and five touchdowns, and he capped his year with a 10-catch, 124-yard, two-touchdown performance in the Hula Bowl, also appearing in the Japan Bowl, as O'Brien had.

'Al is one of those receivers you can throw high and outside to and have confidence he's going to catch it,' said his former college quarterback, Randy Wright. 'We designed plays for him to make spectacular catches.'[6]

Toon's competition as the top receiver in the draft was Mississippi Valley State's Jerry Rice, who had put up gaudy numbers as part of the 'Satellite Express' offense. His senior year saw him catch 112 passes for 1,845 yards and 27 touchdowns. Neither of the two were burners – various sources gave Rice 40-yard dash times between a respectable 4.45 seconds and a pedestrian 4.71, while Toon was clocked at between 4.5

and 4.65. What stood out, literally, was Toon's size. At six-foot-four and 205 pounds, he was physically imposing, with a huge catch radius.

Still, not everyone was convinced that a new receiver was the way to go. With the switch to a 3-4 defense, a pass-rushing linebacker would have been awfully helpful, and the Sporting News mocked Pittsburgh's Chris Doleman to the Jets with the No. 10 pick (they had Toon going the pick before, to Cleveland, and Rice going 14th). Doleman would have been a fine selection, totalling 150.5 sacks in a 15-year career, but he was snapped up by the Vikings with the fourth overall pick. The Jets had no doubts when their turn came. Al Toon was coming to New York.

'Al has outstanding size, excellent speed and hands,' said Mike Hickey, the man responsible for the selection. 'He lays out for the ball, runs every pattern hard, is durable, will catch over the middle and is a great blocker downfield. The thing that impressed us the most was that he just loves to play football.'[7]

Walton was pleased with the new weapon for his offense, although he may have initially underestimated the impact the rangy receiver would make.

'Al gives us a big, strong, durable WR that everyone looks for,' said the coach. 'He played against good competition and has another dimension having played his college career in cold weather. Al should be an excellent third-down possession type receiver.'

One of his old college coaches had no doubt the Jets had snagged themselves a special player, one who could elevate those around him as only the best do.

'Every game Al's played he's had two, three and sometimes four defenders watching his every move,' said Wisconsin's receivers coach, Fred Jackson. 'For Al, it's an invitation to go out and beat those guys, to get to the open hole. All the attention does not frustrate him because above all else, Al is a complete team player.'

Toon was a welcome addition to a depleted receiver corps that had been devastated by injury in 1984. He was not the only new target being brought in for O'Brien. Doug Allen (Arizona State, fourth round), Tony

O'Brien in training camp, 1985 (AP Photo/Lance Jeffrey)

Smith (San Jose State, fifth round) and Bill Wallace (Pittsburgh, 12th round) were also selected in the draft – but not one of them would play a single down of professional football. More intriguing was the return to the NFL of one of the Jets' former draft picks. Jo-Jo Townsell had been drafted in the same year O'Brien joined the Jets, but he had opted to play in the USFL. After three productive seasons with the Los Angeles

Express (126 catches for 1,192 yards and 16 touchdowns) he was finally coming to New York. The new faces inevitably meant some older ones had to make way. Derrick Gaffney, who did not fit in with the youth movement at the age of 30, was not asked to training camp (he would return for a brief stint in 1987) and the enigmatic Lam Jones' career was hanging in the balance after five seasons of promise and disappointment.

The big stories as training camp opened, however, were not about the players who were with the team… but those who weren't. Offensive tackles Marvin Powell and Reggie McElroy were holding out, while Toon had not signed a contract and was not allowed to attend the camp as per league rules. As the team began to take shape for a new campaign, three critical pieces were missing from the offensive side of the chess board.

Also up in the air was the overall philosophy of the team. Walton had relied on veterans in his first season, then had purged them before his second. The results had been identical 7-9 records, and now he had no choice but to continue with his youth movement because the Jets were traditionally wary of spending draft capital to bring in veterans via trade. In a nod to the feelings of his players, Walton did promise that training camp would not be as physically demanding, the hope clearly being that the team would not start to wear down by midseason.

The early feedback from training camp was unpromising. Klecko suffered another hamstring injury during sprint drills and was expected to miss a couple of weeks. After his problems the season before, this did not bode well for the heart of the defensive line. Lam Jones damaged a tendon in his right index finger after a heavy hit from Harry Hamilton and was ruled out for the first month of the regular season at least. It was a depressingly familiar story for the oft-injured player, but at the time nobody suspected that he had played his last down of professional football.

The media were keen to get a look at Pat Ryan's modified throwing motion. Under the tutelage of Bratkowski, and in an effort to avoid the problems of the previous season, Ryan had overhauled his delivery.

O'Brien, though, was the clear starter, and he was enjoying the role. Bratkowksi was coaching him up on improving his footwork (skipping was one of his new drills) in an attempt to make his dropbacks smoother and quicker, and help him avoid pass-rushers more easily. During the offseason, before the official camps, O'Brien had been able to throw passes to Walker and Sohn three times a week, and Bratkowski had added in challenging elements, getting O'Brien to play from the 20- or 10-yard lines, so that he could gain experience of the limited space in those situations. He worked with the Jets' strength coach as well, getting stronger as well as more agile, and he became a film rat, devouring the stuff in his quest to get better. Walton did not exactly gush about his young quarterback, but that was not his style. He was, however, positive.

'Ken made progress last year, but he still has a lot to learn yet,' he said. 'He is very intelligent and proved he can throw the football, now he just needs to play and experience the things that happen defensively.'[8]

At the same time, Walton was careful to make sure nobody forgot about Ryan, aware that it would have stung to lose the starting job through injury.

'Pat proved he can win in this league, displayed excellent leadership and was always prepared to play,' Walton said. 'His concussion during the season set him back, but he made tremendous progress last year which should help him in the future. Our QB situation is more stable because of Pat.'[9]

Walton's plan to give his players a less-demanding camp quickly ran into a problem – the defense seemed intent on making it as physical as possible and skirmishes broke out regularly. For new offensive line coach Bill Austin, the camp was a nightmare. Austin, who had served in the same role with the Giants' before a spell with the USFL's New Jersey Generals, was trying to patch together a line despite injuries and holdouts. With both starting tackles absent, Joe Fields injured and a second-year man (Jim Sweeney) at the left guard spot, the Jets were desperate for help. Billy Shields, an experienced, capable veteran with 117 starts under his belt, was brought in to shore things up.

The physicality of practices was raising eyebrows. Harry Hamilton, who put Lam Jones out of action early in the camp, had earned the nickname 'Harry Callahan' from offensive players, after the movie character better known as 'Dirty Harry'. Hamilton, eager to make an impression, was throwing himself around with abandon. Gastineau, finally free of his community service commitments stemming from the Studio 54 incident, was a man possessed, tearing the facemask off the helmet of offensive lineman Dave Pacella. Pacella was injured later the same day and missed the entire season, yet another injury to contend with in the trenches.

The preseason opened with a defeat to the Eagles, but O'Brien looked good and the team was leading when he left the game. Against the Bengals (a second defeat) the Jets lost receiver/returner Bobby Humphery to a fractured wrist, left tackle Shields to a knee injury and starting safety Darrol Ray to a separated shoulder. Less serious, though still concerning in the big scheme of things, was a knock that forced stand-in right tackle Ted Banker from the game.

With a roster cutdown imminent, the Jets were facing some difficult decisions, but their response was still shocking. Ray, and long-time linebacker Greg Buttle, both of whom had started the Bengals game, were cut. Bob Crable, recuperating from knee surgery, was placed on the PUP (physically unable to perform) list, ruling him out for the first five games of the regular season. Promising second-year tight end Glenn Dennison would not play in 1985, being placed on injured reserve (there were only two more receptions to come in his football career, both with Washington in 1987) and long-time fan favourite Bruce Harper, the scrappy little utility back and return man, was also out. In an eight-year career he had piled up 11,429 all-purpose yards. Four of the Jets draft picks from just a few months earlier were also let go, along with two linebackers who had started games for the Jets – John Woodring and Bobby Bell.

The linebacker situation was alarming, but it was the offensive line that was the biggest headache, with protection for O'Brien of paramount importance. By the time the preseason matchup with the Giants arrived, the Jets were bringing in just about any big man with a pulse and two healthy knees. Sid Abramowitz and Steve August joined the team just days before the game. Rookie Greg Gunter started at center because Guy Bingham, filling in for the absent Fields, had to slide over to fill Shields' spot at tackle. The football gods still did not think the Jets were suffering enough, so they gave Gastineau a fractured thumb, sustained in practice because he was trying to show the coaches how hard he was pushing. He would play with his right hand in a cast for the foreseeable future.

Both O'Brien and Ryan were under siege in the Giants game, going down under a combined seven sacks, but there was hope within the 34-31 loss, their third consecutive defeat. Townsell looked like a legitimate addition to the receiver corps, catching five passes for 62 yards, including an 11-yard touchdown, one of two scoring passes from O'Brien in a solid first half. Of particular note was the fact that he had not thrown an interception in 48 attempts over three games, despite often running for his life behind the patchwork line. The line, incidentally, was weakened still further when one of the new arrivals, Steve August, sprained a knee – after one appearance for the Jets, he was on injured reserve.

Bubbling away under all of the turmoil was the fact that Toon had still not signed his rookie deal. The Jets had a reputation for being difficult to negotiate with and in the days before rookie salaries were more or less carved in stone automatically, there was room for acrimonious disagreements. Toon and his agent, Ralph Cindrich, were disenchanted with the Jets' offer, which was an estimated $400,000 less that the package received by Russel Carter (also drafted 10th overall) the year before. On August 28, Toon, by then the only first-round draft pick not to have signed with his team, was publicly requesting a trade. The team's desire to save a few hundred thousand dollars was costing Toon valuable practice time and preventing O'Brien from developing chemistry with one of his starting receivers – and things only got worse. In the Jets' final preseason game they finally got a victory, but they lost Walker for the first four weeks of the season after he suffered a sprain to his right knee. It took a lot of the luster off a strong performance from O'Brien, described as 'dazzling at times'[10] by Gerald Eskenazi in *The New York Times.*

Expectations, at least outside the club, were not high as opening day approached. According to a leaked report, the Jets had the highest payroll in the game, but a chaotic and injury-plagued training camp and preseason did not suggest there would be much of a return on the investment. It was an era of spiralling costs, fuelled in part by competition from the USFL – average player salaries had increased 25 percent from 1983 to '84.

The Los Angeles Raiders were waiting on the other side of the country as the Jets limped their way to the starting line. All teams have to contend with injuries, even in week one of the season, and the key is how much depth is available to compensate. The Jets, however, were more like a M*A*S*H unit than an NFL team. The official injury report submitted prior to the opening game listed 12 players, and that was on top of the absences of the starting offensive tackles and the top draft pick. A league-leading 18 players were already on injured reserve, including the anticipated starting wide receiver pairing. Sohn and Townsell, neither of whom had started an NFL game, were stepping in for Jones and Walker.

A little good news came from the two Joes, Klecko and Fields, who were returning after spells out with injury. If there was hope, it lay in the promise shown by O'Brien, who had looked notably quicker in his preseason action as well as showing off his accuracy and arm strength. If the team could hold together through the early games, most commentators seemed to think, they might put together an 8-8 season. Or maybe a third consecutive 7-9 mark.

Modest though that target sounded, it appeared wildly optimistic after the debacle of week one's encounter with the Raiders. Questions get answered quickly in the NFL, and the Jets did not like any of the answers they received in a 31-0 drubbing. Would the makeshift offensive line hold up against a fierce pass rush? No, it would concede 10 sacks. Would the decimated receiver corps be able to take advantage of O'Brien's improved play? No, Townswell was the only wide receiver to catch a ball all day. Would the ground game be able to take the pressure off the passing game? No, Freeman McNeil gained just 44 yards on 17 carries and the Jets as a whole rushed for just 62.

The Jets did get a near-300-yard performance, but it was from the newly acquired Dave Jennings, who had a busy day with seven punts. Other patches of daylight in an overwhelmingly silver and black day were seven catches from Shuler and a pair of sacks by stand-in defensive end Barry Bennett. Gastineau, though hampered by his thumb injury, also grabbed a sack in limited playing time, and Klecko marked his return with the team's fourth take-down of a Raiders quarterback.

As bad as things had been on the field, the players were braced for more humiliation when they got back to New York. Surely, Walton was about to tell them exactly what he thought... the coach therefore surprised everyone by taking a much more measured approach. The man who had once harangued his players during the team's annual Thanksgiving meal toned down his act and spoke to his players in a calm and philosophical manner, appealing to them to put the game behind them and do better next time.

The new approach may have had an effect, but of more tangible value was the return of the two starting offensive tackles and the long-overdue arrival of Toon. McElroy and Powell promised to bring instant credibility to the Jets' offensive line. The duration of the holdouts (Powell had been in dispute with the team for six months) was puzzling given the team's willingness to throw around big contracts the season before. The Jets front office often puzzled its own players – they had signed a veteran stopgap, Billy Shields, and had given him a bigger salary than they were asking McElroy to accept. Whatever the underlying reason for the financial eccentricity, the Jets had jeopardised the development (and even the health, considering he had taken 10 sacks in the first game of the season) of their top quarterback. The day after the two top tackles returned to the fold, Toon signed his rookie contract, believed to be worth around $1.9 million over four years.

How much of an impact the new arrivals could have with less than a week before the second game, at home to Buffalo, was up for debate, but for the first time since he had arrived with the team, it looked like O'Brien was being set up for success rather than failure. He would repay the Jets with 20 wins (19 as the starter) in his next 25 regular season appearances, the best return from any quarterback in Jets history over a 25-game span.

If O'Brien was pleased to see the return of his two offensive tackles, then Freeman McNeil was even more so. Stymied in the first week, he cut loose against Buffalo to the tune of a career-high 192 yards on just 18 carries, part of a Jets rushing attack that piled up 288 yards on the ground.

'Freeman was playing like Superman out there,' [11] O'Brien commented after the game. The dominating ground attack made life easy for O'Brien, who completed 16 of his 24 passes for a modest 181 yards and two scores. Perhaps the most important pass of the day, however, was thrown not by O'Brien, but by Ryan. In the second half, with the Bills on ice, Ryan was given a chance to flex his arm and responded with the first completion to Toon.

Toon, rather disarmingly, had once thought the fans at Wisconsin were booing him, until he realized they were simply calling out 'Toooooon' every time he made one of his many receptions. After taking his first catch as a Jet for 50 yards, he heard the 'Toooons' for the first time as a pro. The coaches were determined to ease him in slowly, a decision his teammates did not universally agree with, and he only saw five snaps in the game, but he had given a glimpse into a bright future. On those five snaps, he was targeted three times and caught all three.

McNeil was understandably the focus of the Green Bay defense the following week, and they held him to 64 yards on 25 carries. O'Brien was unable to take advantage, completing barely 50 percent of his passes for just 138 yards. For the second straight game, however, he did not turn the ball over, allowing the Jets defense and special teams to control things.

Five sacks of Packers' quarterbacks, a pair of interceptions and a fumble return on a fake punt (giving Tom Baldwin the first touchdown of his life) kept Green Bay under wraps as the Jets eased to a comfortable 24-3 victory. The defense had not given up a touchdown in 10 quarters, and part of the credit was given to a new style of jersey – a form-hugging, slippery nylon of the type worn for years by running backs.

With the defense taking the pressure off, the Jets prepared to host Indianapolis. It was against the Colts the previous season that Ryan had made his last start as quarterback, and a 5-9 defeat had been the dispiriting result. This was a different Jets team, however. The Colts insisted they would not try to copy what the Raiders and Packers had done on their way to containing McNeil, but perhaps they should have, as the Jets running back had his second big game of the year, rushing for 115 yards on 25 carries.

The passing attack was operating efficiently, even without Walker (still injured) and Toon (still a rookie). With O'Brien completing two thirds of his passes, it was Sohn (eight receptions for 112 yards, the best stats of his career) and Shuler (seven grabs for 67 yards) that did the damage. The Colts hung tough, but a 25-20 result was the New Yorkers' third straight victory.

Amid the understandable excitement, there was caution. Two weeks down the line, the Miami Dolphins were coming to town, in a Monday Night Football match-up that would go a long way to telling if the Jets were for real or not. The Jets hadn't beaten their divisional rivals since 1981, and until they did they would not be considered a legitimate threat in the AFC East. The week five encounter with Cincinnati, therefore, was a potential trap game, and it duly turned into one of the messiest games of the season.

'This was not a good day for the sport of football,' Bengals head coach Sam Wyche said after a game that saw the teams commit a combined 29 penalties and one Bengals player ejected for kicking an opponent. 'I think it hurt the sport a little bit.' [12]

Wyche was probably overstating things a little, but it was a sloppy game. O'Brien made the most of an improved receivers stable following the return of Walker, hitting both him and Sohn on deep, perfectly timed passes for big gains. The game began to get fractious after two roughing-the-passer penalties against the Jets on the same drive. The Bengals returned the favour on the Jets' next drive, and things really heated up in the third quarter.

With the Jets leading 17-13, commentator Don Criqui pointed out that O'Brien had not been intercepted in nearly four games. Sure enough, he was picked off on the very next play, after Tim Krumrie applied a hit to prevent him from following through on a deep pass to Walker. Bengals defensive back Louis Breeden ran into his own end zone with the ball and was tackled there by Walker.

'That will be a touchback,' said Criqui, 'momentum carried him in.'

But Criqui was wrong. Having caught the ball outside the five-yard line, the touchback was not an option. Color commentator Bob Trumpy then explained at length how the Bengals would get the ball at their own six-yard line, but Trumpy was wrong as well. The officials called a safety as Bengals players surrounded them, arguing incredulously.

'Holy Toledo!' said Trumpy. 'That means the Jets get the ball back!'

O'Brien's first interception since week one therefore scored two points for the Jets and they got the ball back from the ensuing free kick. Trumpy continued to rail against the decision, but the officials had ruled that Breeden ran deliberately into the end zone, rather than going there under momentum. It was a huge call and turned the game.

Kirk Springs returned the free kick to the Cincinnati 18-yard line and with the game threatening to get out of hand as the crowd booed and Bengals players continued to complain, O'Brien hit Shuler from the seven for a 26-13 lead.

The game became increasingly chippy, leading Criqui to quip, 'We're here at the fights and a football game broke out.' Despite the turmoil, O'Brien kept his cool, leading the Jets to another field goal amid a flurry of yellow flags. They ran out 29-20 winners and found themselves tied for the lead in the division with the 4-1 Dolphins.

There was much discussion in the days leading up to the Monday night clash with Miami. Were the Jets for real? Under Walton, they had a habit of beating the bad teams and losing to the good ones (their four victories so far in 1985 had come against teams with a combined 7-17 record), but the team was brimming with confidence.

It wasn't just the suddenly potent offense that inspired that confidence, it was Bud Carson's new, attacking defense. The Jets were earning a reputation as a team that was willing to cross the line to intimidate an opponent, and it was bearing fruit. In fact, such was the desire for defenders to play with abandon, Ron Faurot found himself waived. The first-round draft pick just a year earlier, Faurot had tried to transition from defensive end to linebacker in the new 3-4 alignment, but simply could not muster the intensity and aggression that the new defense demanded.

The Dolphins came into the game with a devastating offense. After losing their first game of the season, Marino had been in imperious form, averaging over 300 yards per game through the air and throwing eight touchdowns in four wins. In the ABC booth prior to the game, both Joe Namath and O.J. Simpson stated their belief that Freeman McNeil would be the key – he had enjoyed big games against the Dolphins in the past.

After their defense forced a quick three-and-out, the Jets came out throwing, with O'Brien hitting Toon on his first two plays of the game. The passes were good for 28 yards… but Toon was only targeted once more in the entire game. The deep-threat potential of Walker was undoubtedly on the Jets' minds, but he and O'Brien were out of sync and the speedy receiver would not catch a single ball all day.

It was a careful start from O'Brien, as the ground game began to establish dominance. Equally dominant was the defense, which was in the mood to terrorize both Marino and his offensive line. On many plays it looked like an explosion had ripped through the Miami line – no sooner was the ball snapped than offensive linemen were strewn all over the place as rampaging Jets defenders slammed into them. Under intense pressure, Marino looked a shadow of his usual self, and when his passes were on target, a Jets defensive back was often there to bat it away.

In the second half, with a 6-0 lead, O'Brien and the offense began to turn up the heat.

'He's big, strong, and he can fire the football with a flick of the wrist,' Gifford had said in the pre-game introduction, and O'Brien was showing all of this. Although frequently pressured himself, he steadily built the Jets' lead, finding Kurt Sohn with a perfectly thrown bullet for a 15-yard touchdown to start the third quarter, and then driving the team to 10 more points after Marino had threatened a comeback.

Asked for his opinion on O'Brien, Namath (who had seen his number retired during a halftime ceremony), said that he was, 'Rapidly improving, definitely becoming one of the better quarterbacks in the NFL.' By the end of the game, Namath was praising a 'brilliant offensive performance by this offensive line for the Jets and Kenny O'Brien.'

Gifford chipped in: 'He's having a sneaky great night on his own, overshadowed by a tremendous performance by Freeman McNeil.'

McNeil had indeed enjoyed a spectacular day, rushing for 173 yards and catching passes for 46 more. Johnny Hector had added another 51 yards on the ground as the Jets chewed up the Dolphins' run defense, but O'Brien had been far from a passenger. Nor had he been simply a game manager – his passes were deadly accurate and he had completed 18 of them for 239 yards and a touchdown. Miami simply had no answer, having been comprehensively beaten in a game that turned out to be far more straightforward than the most optimistic of fans could have hoped for. The Jets were 5-1, and they were alone on top of the AFC East.

The game had exacted a toll, however. In one of the more bizarre injuries of the season, Tony Paige sprained an ankle while celebrating his fourth-quarter touchdown that iced the game. Johnny Lynn, who had made his first start at safety, suffered a knee injury and was considered doubtful for the next game and McNeil, who had looked to be in pain several times against the Dolphins, was so battered that he was unable to practice during the week and eventually did not play against the Patriots.

There was a feeling among fans and observers of the game that the Jets could not yet be trusted. Beating the Dolphins was good, but they needed to follow up that win against two tough opponents. The Patriots were only 3-3, but as divisional rivals they always brought a little extra to a Jets game, and they had beaten the New Yorkers twice a year earlier. Then came the Seahawks, who had some sort of hex over the Jets, who had never beaten them in seven previous games.

Sure enough, the Patriots proved a handful. Although Tony Eason was out with an injury, veteran Steve Grogan had a fine history against the Jets, compiling a 10-3 record and once throwing five touchdowns in a single game. He was going to be rusty (he hadn't started a game for 13 months) but he'd looked sharp the previous week, when relieving the injured Eason. The rust showed, as Grogan completed barely a third of his passes and put together a miserable 50.4 passer rating... but as if to prove that the rating formula is not foolproof, this was enough to beat the Jets, because on just 11 completions, Grogan piled up 171 yards and a touchdown, and his old legs added the game-winning three-yard run late in the final period.

The defeat came on the back of a mixed showing from O'Brien, who completed less than half of his passes. The disjointed nature of the Jets receiving corps was an issue, though – they had not yet been able to fire on all cylinders. Against the Patriots, Walker had a huge game, with six catches for 140 yards, including plays of 52 and 49 yards, but Toon was invisible.

The receivers were not yet being unleashed in tandem, but the Jets were beginning to feel their way towards the explosive passing offense that would soon be their trademark. As well as Walker's two huge plays, O'Brien tried to find him several other times on long bombs as Walton developed trust in his quarterback. On a third-down play from their own five-yard line, Walton called a deep pass to Shuler and O'Brien delivered, dropping back into the end zone and firing a pass to Shuler for a 28-yard gain.

'If you ever want to question Joe Walton, what he feels about his young quarterback, O'Brien, this tells you a lot,' said color commentator Bob Griese. 'Backed up inside your own five-yard line, [Walton] calls a big play to get them out of the hole.'

The deep passing was not quite enough. After Walker's 52-yard catch, which placed the ball inside the Patriots' one-yard line, the Jets failed to get into the end zone, Tony Paige fumbling after a reception and handing possession back to New England. The absence of McNeil was undoubtedly a factor. Hector did well in reserve, rushing for 80 yards on 21 carries, but the mere presence of McNeil appeared to make the team better.

'Freeman is the pulse of our offense,' Walton had said prior to the game. 'All the guys look to him and when he's not there, we feel the void. His health is the key to our offense.'

That was underscored against the Seahawks, where McNeil returned and posted his fourth big game of the season, rushing for 151 yards on 22 carries. Even with McNeil on form, the win required a second-half comeback after Seattle eased out to a 14-0 halftime lead. O'Brien had led the Jets to just 80 yards through the air but they remained patient, even so far as running the ball twice to convert a first-and-20 after a penalty. Eventually, momentum shifted and O'Brien had the chance to orchestrate a comeback. Trailing 14-10 with just over nine minutes remaining, the Jets started a drive at their own eight following a good punt from Seattle's Dave Finzer.

O'Brien proceeded to put together a perfect drive for the winning score. With Walton alternating run and pass plays, he completed four of four for 13, 12, 33 and 15 yards, the last 15 going to Walker for the go-ahead touchdown. The game was significant not only because it gave the Jets their first ever win over Seattle, but because it was also the first game in which both Walker and Toon caught passes. Although neither player was prolific (Walker's scoring reception was his only catch of the game and Toon caught just three balls) both players grabbed a pass on the game-winning drive.

'It's a great feeling,' O'Brien said after the game. 'It's not really a

O'Brien about to be sacked by the Seahawks' Terry Jackson (Kevin Reece: Icon Sportswire via AP Images)

pretty win, but it's a big win. It's much more meaningful to come back and win a close one like that, than to win 42-0.'[13]

At 6-2, the Jets remained atop the division, but a worrying trend was developing. O'Brien, who had been doing a decent job of avoiding sacks following the week one disaster, was suddenly being hunted down. The Patriots had sacked him five times, the Seahawks seven. Two of the biggest hits he took were on the last two plays of the game-winning drive against Seattle. First, he was levelled after a 33-yard pass to Kurt Sohn.

'Let's give him [O'Brien] high marks right here,' commented Merlin Olsen. 'Tremendous pressure. He knew he was going to take a lick. He stayed right in there, he delivered that football on target and just got buried back there, but a gutsy play, a fine play by Ken O'Brien.'

'That's an unusual connection, collegiately,' added Dick Enberg in one of his whimsical moments. 'The University of California Davis to Fordham for a big gain and a first down.'

Two plays later, O'Brien took another huge hit after delivering the touchdown pass to Walker and looked shaky as he walked off the field. Noteworthy was the fact that Klecko, one of the toughest guys in football, came out to check on O'Brien as he shuffled off the field. Plays like this were earning the respect of his teammates, and of the commentators.

'Another pinpoint pass,' Olsen enthused. 'Again buried as he threw the football. Let's give him another nod for great courage.'

O'Brien had now been sacked a league-leading 33 times. The following week, Walton gave him a day off from practice, citing a bruised right elbow, but he was bruised and battered all over. He was young and strong, but the cumulative punishment would inevitably take a toll. For now, youth and strength were winning out, and O'Brien's star was rising. In fact, he was about to embark on one of the best streaks of his career.

From week nine to week 14 of the 1985 season, O'Brien put together six consecutive games with a passer rating over 100. The streak included a 62-28 demolition of Tampa Bay in which the

Jets gained revenge for the perceived lack of respect shown by the Bucs in that controversial 1984 game. Extrapolating statistics is a dangerous game, but it is tempting to look at just how good O'Brien was during this six-game spell, a sequence in which he established himself as one of the top quarterbacks in the NFL, despite having less than a season's worth of starts under his belt at the start of the streak.

Against Indianapolis, Miami, Tampa Bay, New England, Detroit and Buffalo, O'Brien completed 133 of 206 passes for 1,886 yards, 16 touchdowns and just two interceptions. Over a 16-game season, those numbers would extrapolate to 5,029 passing yards, 43 touchdowns and five interceptions, for a passer rating of 116.5. Nobody would beat that in an actual season until Peyton Manning registered 121.1 in 2004. The streak included four 300-yard games, having managed just one in his previous 13 starts. Against Indianapolis he threw three touchdowns in a game for the first time, then threw five against the Buccaneers two weeks later and three more against Buffalo to end the streak.

There was one stat to give pause, and it might just have been the most important stat of all – he took 22 sacks during the six games, which would equate to 59 in a full season, a number that would lead the league in most of the seasons O'Brien played in the NFL. Despite his fine play, the Jets were only 4-2 in the six-game run, and a loss to Miami in week 10 was particularly heartbreaking. With a chance to drive a stake into the Dolphins' hearts (a Jets win would have put them three games clear of their main divisional rival), the Jets had mostly controlled the game, enjoying more than 34 minutes of possession as O'Brien passed for a then career-high 393 yards and McNeil rushed for 107.

O'Brien had put the Jets ahead by three points with less than two minutes to play, after hitting Rocky Klever for a 20-yard touchdown at the end of a desperate drive that included a fourth-down conversion. But the Dolphins had a great passing duo of their own, in the 'Marks Brothers' – Mark Clayton and Mark Duper. It was Duper, recovered from a broken leg he had suffered in week two, who torched the New York secondary for the 50-yard touchdown that won the game.

The bitter defeat was a coming-out party for Toon. Having caught just nine passes in his first eight games, he exploded for 156 yards on 10 receptions in Miami. He followed up with six for 133 against Tampa and was off and running on a streak of his own – he would catch at least three passes in 52 straight games.

Walker and Toon were in harness for the entire string of games, and rapidly becoming one of the top pass-catching duos in the league. Nothing epitomised the strike capability of the new-look Jets better than a drive against the Bucs in week 11. Starting at his own six-yard line, O'Brien completed a 16-yard pass to Walker and then a short pass to Toon (making his first career start), who broke away from three tacklers to score on a 78-yard play as cries of 'Toooon' rained down from the stands. The 62-28 shellacking was the biggest win in Jets history, and O'Brien passed for four touchdowns in the first half alone. The Jets almost pulled off something unheard of – holding possession for an entire quarter. In the fourth period, buoyed by an 18-play drive that devoured more than 11 minutes, they held possession for all but 23 seconds.

'I believe in myself,' O'Brien commented after his record-setting display. 'I believe I can complete any pass I throw.'[14]

His confidence was justified – he hit on 12 consecutive passes at one point, but saw that as just a beginning: 'I believe I can do 12 in a row or 20 in a row,' he said as the belief surged through him. 'I want to be the best. You can't be the best if you make mistakes. Some days are like this. You must take advantage of what develops.'[15]

The Buccaneers game was significant in another way. It was O'Brien's 16th game as starter, and pro football prognosticators now had some hard data to chew on. The stats made appetising reading. O'Brien had completed 60 percent of his passes for 3,815 yards, 24 touchdowns and 13 interceptions. For the 1985 season, O'Brien was leading the NFL in terms of passer rating, measuring 97.3, significantly ahead of Marino's 79.5.

'Even to statniks, the NFL rating system for passers is somewhat convoluted and confusing,' wrote Dave Anderson in *The New York Times*.

'But his No. 1 rating this week indicates that Ken O'Brien is now a prize instead of a prospect, a bargain instead of a bust.' [16]

O'Brien was drawing serious attention for his play (as opposed to his draft status or off-field issues) for the first time as a Jet, and the media was having trouble figuring him out. Though undeniably competitive (the fire would occasionally reveal itself after a big completion or touchdown) he was mostly an even-keeled player, one who refused to talk about his own play and instead emphasised the collective nature of the game. If ever a reporter wanted to provoke a flash of emotion, they might bring up the Studio 54 case, ancient history by now but still enough to trigger a momentary burst of frustration. Soured on the criminal justice system, O'Brien (a pre-law student at UC Davis) no longer planned for a career in law after his playing days were over.

Zeke Bratkowski was becoming more and more impressed with his young charge as the rough edges were smoothed out. And there were still a few rough edges – a tendency to speak quickly carried over into the huddle, where O'Brien's near-perfect recall allowed him to bark out a play in a flurry of words that teammates sometimes struggled to follow.

'I've never been around a QB who has the recall he does,' Bratkowski commented. 'Not too many things get him rattled. It's because he studies so hard. Kenny knows the stuff so well, it comes out like a computer in the huddle.' [17]

As the season progressed, this tendency was curbed.

'You can tell Kenny is more in command by the way he controls the huddle,' Joe Fields claimed. 'You can tell by the tone of his voice. He tells us what we're going to do and tells us to be aware of certain things that could happen.'

In short, he was becoming the leader of the Jets offense. After taking out their frustrations on Tampa Bay, O'Brien led the Jets into a critical divisional match-up against New England. Once more they would face their old nemesis, Steve Grogan, a throwback who called his own plays. He didn't get to call many, as he was rolled by Ben Rudolph after a pitch-out, breaking his leg. Tony Eason played the rest of the game, and he did well, but the game turned on a combination of plays. First, the defense forced a fumble as Irving Fryar went airborne looking for the end zone. Harry Hamilton recovered the ball and after a short dive from Hector, O'Brien hit Walker on an 88-yard touchdown, the third-longest completion in team history.

'What a perfect throw,' Merlin Olsen said, simply.

The game was not won, as the Patriots came back to tie things up at 13-13 and force overtime, but then a forgotten man made his contribution. Since the emergence of Toon, Kurt Sohn had been seeing less and less of the ball (he would catch just five passes in the last five games of the season), but he was a capable punt returner and was given the job after injuries to Kirk Springs and Jo-Jo Townsell. In overtime, he got his chance. Fielding a 51-yard Rich Camarillo punt, as the game fizzled towards an anticlimactic tie, Sohn eluded the first coverage, ran left, then cut hard upfield, ripping off a 46-yard return that set up Pat Leahy's game-winning field goal. The Jets had the division lead to themselves once more.

The other defeat in the streak of games was a Thanksgiving Day disaster in Detroit. The Lions were a decent team, but the Jets had fallen into a habit of getting behind early in games. Against Seattle and Tampa Bay they had been able to rebound from 14-0 deficits, but they had failed to overhaul the Dolphins after going 14-3 down. They trailed by 14 at halftime against the Lions, and were once more unable to reel in their opponent. O'Brien suffered seven sacks, but the most punishing hit came after he had delivered a pass in the second quarter, a brutal hit in the small of the back from Randall Gay that nearly cut O'Brien in half and resulted in a penalty. After the disappointing loss, O'Brien responded with another demolition, this time of the hapless Bills. Three touchdowns (including a team-record 96-yarder to Walker) and 370 passing yards eased the New Yorkers to a victory that put them at 10-4 and in a three-way tie at top of the AFC East.

The streak of fine games ended, as many streaks did that season, against the Chicago Bears. In the run-up to the game, the Jets had made it clear they were aware of the challenge posed by a Bears defense that was playing at a historically high level.

'We might have to try some things,'[18] Walton said, enigmatically, in the days leading up to the game. It suggested the Jets would unveil some trickery, or at least a few new wrinkles, and O'Brien added a little more insight.

'I haven't done a whole lot of rollouts,' he said, suggesting he might be trying a few. 'They [Chicago] are one of the best defenses and it can carry their team.'

Chicago had lost just one game all year going into the week 15 clash, and the Dolphins had exposed a potential weaknesses in the Chicago system with their stunning victory – Marino had repeatedly rolled out, behind pulling offensive linemen, to buy time for his speedy receivers to find holes in the Bears' secondary. It was a blueprint that offered hope – O'Brien was not known for his mobility, but neither was Marino.

'When Miami beat them, they executed every play the way they wanted to,' O'Brien said. 'They didn't make mistakes. We have to do the same. I think we're coming on and playing good football and not making the mistakes we made earlier on offense.'

As well as the Bears' defense, there was also the matter of handling Walter Payton at the top of his game. He had rushed for at least a hundred yards in nine consecutive outings. Payton's streak came to an end against the Jets, as he was held to just 53 yards on 28 carries, but with the Jets needing a near-perfect game on offense, they got off to the worst possible start. O'Brien found Shuler to convert their first third-down of the day, but Shuler fumbled the ball before taking any contact, and the Bears recovered to set up their first score, a Kevin Butler field goal.

The offense settled down on their next possession, moving the ball smoothly. O'Brien had completed his first four passes, three of them to Toon, and John Madden, covering the game for CBS, commented on how much O'Brien loved his big new receiver.

'Ken O'Brien was talking yesterday about Al Toon,' said Madden, 'and telling us how much he liked him. He said that right now, he's one of the best in the league, and he said someday he's gonna be the best in the league, he said the best of all the guys, once he gets this whole thing figured out.'

The Jets put together their best drive of the day, helped by a pass interference call on Dave Duerson, and were poised to score after McNeil gained eight yards with a strong run to the six-yard line. O'Brien's first incompletion of the day followed, as he tried to find Toon in the end zone. A near-perfect lobbed pass on third down was then batted away by Duerson at the last moment, and Walton settled for a field goal to tie the game. A turning point came when an interception by Kirk Springs was wrongly ruled to have been incomplete – this was before instant replay and there was no way to challenge the clear mistake. Instead of the Jets taking over, the Bears continued their drive and scored the only touchdown of the game, a seven-yard pass from Jim McMahon to Tom Wrightman.

The Jets offense had looked efficient and potentially dangerous, but there was little of the tactical chicanery hinted at prior to the game. They played conservative football and O'Brien's dropbacks were mostly conventional. Uncharacteristically, his passes were often inaccurate, and he sometimes appeared to be out of sync with his receivers – Toon did not catch another pass after snaring three in the first quarter. A swirling wind, with gusts reaching 30 mph, was hampering quarterbacks, kickers and punters alike.

On the Jets' first offensive play of the second half, Walker was open for a touchdown, but O'Brien's pass fell short. Though not under pressure, he did not set up properly, hopping into the air to throw, as if anticipating pressure that had not materialised. Against the 1985 Bears, chances like that could not be missed and Chicago duly improved to 14-1 with a suffocating, 19-6 victory. The Jets were held to just 11 first downs, while O'Brien was sacked four times (he lost the ball twice) and managed just 122 passing yards. The offensive line had struggled, as many did that year, to contain the aggressive Bears' defense. Reggie McElroy, working against Richard Dent, had a particularly rough day, giving up two sacks.

The loss left the Jets in second place in the division and threatened much worse – if they failed to beat Cleveland in their season finale, they were at risk of missing the playoffs for the third straight season.

Cleveland were in contention for the AFC Central title, despite their modest 8-7 record going into the last game of the season. The Jets were favored, but they were also hurting. McNeil had been banged up all year and O'Brien was becoming increasingly battered. Factoring into the wear and tear was Walton's reluctance to rest his stars even when a game was beyond doubt. The Jets had led Indianapolis by 35-3 at halftime in week nine, but McNeil, nursing a broken rib, had more carries in the second half than he did in the first, and O'Brien was left in despite having been given a day off practice the week before because he was so banged up.

For the second straight season, the defensive secondary was a catalog of walking wounded. On the critical Duper touchdown against Miami in week 10, the Jets had just five defensive backs left out of the eight who had started the game, and were unable to put double coverage on the dangerous receiver, trusting instead to a blitz to get home. The blitz did not get home and the game was lost.

'I'm not one to make excuses for losing because you are what your record says you are,' Ted Banker would later recall when looking back on this period. 'But we always had a lot of injuries at the end of the season. We did practice an extreme amount with full pads – where a lot of other teams just didn't do as much as we did.'[19]

The punishment taken by O'Brien was the most concerning. With a game still to play, he had tied the NFL record for sacks endured by a quarterback in a single season, with 59. Many of them had left him clearly shaken up, but each time he had shrugged them off. The Jets' nightmare was a hit that he would not be able to shrug off, and that dire scenario had appeared about to play out in the second half of the Bears game, where O'Brien came under intense pressure and repeatedly landed on his right arm after taking hits, often laying on the hard Meadowlands turf for a few moments, in obvious pain.

The sight of their quarterback clutching at his right elbow after getting back to his feet was a warning, and it was heeded. After his poor performance against Chicago. McElroy was benched for the final game of the season. Ted Banker had given McElroy a breather a couple of times against the Bears, but now the change was more substantial. Also feeling the heat was first-year offensive line coach Bill Austin, one of the slew of new coaches brought in by Walton. Most seemed to have settled in, some spectacularly (as with Bud Carson), but Austin's unit was the team's weak link, and it was threatening to derail the season.

A battered quarterback was not the only consequence of the line's struggles – the ground game had also lost effectiveness. In the first half of the season, McNeil had rushed for 796 yards in seven games. Since then he had managed just 461 in six games, and his average had dropped from 5.1 to 4.1. Walton was vocal about his dissatisfaction with his line, but there was little that could be done apart from trying Banker at tackle.

The game against Chicago had been cold. Against Cleveland a week later, it was even colder – 24 degrees, with a wind chill factor that made it feel like 12. The combination of numb hands and a hard ball would make things interesting all day. The defense made a statement on the opening play, Gastineau tackling Kevin Mack for a five-yard loss to set up a three-and-out. After the Browns punted, O'Brien ran onto the field with breath plumes billowing from his mouth in the frigid conditions. He was also wearing a pad just below the elbow, on his right forearm, the first time such extra padding had been visible.

Walton unveiled a no-huddle offense, obviously keen to get his team playing rather than thinking, but after a second-down incompletion, the experiment was abandoned. A faltering start got worse when McNeil fell into the back of Banker's leg, breaking it and bringing McElroy back into the line after just six offensive plays. McElroy's first series was rough. On third down, he gave up a sack that was almost a safety, almost a fumble, but somehow avoided being either.

'The 60th time he's been down this season,' Bob Trumpy commented on O'Brien. 'He's been on the mat more than Hulk Hogan.'

A short punt by Dave Jennings, from the back of his own end zone, then set up Brian Brennan for a 37-yard touchdown return and the Jets were struggling. Humphery fumbled the ensuing kickoff return but managed to recover it himself. McElroy then came close to allowing a second sack, Carl Hairston getting to O'Brien a split second after his arm began moving forward – for a moment it looked like a sack and a fumble, but it was ruled an incomplete pass. On the very next play the Jets got another slice of luck. An overthrown ball from O'Brien was easily picked off by Don Rogers, but Kurt Sohn alertly ripped the ball out of his hands (Rogers was playing with one hand in a cast) and galloped into the end zone for a 39-yard score. On the sideline, Walton looked angry, and O'Brien was clearly seen arguing his case about the near-interception, but the head coach turned away. Sohn later admitted that he had run the wrong pattern on the play, cutting to the inside instead of the outside.

As the Browns closed in on the field goal that would tie things up at 10-10, the game was developing into a curious one. In the first quarter, the teams had almost equal time of possession and equal offensive yardage, but how they were getting it done could not have been more different. The Browns had 88 rushing yards and zero through the air, while the Jets had just eight yards on the ground and 71 passing yards.

McElroy gave up another sack on the Jets' next drive, Curtis Weathers taking O'Brien down. Again, he came down on his right elbow and seemed to clutch at his forearm as he sat on the turf. McElroy was getting beaten consistently on pure speed rushes, defenders simply running by him before he could engage. He would later admit to being distracted by unspecified personal problems during the first half.

'I think the Cleveland Browns have found a weakness,' said Trumpy. 'Watch Reggie McElroy on Weathers. Now that's an offensive tackle at 280 pounds against a linebacker [who] just shoves the offensive tackle out of the way and O'Brien [is] on the ground for the 61st time this season.'

The sensitivity of O'Brien's elbow was becoming an issue. Don Criqui referred to him suffering from a 'dead elbow', which was the sort of injury that would flare up and worsen each time he took a blow to the injured area. As always seems to be the case when you are nursing an injury, O'Brien was falling on his right elbow repeatedly.

Only good fortune was keeping the Jets in the game. On third-and-long after the latest sack, McNeil fumbled following a nice gain, only for the ball to bounce right into Hector's hands. As if sensing they needed to take control of the game, Walton called a fake punt on the next play, which Tony Paige turned into a 30-yard scamper up the middle to set up a first down, but two plays later, McNeil fumbled again and this time the Browns recovered. It looked like it was going to be one of those days.

With New England in control of their game against Cincinnati, and the Broncos having won the day before, the Jets now needed to win to make the playoffs – they had run out of scenarios where they could lose and back in. But O'Brien was under siege. Bob Golic flattened him after an incompletion and he had to scramble to the left on the next play to avoid more pressure, again throwing incomplete.

His statistics over the previous six games were flashed up on screen and Don Criqui commented on how well he avoided interceptions.

'Oh, he has paid a price though,' Trumpy chipped in. 'They gotta put some extra pads on the seat of his pants cos he's seen this turf a lot.'

The Jets defense was returning the favour, Gastineau sacking Bernie Kosar to set up the go-ahead score (a five-yard Hector run), but the mood in Giants Stadium was nervous. O'Brien continued to take hits, and Trumpy expressed his sympathy after he was drilled by Chip Banks after throwing an on-target pass that was dropped by McNeil.

'I wonder what that feels like,' he mused. 'You're a quarterback, you gotta try to get the ball off and you're staring right into the facemask of one of the hardest hitters there is in the game. I guess it's like standing out in the middle of the rush-hour traffic, right?'

The traffic proved especially dangerous a couple of plays later, as Hairston easily beat McElroy again and levelled O'Brien, as well as hurrying him into an inaccurate pass that was intercepted. O'Brien could be seen doubled up in pain after getting back to his feet, cradling his right elbow with his left hand. As the teams went into halftime with a 17-10 scoreline in favor of the Jets, it was clear that both their season and the health of their quarterback were very much up in the air.

Interestingly, O'Brien came out to start the second half without the padding on his right forearm. Another huge hit from Hairston on the first drive left the Jets quarterback on one knee, surrounded by staff, as Pat Ryan pulled his helmet on. O'Brien walked to the sidelines, looking shaky after taking a shot directly to his right ribs after delivering the ball, but he was back in after one play, having officially had the wind knocked out of him.

A leaping catch from Toon and another leap from Hector, this time a dive into the end zone, gave the Jets breathing room for the first time. Two Leahy field goals put them 20 points clear in the fourth quarter, but when the Jets got the ball back, with just over eight minutes on the clock, O'Brien was still under center and McNeil was still in the backfield. The star running back, who had been banged up for most of the year, was given the ball on four of the first five plays of the drive, causing Trumpy to question Walton's thinking.

'Don, I read an article in preparing for this football game… Joe Walton himself said, "We've got to guard against over-using Freeman McNeil." I read the scoreboard 30 to 10, I wonder why Freeman McNeil is still getting the ball, now his 24th carry, 75 yards… and they play next week. They need McNeil as fresh and as healthy as possible.'

The same could be said of O'Brien, who had been battered throughout the game and yet was still dropping back under pressure to find his receivers. After the two-minute warning, O'Brien hit Mickey Shuler with his 76th catch of the season to set a Jets record, and Tony Paige scored from a yard out to make the final score 37-10.

After the game, Walton offered three main reasons why the Jets were better than a year ago. First he cited the health of the team, then the improved play of O'Brien, and then the impact made by Bud Carson. People might have taken issue with the team being healthy, given how banged up the two biggest offensive stars were, but there was no doubt

Carson had turned the defense around, and O'Brien had established himself as one of the top quarterbacks in the game.

'Ken O'Brien played well all year,' Walton said. 'He became our leader and will be a great one for years.'[20]

The Jets had made the postseason for only the fifth time in their history and would be playing their third consecutive game in the harsh environment of Giants stadium. It would be a short week, as they would face the Patriots in the AFC wild card game the following Saturday. The tight schedule presented a challenge. Raymond Berry, coach of the Patriots, chose to give his players time to recover as best they could from a hard regular season. They had Tuesday off, just as they did every week. In contrast, Walton moved the calendar forward a day and treated Tuesday like a Wednesday, meaning his players were practicing.

The wild card game pitted two of the original AFL franchises against each other for the first time in the playoffs. It also matched up a pair of childhood friends and fellow Quarterback Class of '83 alums. O'Brien and Eason had been linked together since their high school days, having first met at the annual Optimist Game, a Sacramento high school tradition, when O'Brien's Jesuit High played Eason's Delta High (although O'Brien didn't actually get into the game). After that, the two young men became close.

'We used to work out together, and both our families are close,' O'Brien said as hype built for the showdown. 'We used to all go out together, and I'd try to get Tony in trouble. It wasn't that hard to do.'[21]

There was respect between the two players as well as friendship.

'I knew how good Kenny was,' Eason said. 'I knew the day the Jets got him they had the right man for their system.'

During the 1985 season, the Jets played 13 of 16 regular season games on AstroTurf, including their last six games, when O'Brien began to wilt under the punishment he was receiving on a weekly basis. Much has been written about AstroTurf, about the fact that it meant you were hit twice on every play – once by the opposing player and once by the turf itself – about the fact that it felt like playing on concrete, about the fact that it would burn off exposed skin if you were unfortunate enough to slide along it. The turf also made the game faster, and Hall of Fame tackle Dan Dierdorf commented that he enjoyed aspects of the playing surface – it's predictability, the fact his feet would not slip out from under him when setting up to block. Dierdorf also had to have both knees and both hips replaced after playing 13 years on the AstroTurf at the Cardinals' Busch Memorial Stadium.

The debate was a complex one, and there were studies that suggested there was no greater injury rate on AstroTurf than on natural grass – but the players almost uniformly loathed it. Until the Jets and Giants installed natural grass in 2000 (it was replaced with the more advanced but still controversial FieldTurf after just three seasons), they had to play on the 'carpet'. And it was about to end their season.

Going into the wild card game, the Jets knew exactly what they had to do in order to have a chance of beating the Patriots.

'We know there's a burden on us to keep the defense off Kenny, to give him the time he needs,' said right tackle Marvin Powell. 'The Patriots come at you hard, with lots of blitzes, and it's always a punishing afternoon against them.'[22]

O'Brien completed his first pass in the playoffs to his most reliable receiver, Shuler taking the ball out from the 16-yard line to the 23, but the drive fizzled after an uncharacteristic drop from the same man on third down. Andre Tippett killed the next drive with a sack on third down and Tony Franklin booted the Patriots into the lead from 33 yards on New England's next possession.

The Jets had yet to pick up a first down, but O'Brien connected with Walker for 16 yards to start their next drive. The camera didn't catch the impact, but O'Brien took a heavy hit after delivering the pass and was in visible pain as he walked up the field, his right forearm held close to his body. McNeil was then shaken up on the next down, leaving the game for a couple of plays. Both of the Jets' key men on offense were hurting.

Garin Veris took O'Brien to the turf for his second sack, but he rebounded with two accurate passes, 21 yards to Shuler and 15 yards to Toon. McNeil ended the first quarter with two jinking runs to gain a first down at the New England 11, and the offense was humming. From there, on the first play of the second quarter, O'Brien threw his first touchdown pass in the playoffs, to Hector.

O'Brien had the Jets marching again as time ran down in the first half, hitting his tight ends, Klever and Shuler for nice gains to set up a first down in Patriots territory. He had completed 10 straight passes and looked to be taking control of the game… then he was intercepted on a poorly judged deep pass to Walker, and Eason hit Stanley Morgan on a 36-yard pass to take the lead.

After a good kick return to the 36, Walton kept his foot on the pedal, and O'Brien avoided a heavy rush to thread the ball to Toon at the New England 48 as the clock ticked below one minute at the end of the first half. The Patriots were keying on McNeil, holding him to 23 yards on 10 first-half carries. He remained the focus of the Jets attack, with a run and a short reception setting up a third down, which is where the game changed completely.

O'Brien was hit by Tippett just as he delivered a pass, taking the blow under his right arm. The camera panned to the pass falling incomplete, but quickly snapped back to the Jets quarterback, who was rolling on the ground in obvious pain. Then he became ominously still, on his knees, head touching the ground, hands on each side of his helmet as if that might stop the ringing in his ears. The seconds ticked by and he was surrounded by staff as Ryan warmed up on the sideline. O'Brien did not want to leave the field, but he did not know where he was.

A replay then showed exactly how hard he had been hit. With Tippet bearing down, O'Brien had cocked his arm to throw, but then reset. The extra split-second this took proved disastrous. Tippett's hit was legal, but the impact lifted O'Brien off his feet and pivoted him in mid-air until he was past the horizontal. In wrapping O'Brien up, Tippett also pinned his left arm, meaning he could not reach out with it to break his

O'Brien is lifted off his feet by Patriots linebacker Andre Tippett...

fall. His left shoulder and head hit the hard Giants Stadium turf about the same time, and they hit it hard. As O'Brien walked to the sidelines, looking dazed, Walton understandably chose to punt on fourth-and-six rather than risk a fourth-down play at midfield.

O'Brien was deemed able to return to the game in the second half, but Walton was being cautious, calling runs on the first five plays before taking to the air for the first time, an off-target throw to Hector. O'Brien later admitted to having called the wrong play in the huddle, from the wrong formation. His thinking had been slowed by what was undoubtedly a serious concussion, and disaster then struck again. After the Patriots drove for a field goal, they forced a fumble on the ensuing kickoff and Johnny Rembert returned it for a touchdown. From a tight 13-7 game, two plays had put the Patriots up 23-7 and the fact that Rembert might have been down by contact on the play was no consolation.

When the Jets came out after another kickoff (Hector almost fumbled the ball again), it was Ryan who lined up under center – O'Brien's day was done, having suffered what was officially termed a 'mild concussion'.

... and then dumped on his head during the 1985 wild card game (AP Photos/Ray Stubblebine)

'He took a helluva hit,' Ryan commented. 'After that he wasn't very lucid.'[23]

'Things weren't clicking in my head,' O'Brien added. 'Obviously the coaching staff was concerned because I wasn't 100 percent sharp mentally.'

Ryan played well, tossing a touchdown to Shuler, but the Jets were on their way to a bitterly disappointing playoff defeat, only the second time they had been beaten at home during the entire season. The defeat put paid to a shot at redemption for the Jets, who would have travelled back to the LA Coliseum in the next round of the playoffs, the place where their season had started with that shocking 31-0 defeat. Instead, they were heading home early, already looking to next year, and the number one priority was clear. They had to improve their offensive line.

The 1985 season had been a success in many ways. O'Brien was voted MVP by his teammates, he earned a vote in the AFC Offensive Player of the Year ballot (open to 56 sportswriters who covered the game) and he made the Pro Bowl as an alternate after Dan Marino was unable to play. He also led the league in passer rating (96.4), finished third in yardage (3,888), sixth in touchdowns (26) and lowest in interception rate (just 1.6 percent).

And yet there was a realisation that another stat might have been the most important. He had been sacked 62 times in the regular season and hit on many other plays. He was tough, but the wild card game had shown that he was not indestructible. With limited mobility, and a tendency to hold the ball for too long while looking for a target to present itself, he did not need good protection, he needed exceptional protection. Walton talked of wanting to halve the number of sacks his quarterback endured.

In the days before free agency, there were limited options when it came to fortifying a struggling line. The draft was the obvious route, but it almost always entailed waiting a year or two for a player to mature, even if you drafted a good one. Rejigging existing resources was also an option, and the Jets would try both of these approaches as they started their planning for the 1986 season. Walton also found a third way to make a change. He fired offensive line coach Bill Austin after just one season. Linebackers coach Dan Radakovich was the rather surprising replacement, especially as he was open about preferring to stay with his linebackers. Radakovich had flip-flopped his entire career, coaching the Steelers defensive line in 1971 and the offensive line from 1974–77 (during which time he helped Pittsburgh win two Super Bowls). A spell as defensive coordinator with the 49ers was then followed by a return to offensive line duties with the Rams, Broncos and Vikings. He was clearly a multi-talented coach and his initial view was that around half the sacks conceded by the Jets were not the fault of the line, but rather due to O'Brien holding the ball for too long. Jim Vechiarella stepped in as linebackers coach, having worked with defensive coordinator Bud Carson before, most recently with the Chiefs in 1983.

For Austin, it was the end of a long and distinguished coaching career that had begun back in 1958 and had included two stints as head coach in the NFL, with the Steelers from 1966–68 (he was succeeded by Chuck Noll) and with the Redskins in 1970.

The first moves had been made to improve the 1986 version of the Jets, but there was one more thing to get through before preparations could start in earnest – the Pro Bowl. It seems unfathomable now that after a gruelling season, the NFL would ask its best players to go out there once more, on the hard AstroTurf of Aloha Stadium in Hawaii, to play a meaningless game. The intensity was toned down, but this was still a full-tackle game. As well as O'Brien, McNeil, Gastineau, Klecko and Lance Mehl made the trip to Honolulu. On one play, Gastineau registered a strip sack and cavorted joyfully, free from the constraints of a regular NFL game and able to celebrate as he saw fit without drawing a penalty. On the next play, O'Brien was fortunate to find Pittsburgh receiver Louis Lipps with an 11-yard touchdown. O'Brien took a hard hit on the play, one of many absorbed during the game, but finally his season was over, having completed eight of 15 passes for 87 yards and the one touchdown. He received just $5,000 for the game, the same as every member of the AFC's losing team (the winning team received $10,000 per man).

With this distraction out of the way, the team could look ahead, and O'Brien could start to recover from a bruising season.

Of the 56 players under contract at the end of the 1985 season, the Jets had acquired 41 through the draft. Trades had been extremely rare in recent seasons, after the team got its fingers burned in several disastrous transactions in the 1970s. The draft would remain the main focus, and the needs were obvious. At least one and possibly two offensive tackles, an outside linebacker with blitzing ability, maybe a quality running back who could team up with Johnny Hector whenever Freeman McNeil was nicked up, and a defensive back who could stay healthy.

The Jets selected offensive tackles with their top two picks. This was laudable as they sought to keep their franchise quarterback on his feet, but the Jets pulled off a major 'who?' pick by taking Iowa's Mike Haight 22nd overall. Haight was undersized, at 270 pounds, but the Jets cited his intelligence and maturity as major plus points – the team was fixated on bringing in men of good character, but even Haight admitted to being surprised when he was selected so high. To make the pick more puzzling, the Jets had spoken to Haight about maybe switching to guard.

After reaching for Haight, the Jets played things straight in the second round, drafting the physically imposing Doug Williams from Texas A&M. Williams was a tackle through and through, and had been hyped as a potential first-rounder.

Nobody could accuse the Jets of not trying to fill their needs – the next three selections were all linebackers. In total, the Jets selected four offensive tackles and four linebackers and clearly felt they had addressed their major issues. A couple of running backs and a defensive back in later rounds filled out what looked like a solid effort to plug the holes in a talented roster. Such was the feeling of confidence after the draft, the Jets felt able to cut starting right tackle Marvin Powell. There were rumbles that Powell's election as president of the players' union had played a part in the decision, but he had declined over the previous two seasons. Still, cutting an experienced lineman with the line a key area of emphasis going into training camp was a surprising move.

The Jets talked about a double-pronged approach. First, they would try a reshuffle – moving Reggie McElroy to right tackle, switching Jim Sweeney from left guard to left tackle and bringing Ted Banker in at left guard. The second approach would see draftees Haight and Williams at right and left tackle respectively, as back-ups at first, but hopefully quickly moving into the starting lineup. To further help, Walton planned to introduce the shotgun formation, to give O'Brien a little extra time to read oncoming pass-rushers and, hopefully, get the ball out of his hands more quickly.

'We have the start of a good program,' Walton said on the verge of training camp. We have the nucleus of a good young team and a good mix of veterans. The experience of playing in tough games last year – winning some big ones and losing some big ones – the experience has to help.'[24]

Walton seemed especially satisfied with the reshaping of his team. It had been a sometimes brutal process, but this was now a team that was built in his image.

'The most pleasing part was that the guys played hard almost every week, almost every game,' he said. 'It shows the good character and the type of people that our organization is trying to put on this team. They're willing to work and play hard. We're headed in the right direction, but we've got to start again in 1986.'

Walton's approach didn't always sit well with his players, but he was getting results, and the Jets were preparing for a new season as a team on the rise, one that demanded respect. Joe Klecko was not the kind of man to pay lip service to anybody, but he spoke out in support of Walton's methods: 'The Jets started to win again after Joe got rid of cocky people, and got people who will work,' said the man who had just become the first player ever to be named to the Pro Bowl at three different positions. There was also no doubt that O'Brien had won the respect and support of his teammates, not only for his play, but for his toughness.

'Joe Klecko said that maybe O'Brien should be playing nose tackle,' tight end Rocky Klever commented. 'Quarterback is not always a standard for toughness, but Kenny is tough.'[25]

'We feel good about Kenny's progress and we're confident he can get better,' was Walton's assessment. 'He displayed physical and mental toughness last year and gained leadership and respect from his teammates.'[26]

Still, that offensive line was a worry. A lot would depend on how quickly the two rookie tackles could make an impact. The team was effusive about both of them. On Haight, Mike Hickey said: 'Mike is one of the most competitive linemen I've seen. He plays with great tenacity and has rare football intelligence. He has the ability to play tackle or guard. Mike is an outstanding person with a great work ethic.'[27]

'Mike impressed us with his pass-blocking techniques,' Walton added, 'and he showed us he has the experience and background to step in and give us help in an area we need it. Mike displayed the ability to finish all his blocks and then give a little more downfield. We've added one more competitive, hard-working type athlete.'

It was clear to see why the Jets had fallen in love with Haight. He was exactly the type of player they were looking for: competitive, hard-working and of high character. An extra plus, in the mind of Walton (who had been a 5'10", 185-pound tight end), was that he was a little undersized for the position. There was nothing Walton liked more than an undersized scrapper.

There was nothing undersized about Doug Williams, the second-round draft pick.

'Doug is a massive physical specimen with good athletic ability and excellent feet for pass blocking,' Hickey said of the 6'6", 290-pound second-rounder. 'He is very strong and can be a devastating run blocker.'[28]

'Doug has the size and great feet that you need to be an outstanding pass blocker, which impressed us at the Senior Bowl,' said Walton. 'He will solidify the competition we need to improve our offensive line.'

There were similarly upbeat comments about other picks. Linebacker Tim Crawford 'can be an excellent blitzer in Bud Carson's scheme'[29] according to scout Sid Hall. Rogers Alexander was 'a tough player who doesn't quit and makes things happen,'[30] in the words of Hickey. Ron Hadley, the third linebacker chosen in succession, 'makes a lot of plays and just loves to play,' according to scout Marv Sunderland. 'He also has great special teams temperament.'[31]

It looked like just the kind of draft the Jets needed. The reality was very different. With an impeccable sense of timing, as the team was primed for big things with the injection of a little more talent and depth, Hickey had delivered one of the worst drafts in NFL history. Simply put, the Jets' 1986 draft was stunning in its ineptitude. Out of 11 players selected, seven did not play a single game for the Jets. The remaining four players combined for 101 games and just 43 starts, and all of those starts came from Haight. The draft class looks a little better when you consider that the cast-offs made a total of 33 starts for other NFL teams, but 17 of those were in the so-called 'replacement' games during the 1987 strike. Hickey had found just one NFL-caliber player in 11 selections, plus one useful special teamer (fullback Nuu Faaola).

It was a draft to freeze a franchise in time, and the repercussions would be felt for years, as the players who should have matured into quality starters and backups simply were not there when they were needed. Late-round misses can be forgiven, but the middle rounds need to offer a supply line of backup-quality players who can fill out a roster. The Jets got a grand total of one game out of the linebacker trio drafted in rounds three through five.

At the top of the draft, of course, nothing but starters will suffice. Haight went on to enjoy a decent career, but as a guard rather than a tackle, which was where the Jets had the greatest need. In contrast, Williams pulled off something remarkable when he was cut before the preseason was over. Despite their focus on character, the Jets scouts had failed to see that Williams was unreceptive to advice, had sluggish footwork and poor technique. He went into a sulk when not drafted in the first round and never came out of it, at least not as a Jet. He made nine starts for the Oilers and that was it for his NFL career.

A draft that could have solidified the team instead gave a lesson in the dangers of drafting for need. In a draft meant to be strong at the tackle position, few players emerged as quality pros, the exceptions being Will Wolford (drafted by the Bills two spots before the Jets) and Steve Wallace (a fourth-round gem picked up by the 49ers). Jim Dombrowski (drafted sixth overall by the Saints) was a solid pro, but spent most of his career at guard. Far better value had been available at linebacker – Pepper Johnson and John Offerdahl went just after the Doug Williams pick, but neither was the kind of pass-rusher the Jets were looking for.

Retrospective deconstruction of a daft class is hardly fair, but the paucity of return from the 1986 class was nevertheless remarkable. In the

1985 draft, the Jets had selected players who would give them 343 games and 194 starts. In 1984 the return was a dazzling 683 games and 444 starts. The miserable 1986 draft impacted (quite literally) on O'Brien, as the Jets had no option but to go with their offensive line reshuffle. As training camp opened, both of the top two draft picks were unsigned, part of a theme around the league as clubs looked to cut wage bills and players resisted – late in July, only three first-round picks had signed contracts.

Haight, pencilled in as a backup at right tackle, signed his deal on 22 July, the day before rookies were to report for training camp. His deal was for less money than the previous year's No. 22 pick (William 'The Refrigerator' Perry) had received, but Haight claimed he did not want to appear greedy. His signing came amid a flurry of deals that left Williams as the Jets' only unsigned rookie. Veterans were starting to drift in as well, although they weren't required to report until 25 July. Many of them, including O'Brien, were sporting cropped hair. Rocky Klever had started the fad, cutting his own hair and then doing the same for O'Brien, resulting in the Jets looking more like military recruits than a football team.

Williams signed on 27 July, and weighed in at 305 pounds, making him the biggest Jet in training camp. There were some eyebrows raised at his weight, and he also made it clear he was not happy with the switch from right tackle (where he had played in college) to the left. With all personnel now in camp, the line would have a week to prepare for a scrimmage against the Redskins on August 2.

At the same time as the offensive line began to introduce themselves, O'Brien was working on the little details that might reduce the amount of punishment he would have to absorb in the new season. Working through progressions more quickly was key. Many of his sacks in 1985 had followed a familiar pattern – he would cock his arm to throw, hesitate, reset… and then get hit. Under the continued tutelage of Bratkowski, he was being trained to dump the ball off underneath if neither of his primary targets was open, and to process the information more quickly.

He was also encouraged to run more. Although that was never going to become a major weapon in his arsenal, it might limit the number of times he was stationary when hit by a blitzing defender.

There was a setback during the Redskins scrimmage, as Haight hyperextended his left knee and was expected to miss up to a week of practice. The development of the line as a whole, however, appeared to be coming along and Walton expressed cautious satisfaction. That tune changed after the opening preseason game, which saw the Packers beat up on both Jets quarterbacks. The Jets' two most experienced linemen (and the highest-paid in the league), Dan Alexander and Joe Fields, were kept out of the game, and pressure poured through the middle of the line repeatedly. Six sacks were registered (only one on O'Brien, although he was also hit four times just after delivering a pass), and both quarterbacks were bruised and battered at the end of the game. Ryan was so beat up he was unable to practice the following Monday.

A ray of sunshine came in the play of Williams, who replaced Sweeney at left tackle and looked solid. Walton insisted he was not ready to start, but the club had to be pleased that he was looking the part. On 16 August, the Jets quietly announced that Haight would switch to left guard when he returned from his hyperextended knee. Williams was now the only chance of getting some new blood at the tackle position, unless one of the later-round picks (seventh-rounder Bob White or 12th-rounder Sal Cesario) became a major surprise Shockingly, Williams would last just two more weeks with the team.

In a preseason victory over the Bengals, O'Brien completed 11 of 17 passes for 137 yards and two touchdowns. Alexander and Fields were back in the starting line-up, but O'Brien still suffered two sacks and numerous other hits. Three more sacks came in the second quarter of the next game, against the Giants, despite Walton having O'Brien roll out of the pocket to give himself more time. Two days later, Williams was cut.

It was the first time in team history that a second-round draft choice had been cut before even starting the regular season. Mike Hickey, attempting to put a positive spin on the situation, suggested that the line was gelling strongly in its reconfigured combination even without the rookie, but that rang hollow. In reality, it was a damning indictment of the team's scouting process, and also raised questions about why the player was given no chance to gain a little experience and improve his standard of play. Several players spoke out about Williams' attitude, saying he never asked any of the veterans for advice and was unreceptive to coaching. Others mentioned his poor footwork. Offensive line coach Dan Radakovich suggested it was a combination of physical and mental deficiencies.

It all added up to a big question mark – not so much over the player, but over the front office's decision to draft him so high. A day later, the Jets pounced on tackle Gordon King, a nine-year pro who had started 51 games for the Giants. He turned out to be a shrewd pick-up, starting nine games for the Jets in 1986.

The preseason ended on an upbeat note. O'Brien was sacked just once in a victory over the Eagles and connected with Toon on a 71-yard scoring pass (the last 60 yards of the play were accounted for by Toon's speed after making the catch, not to mention a fine block from Walker). The season was about to start, but on the Tuesday before the opening game, Mike Haight was placed on injured reserve, never having fully recovered from his knee injury. The move meant the Jets had achieved a dubious distinction. Not one of the 11 players they had drafted back in April was on the 45-man active roster on opening day. Walton, who had seen what standing pat had achieved back in his first season as head coach, had been determined to inject new blood to keep the Jets moving forward, but aside from some minor moves, he had been foiled. The Jets were essentially running back the same team they had in 1985.

The first game of the 1986 regular season would be a short road trip to play the Bills. The arrival of Jim Kelly, after two prolific seasons in the USFL, added spice to the game – the AFC East was now home to four of the five quarterbacks taken in the first round of the 1983 draft. The Jets would also be playing Denver, in week six, so O'Brien would be measured against four of his fellow 1983 draftees.

Jets players had indulged in a little gentle ribbing of O'Brien prior to the game. They had taken to wearing t-shirts bearing the slogan 'If you can read this, throw the ball' underneath their playing jerseys. The reminder to get rid of the ball rather than taking sacks was playful, but it was also critical to the team's hopes in 1986.

The Jim Kelly era started in ominous fashion, with a 53-yard drive culminating in his first touchdown pass as an NFL player. He would become a destroyer of the Jets, but for now he was still an unknown quantity. O'Brien found Paige and Toon with short passes as the Jets tried to respond, but the drive stalled as O'Brien was flushed from the pocket on a third-down play. Encouragingly, he showed good mobility to avoid the sack and then did what everyone had been asking him to do for a while – he threw the ball away. O'Brien was once more wearing padding on his right elbow, suggesting it was still a problem.

The Jets' special teams then struck. Rushing up to field a short punt from Dave Jennings, Walter Broughton muffed the catch and after the ball bounced around for a while, the Jets recovered at the Bills' 15. Paige scored from the one to tie the game up and after a second Bills turnover the Jets had possession again at their own 27. The Jets were passing on first downs, a clear change from their offensive philosophy the previous year. As part of a concerted effort to keep McNeil healthy (he had barely played in the preseason), the change also put O'Brien in fewer obvious passing situations, where a defense could tee off on him. Nevertheless, he took his first sack of the season on a third-and-three, Eugene Marv coming free on a blitz to bury the Jets quarterback for a 10-yard loss. On the sideline, Walton was incensed, but O'Brien had been offered the merest of windows to throw the ball away and had not taken it. Later, Bratkowski and Ryan could be seen talking to O'Brien in a more measured way, but the message was almost certainly the same.

On their next drive, the Jets set Buffalo up for the deep pass. Three straight running plays put them at the Bills 46, and just as commentator

Bob Griese remarked that the Jets were looking good on offense but failing to put points on the board, Toon streaked downfield on first down and O'Brien lofted a perfect pass that was caught at the 10. Toon took the ball into the end zone and the Jets' deep-passing game had clicked for the first time in 1986.

'That's the quickest way to quiet a crowd down,' Griese commented.

O'Brien had recognized a blitz package and knew he had to get the ball out of his hands quickly.

'If you're going to blitz, Al Toon is a big horse out there,' he said after the game. 'Everybody rushed me. I don't know how I got rid of the ball so quickly.'[32]

The Jets were in control, but they were getting a glimpse into the future. Kelly was impressing, and a second-year defensive end called Bruce Smith was beginning to make an impact. A Smith sack ended the Jets' first drive of the second half, and Kelly hit another rising star, Andre Reed, for the 55-yard score that put them in front in the final quarter. Kelly, Smith and Reed were to torment the Jets for years, and with the addition of Thurman Thomas in 1988, they would begin a period of dominance over the entire AFC.

For now, the Jets still had a little too much for them. O'Brien displayed some unexpected elusiveness when Smith next came calling, after beating Jim Sweeney to the inside and bearing down on the quarterback. O'Brien calmly stepped to the side and flicked a short pass to Tony Paige for a nice gain.

'We know how many sacks O'Brien took last year, 62,' said Griese. 'Maybe this is a little bit of his movement in the offseason. He moves around a little bit, moves in the pocket, gets rid of the football, turns a busted play into a positive play.'

The play kick-started a drive that retook the lead on Hector's one-yard run, and another long touchdown play then more or less sealed the game. Bills defender Derrick Burroughs went for the interception on a short pass to Walker, leaving the Jets receiver free to scamper for a 71-yard touchdown.

'He gambled and lost,' O'Brien commented, succinctly.

As a season-opener, there were many positives, and O'Brien's performance (72 percent completions and two touchdowns) had been quietly impressive. His play had caught the attention of Frank Gifford, who handled the Jets' game in week two. It was a short week for the Jets, with ABC's Monday Night Football crew working the Thursday night game. Gifford was full of praise as the teams were introduced.

'Kenny O'Brien is a special young man,' he enthused. 'This will be his 24th start and he plays this game like he's been playing it forever. He is solid, he is strong, he'll stand there, and sometimes he'll stand there just a little too long looking to get something done. Last year he was sacked a record 62 times and believe me, that can smart.'

Whether it was the short week that threw the Jets off (although of course it was the same for both teams) the game was a nightmare for the New Yorkers, as they interspersed good plays with mistakes, penalties and turnovers. While it was still close, Gifford and his new booth partner, Al Michaels, commented on the fact that the Patriots' Tony Eason had set the previous NFL record for sacks in 1984, with 59.

'I find it amazing they're both walking around,' quipped Gifford.

On the next play after Gifford's comments, McNeil carried the ball on a routine run, but stayed on the ground afterwards. A replay showed how he had flailed with his right arm in an attempt to maintain balance, falling awkwardly on it in the process. His elbow was dislocated and he would miss four weeks. When he was taken into the trainer's room, McNeil was greeted by the sight of safety Harry Hamilton being stitched back together. After making a tackle, he had been driven head-first into the ground, inadvertently, by teammate Kyle Clifton. The shuddering impact had driven Hamilton's helmet into the skin of his forehead, leaving a gash along his scalp that would require 27 stitches and leave him blind for several days because of the amount of swelling. He had walked to the sideline pressing a towel to his forehead to hold it in place, his uniform spattered with blood.

'It does appear to be some kind of a laceration. Highly unusual with the sophisticated headgear that they wear,' commented Gifford, unaware that it was the headgear itself that had caused the laceration.

Ironically, in one of his worst games for some time, O'Brien mostly enjoyed excellent protection against a fierce Patriots pass rush. There were some puzzling moments though, like when the Jets coaches asked Hector to block Andre Tippett one-on-one. Tippett, the man who had knocked O'Brien out of the wild-card game the previous season, duly threw the smaller back out of the way and sacked O'Brien.

As the game progressed, it was clear that O'Brien's radar was off. He was intercepted twice and could easily have been picked off three or four more times if the Patriot defenders had taken their opportunities. Several of his completions were also thanks to great catches rather than accurate passes, and his deep ball was badly out of sorts – he was intercepted heaving the ball up for Shuler and overthrew Walker on another pass that might have been a touchdown.

The dispiriting defeat was notable for one reason. With instant replay introduced for the first time, the game saw the first overturned play as the result of a review. Teams were not able to ask for reviews themselves, and all challenges came from the replay booth. The league had announced it expected reviews to take around 20 seconds, but fans at Giants Stadium were treated to a three-and-half minute delay while it was decided if the Jets were facing fourth-and 14 or fourth-and-18 after a potential four-yard catch from Toon. He was eventually awarded the meaningless catch, while Gifford and Michaels had some fun talking about the delay as an official held a walkie-talkie to his ear waiting for the call.

'I'm sorry, that's kinda funny,' Gifford said.

'Funny unless you have a plane to catch,' Michaels replied.

The game ended with the Patriots firmly in control, and the 20-6 scoreline flattered the Jets, who had been comprehensively outplayed. They now had to face the Dolphins, and without McNeil, O'Brien would need to carry the team. He responded with his most famous game as a pro.

The 1986 week three encounter with Miami has gone down in legend as the archetypal 1980s shootout. The rivalry between the two teams had already been intense for years, but now it was elevated to a level that few rivalries have ever matched. O'Brien would later reflect on why the Jets-Dolphins games during his career always seemed to be so special and he admitted that it was simply because Miami, and Marino, forced the Jets to be at their very best, and even lifted them out of their comfort zone.

'We would always run – we were more fifty-fifty,' he said of the Jets' usual offensive philosophy. 'But then once you get behind and you get in a shootout, you've got to score, you've got to throw, and you do things that maybe are a little different for you. And it seemed like against Miami, that was always the case. It was great for a quarterback because you can go do everything you can and lay it on the line, and put the ball in your playmakers' hands, and let them go up and make catches.'[33]

As time was running out in the game, with the Jets trailing 45-38, O'Brien had put the ball up 39 times and his receivers had made 25 catches, good for 390 yards and two touchdowns. It had been a great game by any measure, but Marino had outgunned him, completing 30 of 50 passes for 448 yards and six touchdowns. With just five seconds left on the clock and the ball at the Miami 21-yard line, few people watching the game would have expected O'Brien to attempt four more passes before it was all over.

Those four passes eclipsed everything that had gone before. In the second quarter, O'Brien had thrown two gorgeous deep balls to Walker, connecting for touchdowns of 65 and 50 yards. The balanced offense alluded to by O'Brien had seen three touchdowns come on the ground, two from Hector and one from Dennis Bligen, but all of that was mostly forgotten – because O'Brien completed those four remaining passes, for 89 yards and two more touchdowns.

Walker had nearly been the villain rather than the hero. It was his fumble that had set up Miami's go-ahead score with just over four minutes remaining.

O'Brien delivers a pass in the Jets' legendary game against Miami in week three of 1986 (AP Photo/Bill Kostroun)

'I was so down on myself,' he commented. 'I thought I lost the game for the team.' [34]

In fact, he said as much to O'Brien, but the quarterback encouraged him to stay positive: 'I told him, "No, Wes, believe we'll come back."'

The first comeback attempt fizzled, and when the Jets got the ball back, there was just a minute and four seconds remaining. They were 80 yards from the Dolphins end zone and they had just one timeout. A few hopeful long bombs might have been expected, but instead Walton kept things calm. A five-yard pass to Shuler and an eight-yard scramble from O'Brien got the ball moving, and then a 'hook-and-lateral', where Shuler caught a short pass before pitching the ball to Hector, netted 28 yards but forced the Jets to burn their last timeout.

'Who was the scriptwriter today?' mused Dick Enberg in the commentary booth.

'Well, he came straight out from Hollywood,' Merlin Olsen replied.

On the next play, Walton went to the hook-and-lateral again, but this time the Dolphins sniffed it out and Shuler was forced to keep the ball, battling through defenders to reach the sideline and stop the clock after a four-yard gain. A 14-yard pass to Shuler then left the clock running, and in the days when a quarterback could not simply spike the ball to stop the clock, O'Brien had to loft it out of bounds as the seconds ticked away.

'Good, smart, quick play,' Olsen said, approvingly, 'but we are down to the last few heartbeats of this game, Dick.'

Enberg then proceeded to give a masterclass in commentating, calmly outlining the situation and then getting out of the way: 'The ball sits on the 20-yard line,' he said (it was actually the 21 but we'll forgive him that one hiccup), 'and this is the play. Sent in by the man who calls it, Joe Walton… Tony Paige, the messenger, gives it to O'Brien, and five seconds to tie it up.'

The play was called '78 Fullback Hide', and involved flooding the right side of the field with three targets to confuse the defenders. If they weren't open, Shuler would float out after blocking to offer an outlet, although it is doubtful he would have made more than 10 yards. On the field, O'Brien took the snap and dropped back. He cocked his arm to throw, reset and took another step up into the pocket, before rifling a pass towards the end zone and a leaping Wesley Walker.

'Walker… *Touchdown! Oh my!*' was Enberg's immortal description of the play. He then remained silent for 24 seconds, a lesson to today's commentators, many of whom think their job is to never close their mouths. (WABC radio announcer Charley Steiner was not quite as restrained. It took four days for his voice to recover after the game.) When Enberg finally spoke again the pure excitement was still evident in his voice. 'Wesley Walker's third touchdown of the game comes with time expired! Now Pat Leahy to kick the extra point necessary for overtime.'

Leahy duly slotted the kick, to a huge cheer from the 40,000 or so fans who hadn't left early.

'Unbelievable!' said Enberg. '45-45… overtime!'

'When I came down, I knew I had to lean,' Walker said when describing the critical play, perhaps the most famous play in Jets history aside from Matt Snell's touchdown in the Super Bowl. 'I couldn't believe I wasn't hit immediately. When I realized I was in the end zone, it was instant shock. I didn't even realize there was no time left on the clock.'[35]

'I dropped back and waited and waited... and just waited for Wesley to get anywhere near the end zone,' O'Brien said. 'And I threw it about as hard as I could and the next thing I knew Wesley was flying through the air and made a great catch and rolled in the end zone. As soon as we won the coin toss I knew we were going to score. Everything was going our way at that point.'

Overtime started with more drama. Having spent three and a half minutes deciding on a meaningless four-yard catch the week before, the replay officials didn't bother to check a fumble by Jets returner Michael Harper on the kickoff that started overtime. The Jets got a play off, a 13-yard completion to Toon, before the replay booth could get involved, and followed with another 12-yard strike to the same player. Slashing runs from Paige and Hector then set the Jets up at the Miami 43.

Overtime rules were simpler in 1986 – the first team to score would win, and O'Brien closed the game out with a perfectly judged deep pass to Walker. The Dolphins had left backup corner Don McNeal in one-on-one coverage and Walker simply ran by him.

'O'Brien going for it all to Walker,' Enberg said, breathlessly. '*Touchdown! Oh my!*'

'Any time Wes gets a step on a defender, he's gone,' O'Brien said of the play. 'I just threw it and the next thing I knew, people were jumping all over me. This should end any talk about Wesley being over the hill. This should answer all the questions. And he's not even 100 percent.'

Walker had come into the game nursing a groin injury, but six catches for 194 yards and four touchdowns was his best return in the pros. Toon had also broken the 100-yard mark, with seven catches for 111, while Hector had filled in well for McNeil, gaining 82 yards on 22 carries and also making three catches for 46 more. For the Dolphins, the Marks Brothers had been explosive. Duper had seven catches for 154 yards and two scores, while Clayton had eight for 174 and one touchdown. The combined net passing yardage, 884 yards, was an NFL record. Walker's performance perhaps should not have come as a surprise, groin injury or not. In 15 previous career games against the Dolphins, he had caught 10 touchdowns.

Olsen mentioned during the telecast how well the Jets offensive line had held up. With perhaps the best protection he had enjoyed as a pro, O'Brien had shown how lethal he could be, and Walton was ecstatic.

'This is the best game I've ever been in,' the Jets coach stated. 'We saw two great quarterbacks. I don't think you'll see better, especially as young as they are.'[36]

In *The New York Times*, Dave Anderson realized the importance of the victory, and especially of O'Brien's performance, when he wrote, 'thank you for proving that you don't have to look over your shoulder at Dan Marino ever again.'[37]

It was September 21. The Jets would not lose again until late November.

One of the most remarkable elements of the Jets' nine-game winning streak in 1986, a streak that had some calling them the best team in the NFL, is how many injuries they had to overcome. Eventually, like a wildebeest with four or five lions hanging off it, the injuries dragged them down, but in the early going, they displayed a knack for shrugging them off.

Lost amid the ecstatic scenes as the Jets left the field following their dramatic win over Miami was the fact that Johnny Hector was limping. Already missing their top running back, the Jets were now asked to manage without their backup. Hector had a sprained foot and was soon hobbling around the team facility in a cast. Dennis Bligen would get the starting nod at halfback in week four, but he was nursing a turf toe injury himself. Both Tony Paige and Marion Barber could expect expanded roles, and Barber would start if Bligen was unable to go, meaning the Jets could go into the game with their fourth-string halfback leading the way. Rocky Klever, the Jets' Swiss Army knife, would fill out the depth chart in the offensive backfield. He was the emergency quarterback too, as well as the stand-in kicker, punter, holder...

In previous seasons, such a targeted blitz of their running backs room would have left the Jets floundering. They still liked to run a balanced offense, but O'Brien's climb to the upper echelons of the NFL meant they could now rely on his right arm rather than McNeil's legs. On defense, Gastineau was dealing with an abdominal injury picked up in practice, and his streak of 108 consecutive starts was broken against Indianapolis. Despite the injuries, and despite the risk of a let-down following the emotional week three win, the Jets dominated in week four, building a 26-point lead and holding the Colts scoreless until the last 14 seconds of the game. O'Brien was subdued, passing for just 184 yards and throwing two interceptions as the Colts played deep to take away the long pass. The story of his season so far was alternating great games with poor-to-mediocre ones. His passer ratings in the first four weeks read 140.8, 43.8, 126.0, 59.9.

Joe Fields, known to his teammates as 'the General', sprained his right knee on the fourth play of the Colts game, struggled through a few more plays and was then replaced by Guy Bingham. Fields was expected to miss up to three games but eventually missed seven. And just as Bligen had cracked the starting line-up, he was knocked out with a knee injury of his own (he would not play for the Jets again in 1986). The loss of Fields was especially troubling for an offensive line that was beginning to find its feet, but remarkably, the line did not miss beat.

O'Brien went into the week five rematch with the Bills as the newly crowned AFC offensive player of the month. Hector was back, and clearly eager to make up for lost time. In one of the best games of his career he rushed for 117 yards, including a 41-yard romp on a draw play, and also made nine catches for another 100, but with the Bills roughing up O'Brien, the Jets trailed 13-7 going into the last minute.

On a four-yard touchdown pass to Al Toon in the second quarter. O'Brien had been hit, low and late, by Darryl Talley. The play drew a personal foul flag, but the 15 yards assessed on the kick-off were no consolation as O'Brien was doubled over on the play, his right knee twisting awkwardly underneath him. Perhaps looking for revenge, Marty Lyons later went after Jim Kelly, triggering one of the most memorable calls from an official.

'There's a personal foul, on number 99 of the defense,' said Ben Dreith, mistaking Lyons for Gastineau. 'After he tackled the quarterback, he's givin' him the business down there, that's a 15-yard penalty.' Dreith's enthusiastic call even included a passable imitation of the blows Lyons had been delivering to the Buffalo quarterback while on the ground.

Such antics aside, time was ticking away when, trailing by six, O'Brien dropped back from the Bills' 33, found nobody open and dropped back further to elude the oncoming Guy Frazier. As O'Brien threw the ball away, Frazier fell on his legs, twisting O'Brien's right knee again. After limping around for a few moments, he was helped off the field by two trainers. It looked like the Jets had just suffered their most devastating loss of the year as Ryan trotted onto the field to take over.

O'Brien missed just one play, but time continued to tick away until the Jets found themselves in a familiar position – at their 20-yard line with less than two minutes to play and needing nothing less than a touchdown. Hector took a short dump-off for 19 yards, following with nine more on a swing pass. Walker then caught a pass at the Buffalo 36 with a minute and five seconds remaining and O'Brien saw a chance to strike. Calling the same play at the line, he locked his eyes on Walker, drawing the attention of the Bills' defensive backs and leaving Shuler completely unmarked. O'Brien found him for the tying score and Leahy then kicked the Jets into a one-point lead that would be enough to win the game.

O'Brien had taken the Jets 80 yards, all through the air, in less than a minute, but in contrast to the jubilation shown after his game-winning toss to Walker in week three, he simply shuffled off the field, clearly in discomfort. Just as against Miami, he had orchestrated a game-winning drive inside the final two minutes. Just as against Miami, he had completed 29 passes, his career-high mark. He had completed 15 straight at one point, another career high that also matched the team record, set by Namath. Still, his body language was subdued at the end of the game as he walked slowly off, clapping his hands to show his appreciation for the fans who had stayed raucous until the end. He knew he was hurt. The only question now was how badly.

The early diagnosis was damaged cartilage, but it would take an arthrogram to be sure. If there was ligament damage, he would be out for a number of weeks. If it was just cartilage, he might be able to play against the Patriots the following week in a knee brace. It turned out the truth was somewhere in between – doctors found no ligament damage, but he was still considered doubtful for the Patriots game. Further investigation, via an arthroscopic exam, revealed he had sustained a slight fracture at the end of his shinbone as well. In a stunning twist, the club reached out to Richard Todd, cut by the Saints after the 1986 preseason, to come out of retirement and act as backup to Pat Ryan for a week or two.

The situation going into the New England game was far from ideal. The starting quarterback had not started a game in two years, while the back-up had been about to embark on a bonds-selling career with Bear Stearns & Company. The Jets had faith in Ryan, but the gameplan was still run-heavy. The Jets were not the only team with quarterback woes – Tony Eason's sore ribs kept him on the bench, meaning it was Steve Grogan who would start. The Jets had lost five of their last six games to the Patriots, the only win coming in the overtime squeaker in week 10 of the previous season.

With Hector leading the way with 40 gruelling carries, the Jets took control, opening up a 24-0 halftime lead. They then had to endure a flurry of Patriots scores in the second half as Grogan enjoyed one of his best days as a pro – 401 passing yards and three touchdowns. Hector's third one-yard touchdown run of the game appeared to seal the win in the fourth quarter, but Grogan responded with his third touchdown and appeared to be driving for the tying score before Irving Fryar fumbled in Jets territory. Harry Hamilton, still bearing his gruesome forehead scar, recovered the ball to preserve the win.

Ryan had been solid (14 of 25 for 148 yards and a touchdown, with no interceptions) and the Jets had survived without their two injured stars. McNeil was now eligible to come off injured reserve, while O'Brien would start practicing again later that week. The next game, against the undefeated Broncos, was not considered a must-win (the Jets had a two-game lead at the top of the AFC East), but stopping Denver and John Elway, on Monday Night Football, would be a statement.

O'Brien practiced on the Wednesday, claiming to feel no ill-effects, and was considered 'probable' for the game. Whether he would start or not was up in the air. McNeil's recovery from what he described as the most painful injury he ever experienced was remarkably fast, partly because he had started to treat himself immediately in the most unconventional way imaginable – after dislocating his elbow, he had fortuitously knocked it back into place with his knee.

As gameday neared, it was announced that both O'Brien and McNeil were bracing themselves to face the Broncos. O'Brien would wear a derotation brace on his knee (the same kind worn by Namath back in the day) while McNeil would wear an elbow brace. Neither was expected to start, and O'Brien would likely not get into the game unless Ryan suffered some kind of injury.

The game developed into the Jets' most complete performance of the season so far. While not matching the fireworks of week three, the Jets' controlled the ball with a power running game, often featuring McNeil and Hector in the backfield at the same time. With Paige chipping in, the Jets ran the ball 44 times against the best rush defense in the league and gained 137 yards and a touchdown.

On defense, Elway was befuddled to such an extent that he completed only three passes in the first half, all to running back Gerald Willhite. Denver had four times as many penalties as first downs in the first half (eight to two) and were 22-0 down at the interval. The last two points had come on a safety, symbolic of the frustration endured by Elway in the first half. By then, Ryan had given way after a brilliant start that saw him complete his first seven passes. A rib injury knocked him out of the game in the second quarter, with the Jets leading 13-0, and O'Brien was forced to step in. He was duly hammered to the ground on his first play, a completion to Hector.

'That really is surprising,' Frank Gifford commented, 'because Joe [Walton] was really outspoken that he would not bring [O'Brien] in… and now we see that Ryan is leaving. He's going inside with one of the trainers.'

O'Brien then walked up to the line on second-and-eight and dropped back again, floating a perfect pass to Walker for a 23-yard score.

'Welcome back,' said Al Michaels, succinctly.

'Remember what I said earlier,' Gifford added. 'You wanna throw the ball deep, you get O'Brien in there. He'll never underthrow it. This is one of your basic blowouts, thus far. Everything working for the Jets.'

'And what touch too,' Michaels said. 'To miss a game, to come in cold off the bench…'

The Jets did not score again (they had not scored a single point in the third quarter in any of their six games), but they did not need to.

With Elway finally knocked out of the game (ironically, it was a collision with one of his teammates rather than one of the five sacks administered by the Jets defense that gave him a concussion), Denver could manage just 10 points as they went down to their first defeat of the year.

'We played our best complete game: offense, defense and special teams,' said a satisfied Walton after the game. 'Everybody worked hard for 60 minutes.'[38]

The team was certainly beginning to feel that something special was developing: 'We're at the top,' Ryan said.

'It says we belong up there with the best of them,' added Barry Bennett. 'The Greek [commentator and bookmaker Jimmy 'the Greek' Snyder] says we can't play 60 minutes. We played 60 tonight.'

It might have been expected that another injury would mar the win, and sure enough right tackle Reggie McElroy was ruled out for at least four weeks with a knee sprain. The revamped line, which had been performing so well, was now down its first-string center and first-string right tackle. Gordon King, a smart pick-up at the end of preseason, stepped into the lineup, having subbed for McElroy when he went out of the Denver game. Former LA Rams tackle Bill Bain, who had visited the Jets eight weeks earlier, was called in as an emergency backup.

Injuries would be the recurring theme of the season and the question was how much more the team could absorb. A pessimist might have been waiting for the Jets to crash back to earth, but they would have to wait. Eventually, the pessimists would be proved right but before that, O'Brien went on a three-game tear that was unmatched in team history.

Time tends to blur things together. Many Jets fans will look back on the 1986 season and remember an endless barrage of long strikes to Walker and Toon, an offensive juggernaut with O'Brien at the controls, dissecting, destroying… but that it was only part of the picture.

The 1986 Jets were resilient in the face of tremendous adversity, and they won in a multitude of ways, depending on circumstances. All NFL teams suffer injuries over the course of a season, and all have to adapt, but the Jets offense lost starters at critical positions – quarterback, halfback, center, offensive tackle. They managed to win with their backups, sometimes with their backups' backups. They brought in former players and cast-offs to pad out their gameday rosters. They won by running the ball, by suffocating the opposing offense, by kicking every field goal that offered itself (Leahy was on a streak of 22 successful kicks by now – he had last missed the previous season.) It all worked.

A lot of this was forgotten when people began to sift through the wreckage at the end of the season, looking for the black box that might tell them where it all started to go wrong. The last thing anyone could remember was a string of improbable performances from O'Brien that became the symbol of the entire year. From week eight to week 10 of the season he was, in the words of former NFL kicker-turned-TV pundit John Smith, 'the nearest thing to perfection in the NFL'.

Against New Orleans, Seattle and Atlanta, O'Brien passed for over 1,000 yards, 10 touchdowns and no interceptions. Against Seattle, he tortured the NFL passer-rating formula until it locked up, smoke billowing, its own eccentric definition of perfection flashing on its interface – 158.3. It was impossible to do better. Extrapolated over a full season, the numbers would still be at or near the top of the all-time lists nearly 40 years later – passer-rating (141.6), passing yards (5,392), passing touchdowns (53), completion percentage (74.2%) – all of them would still be remarkable in the modern, pass-happy NFL. Of course, O'Brien was not able to maintain those standards for a full season, but for a few weeks, Jets fans were able to dream. The Jets looked unstoppable.

Statistics also only tell part of the story. The Saints game did not start with perfection – in wet conditions, O'Brien fumbled after a sack on the third play of the game and New Orleans took the lead on a Morten Andersen field goal. McNeil then coughed the ball up on the next drive and the Saints had two turnovers in the first seven minutes.

Strong play in the Jets secondary (Jerry Holmes and Harry

Hamilton both knocked away accurate passes from Dave Wilson) stopped the Saints from doing more damage than another field goal, but after the defense forced a third-down incompletion, the Jets' leading tackler, Lance Mehl, was left rolling on the turf. While trying to slow up to avoid running into Gastineau, Mehl had taken an awkward hop and caught his cleats on the turf. His knee buckled, and although he walked off the field to cheers from the fans, the Jets had just suffered their worst injury of the season so far. First reports, in the days after the game, would say Mehl was expected to miss up to six weeks. After surgeons got a look at his knee, that diagnosis changed. Following major reconstructive surgery, which included a tendon transplant, it was announced that Mehl would not be back for at least a year, if ever.

The Jets were still struggling against the Saints and looked badly out of sync. The first play of their next drive should have resulted in a third turnover – O'Brien's pass, intended for Tony Paige, went straight through the hands of Sam Mills. Despite a few short completions (and a hopeful chant of 'J-E-T-S, Jets! Jets! Jets!' from the crowd) the Jets' third drive ended with a sack.

Defense was keeping them in the hunt – Wilson did not complete a pass in the Saints' first three drives, and their fine rookie running back, Reuben Mayes, was knocked out of the game after just four carries. Special teams then got in on the act, when Dave Jennings landed a punt on the wet turf in front of the Saints' return man, Eric Martin. The ball skidded through Martin's legs and was recovered at the Saints' 12-yard line by Michael Harper, despite Martin's protestations that he hadn't touched the ball. Instant replay could not find enough evidence to overturn the call and the Jets had the shot of good luck they needed. From the 16-yard line, after a penalty, O'Brien fired a high pass into the end zone, which was brought down by a leaping Al Toon. The Jets had tied the game and Leahy's extra point gave them a lead they would not relinquish.

A CBS scoring update then threw up an interesting titbit – Mike Moroski, long-time Atlanta backup, was starting at quarterback for the 49ers in their game with Green Bay. Although struggling early on,

Al Toon catches O'Brien's third touchdown against the Saints (AP Photo/Ed Bailey)

Moroski would go on to enjoy a solid outing and earn the win, making this the only day in NFL history that two UC Davis quarterbacks started and won on the same day.

Back at Giants Stadium, the Jets offense was starting to wake up. O'Brien was basking in solid protection, his knee healed enough that he no longer needed to wear a brace. He connected on his first deep pass of the game midway through the second quarter, before McNeil capped the drive with a one-yard run, his first touchdown of the season. As the Jets prepared to kick off after taking a 14-6 lead, Hector was seen walking towards the tunnel and first reports were that he had a sprained thumb.

The rain started to fall with a purpose, but O'Brien struck again just before the half. The drive started with a rerun of the hook and lateral play from week three, Shuler catching a short pass and improvising a pitch out to Paige, who took the ball to the Jets' 37. John Madden called it 'one of the darnedest plays you're ever gonna see,' but amid the jollity, Gastineau was shown also heading into the tunnel. The football gods now seemed to be demanding a toll on any successful play, not merely a touchdown – or perhaps they were simply collecting in advance. On the next play, with 31 second on the clock, O'Brien found Toon at the Saints' 45. The willowy receiver spun his way through two would-be tacklers and shrugged off two more on his way to a 62-yard touchdown that had Madden in raptures.

'I think this play shows every reason why Al Toon is a great player,' said Madden. 'One, it shows that he's tough, that he'll go to the inside and he'll catch the ball in the middle. Two, it'll show that he's strong and can break a tackle, and three, it shows that he has speed and can outrun everyone. That's one play, an example of everything you have to have.'

As the last few seconds ticked away before halftime, Madden mused that the Jets might be on their way to the Super Bowl.

'I tell ya, this Jet team could very well be the team in the AFC,' he said. 'I know a few weeks ago when we saw the Denver Broncos, I thought that maybe they were the best team in the AFC. And then I watched these Jets beat the Broncos and the way they play, I don't know, they could be the AFC team.'

Toon's third touchdown put paid (just) to an annoying stat that was beginning to bug the team. With the final period just seconds away, the Jets got their first third-quarter points of the season on a six-yard pass that pushed their lead out to a healthy 28-6. They weathered a strong Saints comeback to grab their sixth straight win, but it had come at a steep price. Not only was Mehl lost for the rest of the year, Klecko picked up a knee injury in the second half and would miss four out of the next five games. Leahy saw his field goal streak end at 22, one shy of the then NFL record held by Mark Moseley, but was still mobbed by teammates and applauded by the few remaining fans when his 46-yard attempt went awry. It was a day for celebrations even amid adversity.

The bandwagon continued to gain momentum the next week. Despite fielding a back-up nose tackle and missing their best linebacker, the Jets' defense put the clamps on Seattle's star running back, Curt Warner, holding him to 31 yards on just nine carries. The Jets' plan – to get on top of the Seahawks early and take Warner (and the rowdy Kingdome fans) out of the game, worked to perfection as O'Brien enjoyed his best day as a pro, completing 81 percent of his passes, for 431 yards and four touchdowns. Toon and Walker both turned in big days. Toon caught nine

Getting a pass away under heavy pressure in O'Brien's first 'perfect' game, against Seattle (AP Photo/Barry Sweet)

passes for 195 yards and two scores, while Walker grabbed six for 161 yards and one score. Not even viruses could stop this team – O'Brien and Toon were both suffering from the flu.

On the first touchdown of the day, O'Brien showed surprising mobility. From his 49-yard line, he dropped back on a 2nd-and-11 play and was instantly pressured up the middle by Seattle's Jacob Green, who had looped inside from his left defensive end position. O'Brien stopped his dropback and moved to the right, parallel to the line of scrimmage, allowing Green to overshoot but putting O'Brien in the sights of right defensive end Jeff Bryant, who had also stunted through the middle of the offensive line. Just as Bryant was closing, O'Brien tossed the ball out towards Toon, the ball reaching him at knee level at the Seattle 35. Toon simply scooped the ball in and outran Terry Taylor to the end zone.

The second touchdown was far more straightforward. From his 17, O'Brien dropped back behind perfect protection and was able to step into a deep throw to Walker, who caught the ball at the Seattle 37 without needing to check his stride.

'83 yards for No. 85,' said Marv Albert, neatly summing up the play.

Toon remained the only Jet able to score in the third quarter, corralling another deep pass from O'Brien to push the Jets lead out to 31-7. It was only on replays that it became clear that Toon, leaping up between two defenders in the end zone to bring in the 36-yard scoring pass, had come down with the ball between his thighs.

When Toon and Walker were both on song, the offense was unstoppable, and McNeil showed signs of kicking off the rust with an 84-yard rushing effort, his best of the season so far. Special teams were holding up their end of the deal as well. Walton had chosen this unit to be introduced before the game, and they responded – Leahy landed a 50-yard field goal, there were good punt returns from Kurt Sohn and Jo-Jo Townsell, and Dave Jennings dropped one of his punts at the Seattle three. There was even a chance for the 1986 draft class to make a belated contribution to the season – when left guard Ted Banker went down with a shoulder injury, No. 1 draft pick Mike Haight stepped in.

O'Brien was back at the top of the NFL passer ratings after the emphatic display – a perfect 158.3 rating will tend to move you up a few notches, but he wasn't simply playing the system. He was leading the league in completion percentage (66.1) *and* yards per pass attempt (8.94), two aspects of the ratings formula that usually see-sawed. A lot of this had to do with the electrifying run-after-catch ability of both Toon and Walker, who were both able to turn medium-range passes into long scoring strikes.

'Everything we tried worked,' O'Brien commented, simply, 'and we did it against a pretty good football team. We got on a little bit of a roll and that made a difference.' [39]

For once, no major sacrifice was demanded of the Jets for their dominating victory. Aside from Banker's shoulder, a sprained ankle for Tony Paige and a shin injury for Sohn, no body parts had to be ritually offered up to the gods. Sohn would miss the next game, but both Banker and Paige suited up against the Falcons. Six players with Pro Bowls on their resumes had missed games for the Jets during the season, but it seemed like they could overcome anything.

There were some rumblings of disquiet surrounding the pass defense, the worst in the league according to the statistics. But once more stats told only part of the story. The NFL was still largely a run-first league, and opponents battered their heads against the Jets' rushing defense for an average of just 67.8 yards per game, while O'Brien, Toon and Walker were lighting up the scoreboard. Through nine games, the Jets had not allowed a rushing touchdown. In the second half, usually facing a big deficit, and with the Jets switching to something approaching a prevent defense, teams were piling up passing yardage that was mostly meaningless.

Against the top rushing offense in the league, led by Gerald Riggs, the Jets' defense would be tested the following week, but they would have Klecko back in the middle. It promised to be quite a confrontation. In the pre-game introduction, Don Criqui spoke of the growing respect around the league for the Jets, calling their win over Seattle, 'one of the great efforts in Jet history,' and adding that, 'right now Dan Henning, the coach of Atlanta said, without question, the Jets are playing the best football in the NFL.'

The game was the first the Jets had played all season on natural grass, and it started well, with the longest kickoff return of the season so far. Bobby Humphery took the ball out to the Jets' 46-yard line, but the offense could not capitalise. Nor could they throughout a scoreless first quarter that had Criqui and co-commentator Bom Trumpy musing that the Falcons must be feeling good about how the game was unfolding.

'Psychologically I think Atlanta feels, hey, we got a chance today,' said Trumpy.

'The longer they keep it close the bigger chance they get,' added Criqui, 'because the Jets have put that KO punch on early.'

The game changed completely on the first play of the second quarter. On third-and-11, Walton eschewed trickery and just had O'Brien drop straight back. Nine yards he dropped, the intention so plainly signalled that Criqui stated, 'Here comes O'Brien ready to put it up deep.' From his 33-yard-line, O'Brien uncorked a perfect pass that sailed 52 yards through the air. Toon was running through defenders as though they were standing still and Criqui's commentary was matter-of-fact, as though the play had been inevitable: 'Puts a lot of top on it... Al Toon's going for the ball, it's going to be a touchdown for the Jets… so the Jets, who banged away at this tough Falcon defense finally go high up, and it's a perfect strike to Al Toon from Ken O'Brien.'

The Jets then conjured up a play that highlighted just how effective they were as a deep-passing team – Walker caught a 46-yard touchdown pass from O'Brien. It wasn't so much the fact that it was a beautiful catch by Walker, running at full speed into the end zone and tracking the ball as it came in directly overhead, it was the fact that it *lowered* his yards-per-touchdown average. When a 46-yard pass lowers your season average, you know you have been firing on all cylinders.

The pass was part of a streak of 17 straight completions, which included a third touchdown pass, the second caught by Walker, as the

New Yorkers took control of the game with a 21-point second-quarter explosion. The commentary team of Criqui and Trumpy had difficulty keeping up.

'Here's another completion to Al Toon,' said Criqui as the Jets were driving to their third score. 'He's down to the 16-yard line. Fourteen straight.'

'That's 15 Don, we missed one,' Trumpy cut in. 'Look at him,' he went on, referring to O'Brien. 'Boy I'm telling you, he's as cool as the other side of your pillow, standing back there. He can find anybody open, he's on a roll. That kid is absolutely on a roll.'

O'Brien's next pass was to Walker, tiptoeing down the back of the end zone.

'Into the end zone they go,' said Criqui. 'Is it a touchdown? It is... so the 16th straight completion is a second touchdown pass to Wesley Walker, a third touchdown throw this day for Ken O'Brien, and the Jets now have taken command of the game, 20 to nothing.'

The completion was a special one. O'Brien showed mobility and unflappability in the pocket. He first cocked his arm to throw to Toon, gathered himself, moved out of the pocket and then had to release the pass high to avoid a leaping Rick Bryan. The pass was deadly accurate, barely avoiding Bryan's outstretched hand, then dropping over a defensive back in the end zone right into Walker's hands.

'It's unbelievable,' Trumpy commented. 'He's just standing back there waiting for somebody to get open, he knows they're going to, he has confidence in his offensive line, he's not worried about pressure, he looks to the left, he looks to the middle, he looks all the way over back to the right, even with Bryan right in his face, yeah… nothing to it. Just go deep, I'll hit ya… It looks easy, and O'Brien makes it look easy.'

Characteristically, O'Brien deflected the praise from his performance onto his teammates: 'I think the offensive line deserves the credit,' he said. 'When I've got that much time, I can get things done.'[40]

Walker was far more willing to speak out about O'Brien's play.

'It's unbelievable what he can do,' said the 31-year-old veteran. 'I'll tell you what, over the years I've played with a lot of quarterbacks. No one throws like he can. He loves to throw the ball, but he doesn't take any unnecessary chances. He's a big reason we're winning.'

The football world was getting used to this new-look Jets team. The deep passing game was becoming their trademark, but this was still a team that liked to keep its offense balanced. Even in the three-game streak where O'Brien set the league on fire, the Jets rushed the ball more often than they passed, 109 times to 98. The sportswriters on *The New York Times* struggled a little to reconcile O'Brien's playing style with his undemonstrative persona. Time after time he would throw a perfect deep ball for a score and shuffle off the field as if he had just thrown the game-losing interception.

Dave Anderson wrote of the 'calm, cool quarterback who, week by week, is earning All-Pro stature', while Gerald Eskenazi described him in three words: 'Unemotional, unexciting, and winning'.[41]

But Eskenazi also made another statement: 'Now, the question is, how did the Jets have the brains to pluck O'Brien out of California-Davis, a Division II school that doesn't even have athletic scholarships?'[42]

Eskenazi had been harsh in describing O'Brien as unexciting. He was mostly undemonstrative, but Jets fans were far from unexcited, as chatter grew about a potential New York-New York Super Bowl. Interviewed by former Patriots kicker John Smith for Channel 4 television in the UK, O'Brien expounded on his breathtaking play, as well as confirming that he had no idea he was close to the NFL record for consecutive passes in the game against the Falcons.

'No, I didn't know that,' he insisted. 'Unfortunately, if I would've made a couple of better throws I probably would've had it but, you know, the best is yet to come. I mean, I think that records are meant to be broken, but I'm going to play a lot better football. I have a long time to play and with everybody I have around me getting better, we should have a great team for years to come.'

Was it a consolation to at least break the previous Jets mark of 15 straight completions, held by a certain Joe Namath?

'He's a great,' O'Brien said, emphatically. 'He was an idol of mine when I was growing up and it's just a pleasure to have been able to come back here and meet him a few times. It's like a dream come true for a little kid to meet his idol.'

On his two receivers, arguably the top receiving duo in the NFL, O'Brien had this to say: 'Wesley has proven that he's one of the best receivers to play the game… I think he's helped Al Toon as much as Al Toon's helped him. Al Toon is just phenomenal. He's a very, very smart, intelligent player. He came from college and it took him one year and he has our system down now, and he can jump to the moon it seems, he can run with the ball and we're really good friends… Wesley and Al… our wives are all good friends… I think that's the kind of atmosphere we have around here. Everyone has a good time together, we kid around and everyone's intelligent enough to know when it's time to concentrate on work.'

Smith's interview ended on a positive note: 'The Jets may or may not make the Super Bowl,' he said, 'but no matter how far they get, they'll get there in style.'

The words would start to seem like the proverbial commentator's curse before the season ended, because the wings were about to fall off the Jets' season.

Chapter Five
The Stall

The last five weeks of the 1986 regular season have their place in Jets folklore, right up there with the Mud Bowl, the Fake Spike, the Butt Fumble and whatever Aaron Rodgers' Achilles tendon injury will be remembered as. The five-game losing streak would have been jarring in any circumstances – the Jets were outscored 183-61 – but it was unfathomable given the way the team had been playing.

In retrospect, there were plenty of potential reasons why the Jets became a shell of their former selves. The team had been dealing with injuries to many of its star players for the entire season. Repeatedly, the backups had come in and done a great job, allowing the winning streak to build. Eventually, however, they reached a 'straw that broke the camel's back' moment, especially on defense. When the Jets faced Miami for a rematch of their week three spectacular, they were missing their entire starting defensive line, as well as their best linebacker.

There was talk of bringing in a free agent, and former 49ers pass-rushing specialist Fred Dean was mooted – but Dean's heyday was in the rear-view mirror (he hadn't started a game since 1983 and had just seven sacks over the previous two campaigns). On top of that, he was asking for $50,000 a game to suit up as a hired gun. The Jets offered $15,000 and talks went no further.

The injury woes on defense go a long way to explaining the 183 part of the lopsided cumulative score over those last five regular season games, but what about the 61? A team that had averaged 27.5 points per game over the first 11 weeks suddenly dropped to 12.2. The line was still missing McElroy at the start of the losing streak, but Fields had returned, and the backups had been doing a fine job in previous games anyway. Hector missed the last two weeks of the season, but in both games McNeil topped a hundred yards.

The one glaring element that stands out in the five-game skid is the play of O'Brien. His completion percentage, which had been up at a league-leading 66.5 percent, plummeted to 54.4 over the final five weeks. At the same time, the deep strikes simply disappeared. A pass offense that had generated touchdowns of 46, 71, 65, 50, 43, 62, 50, 83, 59 and 46 yards in the first 11 games, could manage nothing better than a 39-yard completion in the final five. In the last game of the season, a game the Jets actually led at halftime before disintegrating in the second, the longest completion O'Brien could muster was 17 yards.

Clearly, something was wrong. The physical abuse O'Brien had suffered down the stretch in 1985, where he had repeatedly been seen cradling his injured right elbow after being flung to the ground, had not been as big a factor in 1986. The elbow was still sore (it was iced after every game) and the extra padding over it was now as much a part of his uniform as his jersey, but the rejigged offensive line had done a good job of protecting him, even with the losses of Fields and McElroy. Now, however, cracks began to show. He was sacked 24 times in his first 10 games (2.4 per game), but 16 times over the last five (3.2 per game). His interception rate went up alarmingly, from 0.8 per game over his first 10 outings, to a disastrous 2.4 over the last five. Touchdowns went in the opposite direction, from 2.3 per game to 0.4. Yards per attempt dropped more than three full yards, from 8.78 to 5.57.

As you would expect, this had a devastating impact on O'Brien's passer rating. In the last game of the season, his rating was 19.0. Just seven weeks earlier, he had registered a perfect 158.3 against the Seahawks. It was almost as if the Jets had stepped into Bizarro World, where everything was the opposite of what it had been. This impression was underscored by a truly strange fact – as the Jets faltered, McNeil, the very emblem of their offense for so long, finally started to produce. He rushed for 440 yards over the last five weeks.

Over at *Sports Illustrated*, Paul Zimmerman, the man wo had commented on O'Brien's selection on draft day in 1983, had his own ideas. His theory was simple and plausible: O'Brien's arm had given out on him.

'Maybe died is too strong,' he wrote. 'It got tired, very tired. It had two, maybe three deep throws in it per game, and that was all.' [1]

Dr. Z cited no sources, and O'Brien remained adamant throughout the losing streak that there was nothing wrong with his arm, but the theory was compelling, and O'Brien did admit that he would need to rethink his offseason training regimen. And there could be no doubt that, however many deep throws O'Brien had in his arm per game, they were not as accurate as they had been earlier in the year. Against San Francisco, in week 14, he threw three interceptions in a game for the first time as a pro. Then he repeated the feat in each of the next two games. The Jets had stalled, and the stall had turned into a nosedive. Whether or not they could pull up before ploughing into the ground was the question now.

The first sputtering of the engines had been heard the week before the stall began. In the win over Atlanta, two defensive stars had gone down – Klecko had aggravated his knee injury and Lyons had damaged a tendon in his shoulder. Klecko would require surgery but was expected back quickly, but Lyons' injury was more serious. He was placed on injured reserve, meaning he would miss at least four games.

Against Indianapolis, the NFL's only winless team, the Jets found the going tough. Things started well. After getting the ball with a short field, O'Brien looked effortless in directing a scoring drive to take a 7-0 lead – three passes, three completions and a 19-yard touchdown to Walker was on the board. Shortly afterwards he found Walker again, this time with a perfectly timed lob from five yards out.

But the hits were starting to pile up. The first sack of the day was wiped off because the Colts had 12 men on the field, but that didn't stop O'Brien from landing heavily on his right shoulder. A few plays later he was levelled by linebacker Duane Bickett, who appeared to launch himself upwards at the point of contact, hitting O'Brien right under the chin. The Jets quarterback stayed on the ground for a few moments, holding his head, before getting back to his feet slowly. All seemed well as he hit Walker with a 47-yard deep ball on his next pass, and then completed another to Paige, but things were about to take a turn for the worse. McNeil fumbled the ball away to kill the promising drive and when the Jets got the ball back, O'Brien was off. Three incompletions were followed by a sack and an interception on a deflection.

The interception proved especially damaging, as it gave the Colts an opportunity to run a few plays in the dying seconds of the first half and on one of them, Gastineau's left knee buckled while running around a Colts blocker. Gastineau had been ineffective for most of the year, registering just two sacks, but his loss (he would miss the rest of the regular season) meant that the Jets' entire starting defensive line was out.

The second half began with O'Brien still struggling. After completing three of his first four passes he threw his second interception of the day, then put together a string of five incompletions in six throws as the Colts continued to get to him. After one hit he sat on the turf flexing his right hand.

It was the running game, held in check for most of the afternoon, that came to the Jets' rescue as they clung to a 17-16 lead. McNeil ripped off a 40-yard run and Hector weaved his way into the end zone from 17 yards out to get some breathing room. O'Brien then connected with Walker for 34 yards and finished the Colts off with his third touchdown pass of the day, again to Walker. It was a win, and the Jets stood at 10-1, but the Colts had shown that if you could hit O'Brien, you could knock him out of his rhythm.

There was a possibility that the Jets had been looking past their winless opponents to a critical Monday Night Football rematch with the Dolphins the following week. The loss of Gastineau meant the defense was highly suspect as they prepared to face Marino. From the booth, Al Michaels and Frank Gifford voiced their concerns as the Dolphins got to work on their first drive, pointing out that Kyle Clifton was the only Jet defender to have started all 11 games of the season so far. Marino was the obvious concern for the Jets – Miami had not had a 100-yard rushing performance from a back in 40 games.

'They will throw the run at you occasionally,' Gifford commented. 'They have to keep it honest, but their game is the pass game.'

As if to prove Gifford wrong, the Dolphins went to the ground often on their first drive, and Lorenzo Hampton churned out some useful yardage before facing a third-and-two. The Jets crowded the line and sure enough, Hampton was given the ball again. Finding a big hole, he vaulted over the first line of defense and found that there was no second line. His run ended 54 yards later, in the end zone.

Miami taking the lead was hardly unexpected, and there were no signs of panic as the Jets came out for their second drive. McNeil and Hector were effective on the ground and O'Brien hit Walker on a 30-yard throw despite heavy pressure in his face. All seemed well as the cameras switched to a young Vinny Testaverde, watching from the sideline in his final year as a Miami Hurricane. He would have his own Monday Night Football experience against the Dolphins 14 years later, but right now the Jets appeared to be driving for the tying score. That changed when Hector fumbled after being hit by two defenders just after taking a handoff. The first quarter ended with the Jets holding an edge in yardage and time of possession, but their next drive ended on an O'Brien interception by Paul Lankford, as he attempted to hit Walker deep while fading left to escape pressure.

Miami capitalised by driving 84 yards to Hampton's one-yard score. 'Jets Crash in Miami' read a sign in the crowd, which turned out to be prophetic. Behind Hampton's 148 rushing yards (he caught five passes for 40 more) and three total touchdowns, Miami rang up their week three score again – 45 points. This time, the Jets could only muster three.

A freakish defeat could be shrugged off, and the Jets looked to have done that in their next outing. Against the LA Rams, back in Giants Stadium, the Jets put together what would have been their most impressive drive of the year. Starting at their two-yard line after a Jerry Holmes interception, they took a step back after a false-start penalty and then moved methodically downfield, converting a third-and-eight with a pinpoint strike from O'Brien to Walker on the sideline. With McNeil gaining prominence, the Jets moved to the Rams' 33, from where O'Brien connected with Walker for the go-ahead score… before Jerry Gray hit him from the side, causing a fumble which the Rams recovered in the end zone for a touchback. The Jets had come that close to getting their mojo back.

Bud Carson, missing his starting line, tried to compensate with blitz packages, and even started the game with a four-man line, Jim Stuckey making his only start of the season at right defensive end. The Rams' picked up the blitzes comfortably, giving Jim Everett, a rookie going through a shaky first season, plenty of time to throw. On a third-and-four, Carson sent seven men against Everett, who calmly found Kevin House for a 60-yard catch-and-run touchdown. The Rams would not relinquish their lead and ran out 17-3 winners.

It was an out-of-character performance by the Jets. Normally balanced on offense, they put the ball in the air almost twice as often as they ran it, with O'Brien attempting 47 passes, the highest number of his career to that point. McNeil had been stymied after his fast start, but still, it looked like Walton was trying to jumpstart his offense by force-feeding pass plays.

'We're just out of sync now,' he said after the game. 'We can't seem to make the play to get us over the top.'[2]

There was now a question: had the Rams shown the NFL how to combat the Jets' deep passing game? In a league where man-coverage was on the rise, the Rams had utilised a zone scheme with the specific aim of neutralising the long strike. It was not a 'macho' system, but the Rams did not care about that.

'The macho may not win you the game,' Jerry Gray said, in effusive mood after the game. 'You can't give them the bomb. We wanted to make them catch it in front of the linebackers, give them the 5-yard catch, not let them catch it behind the linebacker. Those guys like to have the big plays and one thing we said coming in was we decided we can't let them have a big play, a bomb.' [3]

A return home might be just what the Jets' struggling quarterback needed, and as preparations were underway for a road trip to San Francisco, he allowed his attention to wander just for a moment. His old college coach, Jom Sochor, was in the running to take over as the head man at the University of California, and O'Brien had no doubts his mentor would be a good fit.

'I think he'd win [at Cal],' O'Brien said in support of Sochor. 'There's no doubt in my mind he'd win. He's very, very thorough, very knowledgeable. He has a way of getting across his system to the people so they believe in him and what he can accomplish.' [4]

It was a nice endorsement, but nothing seemed to be going right for O'Brien at the moment. The job went to Rams running backs coach Bruce Snyder instead.

In the build-up to the San Francisco game, 49ers coach Bill Walsh had some thoughts on what might be the problem with the Jets' offense, which had not scored a touchdown in two straight games.

'Those kind of things happen,' said the man widely hailed as an offensive genius. 'I think they've been shaken badly as teams move the ball so well on them and then [they] left their game play very quickly, figuring they had to catch up. So often you are involved in a game, your play-calling offensively is related to how well the other team is moving the ball. And in this particular case, the Jets may have gone quickly to things that they don't necessarily do and lost their continuity.'[5]

Walsh may have been onto something considering the 47 passes thrown by O'Brien against the Rams. Against the Niners, however, things were even more out of balance. The pass-run ratio against Los Angeles had been almost 2:1. Against San Francisco, it was more than 3:1. With the Jets facing a pair of rookie cornerbacks in Tim McKyer and Don Griffin (third- and sixth-round draft picks, respectively), there was some justification in the imbalance, but it also felt like the Jets were pressing.

Back in California for the first time as a pro, O'Brien endured a nightmare homecoming. His first pass was perfect and should have been a 20-yard pick-up to Toon, but the league's leading receiver unaccountably dropped the pass. O'Brien missed on his first nine passes and went on to endure his worst outing so far as a Jet – three interceptions for the first time in his professional career, a 45 percent completion rate and just one score, a 10-yard consolation touchdown to McNeil when the game was already over. Four sacks added pain to the humiliation, and the fact that his family and friends (not to mention coach Sochor) were watching was the crowning indignation.

The defense was not overwhelmed, but simply ran out of steam as San Francisco piled up over 38 minutes of possession with its West Coast offense. Joe Klecko had been expected back for the Jets after successful knee surgery, but the knee had swollen up on the cross-country flight and he had to content himself with prowling the sideline. He appeared in just one play.

'The Jets are out of sync,' said Merlin Olsen from the commentary booth. 'You just have the feeling that the timing is not there. One of the problems cold-weather teams have this time of year is practicing in the cold and the snow and the wind. It's apparent that they are just not crisp.'

The weather may have been playing a role during Jets practices, but more important in this game was the fact that the 49ers had copied the Rams: 'We were determined not to give them the big play,'[6] said McKyer, who helped keep Toon and Walker to a combined six receptions for just 83 yards. This statement was confirmed by the Niners' defensive coordinator, George Seiffert, who revealed that he had ordered his defensive backs to play the Jets receivers a little softer than usual, ensuring they did not get loose behind the secondary for the big gains that had become their trademark. With the San Francisco pass rush also able to pressure O'Brien without resorting to the blitz, a blanket of coverage was laid over the field that the Jets proved unable to unpick.

The Jets had reached a crisis point. Even the unflappable O'Brien was badly shaken by the manner of the defeat. After the game, he sat in front of his locker looking dazed, ignoring the reporters who wanted answers to the all-important question: what the hell had happened to the Jets? Other players were more able to express their feelings, but Walton seemed just as stunned as his quarterback, repeating the phrase, 'We're just not playing very well.' [7]

Mickey Shuler noted how badly O'Brien was taking the defeat, and his own lackluster performance: 'That's as devastated as I've ever seen him,' he said. 'but a lot of us are devastated.' [8]

After sitting in silence for more than 15 minutes, O'Brien finally stirred out of his reverie, but still appeared shellshocked as he gave the gathered reporters something to write about.

'I played terribly,' he admitted. 'I'll just let my play do the talking.' But he was unable to leave it at that. Having started to speak, the words kept coming: 'I expected a lot out of myself today, in front of a lot of people I know and all, but I just couldn't get it done.'

'Right now we feel like we're in a dream,' said Shuler, who instantly corrected himself. 'A nightmare. We have to put a stop to it, wake up and get back to having confidence in ourselves. Any time you lose the way we have, it can cause fear, and that's what we have to guard against.' [9]

Several players went out of their way to defend O'Brien, aware that the bulk of the scrutiny for the three-game skid was focused on him.

'I have complete confidence in Ken,' said Wesley Walker. 'The whole team does. If you don't, you shouldn't play football.'

'Ken is a competitor,' Shuler added. 'All through the game, he kept motivating us and pushing us. We're just not coming up with the plays right now, and it's not fair to blame one person.'

Walton did not blame one person, but he moved decisively to halt the slide. Charles Jackson, having started 13 games at linebacker, was cut outright. He had not been performing at a high level, but it was still a stunning move. Walton explained that as Jackson did not play special teams, his value to the team was eroded too far to keep him on the roster if he wasn't starting. The linebackers were rejigged, with Bob Crable taking Jackson's slot and Kevin McArthur, who had been cut in August three years in a row, taking Crable's old position at right inside linebacker. Klecko and Lyons returned to the starting lineup, although neither was fully healthy, and the hope was the changes might wake up what had once been the league's stingiest run defense. They had been far from stingy in their three-game losing streak, surrendering 525 yards on the ground.

Changes came on offense as well. Guy Bingham would be alternating at center with Fields, who was struggling after his knee surgery. McElroy was back at right tackle with King, who had been playing well at that spot, switching to left guard to replace Ted Banker, another player struggling due to injuries. Nuu Faaola was given the starting nod at fullback, supplanting Tony Paige.

'I don't think we're playing that well,' Walton said to explain his moves, 'and if something is not working you try to fix it.' [10]

The changes were dramatic. Some might say desperate. Barry Bennett spoke for the team when he said of Walton: 'I don't think he'd sacrifice someone for the shock effect, but there's no question he got a shock effect. There are 50 guys in here (the locker room) who are shocked. I hope it has a good effect. We need something.'

The effect seemed to be immediate. On a cold Saturday, McArthur made a solid stop on the Steelers' first offensive play, helping to drop Earnest Jackson for no gain and drawing a roar from the crowd and congratulations from his teammates. The defense had responded to

Walton's changes, now it was time to see the offense for the first time. The decision to start Faaola had been reversed, and Paige was in at fullback, along with two tight ends (Shuler and Klever). Having attempted the football equivalent of a defibrillation machine the last week, trying to shock the offense back into life, Walton was now opting for the more patient CPR approach. He would try to establish the run and stay in the game until the unit rediscovered its confidence.

O'Brien hit his first pass, a 10-yarder to Toon to convert on third down. His second was a dump-off to Paige, who ran for seven, but the drive stalled after two short runs. Still, the Jets had set out their stall – they would be conservative on offense, while their defense was playing with passion. The conservatism lasted two drives, until Walton called for a deep pass. O'Brien dropped back and threw in the direction of Walker, who had a step on two Steelers. With a strong wind behind him, O'Brien appeared to take something off the ball, expecting it to carry further than usual, but instead it fell well short and was intercepted. As the first quarter ended, the stats were ominous. Hoping to stifle the Steelers' ground game, the Jets had given up 76 rushing yards. Hoping to establish a ball-control offense, they had gained 22 yards of their own, just six of them coming on the ground.

As the second quarter started, the Jets lost Klecko again. Walton had taken a calculated gamble in putting him back in the starting lineup just a month after his left knee had been scoped to remove torn cartilage, and the gamble had backfired. But then, amid the cold, blustery conditions, hope suddenly blossomed. A 24-yard touchdown to Kurt Sohn made it apparent how much his teammates wanted O'Brien to pull out of his slump. Even Walton took a few steps out onto the field to congratulate his embattled quarterback.

The score gave the Jets life, and on their first possession of the second half they came out swinging. A sharp 10-yard pass to Shuler was followed by another of the tight end's improvised laterals, this one going to Sohn and tacking on an extra 12 yards. McNeil ripped off a 30-yard run, which made him the Jets' all-time leading rusher. The ball-control offense had cranked into life, but on fourth-and-goal from inside the Steelers' one, Walton called for a field goal rather than trying for the go-ahead touchdown, and the fans booed even as the game was tied at 17.

A chance to grab momentum had been lost and the game turned on a brutal fourth quarter in which the Steelers scored three touchdowns against a wilting defense and added a fourth on a 67-yard interception return. The football gods no longer had the good manners to offer the Jets a victory as payment for their injuries. Klecko would not play again for 11 months. Linebacker Rusty Guilbeau also went down to a knee injury and would never play for the Jets again. McElroy was knocked out of the game with a knee injury. O'Brien had the wind knocked out of him after one of the many hard hits he was subjected to, and was replaced by Ryan. As if that wasn't enough, he also had his throwing hand stepped on after fumbling the ball away. He would claim that it wasn't a significant injury, but he visibly reacted on the field as Keith Willis landed with full force on the hand, and he was later seen cradling it on the sideline.

O'Brien had thrown three interceptions and could easily have had three more. He had also lost the fumble and by now the talk was getting louder. What was wrong with the Jets' quarterback? He was taking a beating once again, having benefited from improved offensive line play during the team's nine-game winning streak. Five times he had been sacked by the Steelers, and many more times he had been flattened after delivering a pass. The state of his right elbow had become a talking point. The team admitted to bursitis, which could be caused by injury or overwork. After each game, and practice, he now wore a pressure sleeve to ease swelling, but the only cure for bursitis is rest, and the Jets were now fighting for a playoff place. In a turn of events that would have seemed unthinkable just four weeks earlier, there was speculation that Walton might give the starting job to Ryan, both to steady the ship and to give O'Brien a little time to recover. Walton would reply without hesitation that O'Brien was his quarterback, but the pressure to do something was growing, and Walton was not the kind of coach to sit and do nothing.

The desperation moves before the Steelers game had backfired.

Klecko and Guilbeau were gone and Walton had to eat a considerable portion of humble pie when inviting Charles Jackson back after his bizarre one-week sabbatical. To Jackson's credit (he had already played enough games to guarantee himself playoff pay if the Jets made it to the postseason), he came back and started again in week 16, putting him in the rare position of starting one week, getting cut the next and then starting a week later for the same team. Such was the growing turmoil around the Jets.

Amid the gathering gloom came a warm ray of sunshine. The day after their fourth straight defeat, the Jets watched Kansas City beat the LA Raiders. The result meant the Jets were going to the playoffs whatever happened in their final game. The nine-game winning streak suddenly began to look good again. At the very least, it hadn't been for nothing.

The guaranteed playoff berth gave Walton an opportunity. He could rest his banged-up quarterback with no major drama. Of course it would make news, but everyone knew O'Brien was hurting. A week off might give him a chance to gather himself both physically and mentally, and with the division title still a real possibility, the rest might even have extended to two weeks.

Walton chose not to make a change, trusting that O'Brien could find his way out of the dark cloud that surrounded him. Instead, he turned in his worst game as a starter. Three more interceptions, a completion rate under 50 percent and just 106 passing yards gave him a rating of 19.0, the lowest mark in his 106 starts as a Jet. The defense also imploded, surrendering a team-record 621 yards as Boomer Esiason tortured them with five touchdown passes and Bengals runners combined for 205 yards on the ground. It was the kind of offensive explosion the Jets had been unleashing just a few weeks earlier.

Despite a wild card berth (New England had beaten Miami on the last game of the regular season to deny the Jets a division title and a much-needed bye week) the tune in the sports pages had switched to a

Joe Walton strikes a defiant pose at the end of the 1986 season (AP Photo/W. Funches)

minor key. Dave Anderson at *The New York Times* quipped that it was a pity the Jets could not trade their playoff berth for an offense. Walton admitted that the nosedive had been the most trying period of his 30 years in professional football, both as a player and a coach.

'It's hard to find anything that's been rougher,' he said, while trying to focus on the positives. 'I still feel very good about what we've done this season. We have accomplished a lot, we beat some good football teams in the course of winning 10 games.'[11]

And still Walton insisted O'Brien was his quarterback… until one day he wasn't. On the Wednesday before the Kansas City Chiefs came to town for the wild card game, O'Brien was benched.

'Kenny is still our quarterback' the coach insisted, 'but I think Pat can give us a shot in the arm. I will continue to strongly support Ken O'Brien as our quarterback. This has been a team thing. I told them right now, I think it is better for him and the team. I felt we needed a change, that it was the right thing to do at this time.'[12]

At the time, a shocked O'Brien had almost no comment: 'I really have nothing to say about it,' was all he would give reporters. Looking back on the decision more than 25 years later, he had more to say.

'I think panic sets in when things are going wrong,' he said. 'You're winning and all of a sudden, you're losing. You start looking for why, and that's the job of the coach. It's ultimately his decision, and he thought it was time to step back and make a change, and bring Pat in. Pat's a great player, and played real hard and real tough all the time. He's a terrific guy, so obviously, I'm going to root for him to do real well. And he did – it was fun to watch him.'[13]

But O'Brien still felt the decision was wrong.

'Do you agree with those decisions?' he asked himself in retrospect. 'Certainly not. But at the other side, it's their job to make those decisions. We should have just played better in the previous game or two, and it would have taken care of itself. But it didn't.'

O'Brien therefore watched from the sideline as the Jets hosted the Chiefs. The benching had made news, and in the build-up to the game NBC ran a piece featuring Dolphins head coach Don Shula and his former quarterback, Bob Griese (who would be commentating on the game). The two men had differing opinions on the situation.

'I would have to, myself, go with Ken O'Brien,' said Shula, 'because he's the guy that got 'em there. And early in the year, when they had that tremendous record, 10-1, he was the hottest quarterback in the AFC, and he wasn't doing it with mirrors, he was doing it with great performance… He is their franchise, so unless there's something physically wrong that we don't know about, I question that decision.'

In contrast, Griese believed O'Brien should have been benched sooner.

'Better late than never,' he said. 'Kenny O'Brien carried this team for the first 11 games. He did it all on his own. He's got that pressure, he's trying to do it and he's trying to do too much and I think Joe Walton maybe could've done it a couple of games ago.'

Griese went on to say he had approached O'Brien before the game with a few words of comfort: 'I said, "It's happened to me. There's life after being pulled and you'll come back and be a good quarterback again."'

Whatever the reason for O'Brien's slump – an injury or the pressure of trying to carry a team with a fading defense – he took no part in the wild card game, although he could often be seen talking with Ryan on the sideline. Ryan played a steady, unflashy game, aided by a great performance from McNeil and a defense that had the luxury of playing the NFL's worst offense. Bud Carson made an adjustment too, reining in his usual aggressive approach and dropping his linebackers into coverage. With Gastineau returning, a four-man line was able to get enough pressure on Todd Blackledge and Bill Kenney, who both saw time under center for the Chiefs.

There were few flashy plays on offense, but Ryan galvanized his team with a 24-yard run on a quarterback draw, converting a fourth-and-six from the Chiefs' 33-yard-line. Griese revealed that offensive coordinator Rich Kotite had said this play was an option because of how wide the Kansas City defensive tackles set up in their nickel formation.

'Right after I took the snap, the defense split wide open,' Ryan said of the play. 'That play really seemed to pick us up. I think we needed something like it to get us going again.'[14]

There was no way Ryan could go back to the bench after such a solid performance. He may only have passed for 153 yards, but he threw three touchdowns and no interceptions. It was the kind of steady, stabilising play the Jets had needed. Against Cleveland a week later, it was Ryan who trotted onto the field for the Jets' first play.

The game will be remembered as one of the most agonising in franchise history. Losing a playoff game is always painful, but losing one in double overtime, having been 10 points ahead with just over four minutes to play, is especially cruel. Ryan had started the game well, hitting Wesley Walker with a 42-yard touchdown pass on a flea flicker in the first period, but after he was buried under a heavy pass rush late in the first half, O'Brien could be seen warming up on the sideline. Ryan had pulled a groin muscle during warm-ups and had aggravated it on the sack.

'You wonder, psychologically what this does to the football team,' said Bob Trumpy as O'Brien trotted out onto the field facing a 10-7 deficit. 'Ryan is the inspirational leader of this offense, they call him Mr. Guts.'

O'Brien hit his first pass, an 11-yarder to Toon, but three straight running plays to McNeil failed to keep the drive going. On the next drive O'Brien took off on an improvised run, gaining nine yards, but then absorbed the first of what would be six sacks. As time ticked down at the end of the half, O'Brien took off again, this time scrambling for 16 yards to set up a 46-yard Pat Leahy field goal that tied the game at halftime. A little strangely, the Jets had kept Ryan in as the holder for the PAT, and he had clearly been in great discomfort as he set up to receive the long snap – the possibility of him returning at any point looked remote.

In the second half, strong running from McNeil set the Jets up inside the Browns' 20, but O'Brien was off target on a lofted pass to Toon that would have taken the ball inside the 10. Another Leahy field goal gave the Jets the lead, but with O'Brien looking inconsistent (he hit his first three passes then missed his next four), Walton became increasingly conservative, feeding the ball to McNeil and hoping his star running back could break free.

Occasionally, O'Brien would remind everyone of how good he had been earlier in the season, such as when he hit Toon for a 31-yard gain, but two downs later he overshot Toon on a play that might have been a touchdown during O'Brien's hot streak. Timing seemed to be the issue, as most of the biggest completions came to stationary receivers who had found a soft spot in the defense – when asked to lead a man downfield, O'Brien's trademark accuracy was just not there.

McNeil could not carry the offense, totalling just 71 yards on 25 carries as the Browns defense collapsed on him. The biggest chunk of those yards, however, looked like they had won the game for the Jets. After a Jerry Holmes interception of Bernie Kosar, the Jets were set up at the Cleveland 25 and McNeil finally found space, jinking through the line before bursting to the outside to go in for a touchdown with just 4:14 to play. The Jets led by 10 and seemed destined to go to the AFC Championship Game.

What happened next is difficult to fathom. The game was slowly petering out as Cleveland were called for a hold on their next drive, setting up a first-and-20. A sack took them back to their 16 and on second-and-24 Kosar's pass fell incomplete with 3:27 to go. They would be facing a third-and-24, needing two scores just to force overtime.

But there was a flag on the field. Gastineau, who had enjoyed a great day, had hit Kosar late on his last incompletion, drilling the Browns' second-year quarterback in the ribs with his helmet for good measure. The 15-yard penalty gave the Browns a first down, and set in motion a tidal wave of misfortune for the Jets. Gastineau's penalty was about to take its place in the pantheon of Jets blunders (he would protest his innocence, but the league would later fine him $2,500).

Kosar led the Browns to a touchdown after the penalty, but the game still looked comfortable with the Jets back in possession and facing a third-down that would seal the victory. Walton, perhaps remembering the success Ryan had with a quarterback draw in the previous game, called up another one… but O'Brien was not as fleet of foot as Ryan and was taken down behind the line of scrimmage. Although a designed run, it counted as a sack, which stopped the clock until the ball was reset, giving the Browns a few extra seconds of life. They tied the game on a field goal and then won at the end of the second period of extra time. The Jets' 1986 season was over in numbing fashion.

Much was said and written about Gastineau's play, but O'Brien, as ever, preferred to see the game as a team effort. Even remembering the play decades later, he refused to put all the blame on Gastineau.

'We can say what we want – it was a stupid play and blah, blah, blah,' he remembered. 'But ultimately, they made the plays they had to. They still had to make a drive down there and kick a field goal – and they did. They were better at the end than we were. Did that play help them? Sure it did. Was it stupid and you wish it didn't happen? Yes. I think Mark and everybody would agree. It wasn't something that was done on purpose, and unfortunately, it went against us and they took advantage.'[15]

One of the strangest seasons in Jets history was over, and the chance for a New York-New York Super Bowl was gone. The Giants went on the beat the Broncos, a team the Jets had manhandled in a game that suddenly seemed to have taken place in a different reality.

Jets and Patriots meet at midfield in a show of solidarity before the 1987 players' strike (AP Photo/Susan Ragan)

Chapter Six
The Strike

In the Walton era, it had become traditional for the aftermath of a season to involve tumultuous change, whether in the player ranks or the coaching staff, but following the 1986 season the coach seemed to be in an unusually philosophical place, publicly declaring that he believed his players had won back the respect they had lost in their five-game swoon.

In a profession where job security was tenuous at best, the situation of Walton was worth consideration. Chiefs coach John Mackovic was fired at the end of a season in which the Chiefs had made the playoffs for the first time in 15 years, so simply making the postseason was no guarantee of holding on to a job.

The Jets moved quickly to avoid any speculation, announcing a new deal for Walton in the middle of January. A statement from the team president, Jim Kensil, simply said: 'Joe and his staff have done an outstanding job overcoming adversity while guiding the Jets to the playoffs the last two years. Our goal is to earn a championship for our fans, and we feel that Joe has shown the ability to help us reach that goal. Stability is an important ingredient in winning. We're pleased to announce that Joe will continue in his role as head coach.'

It was a vote of confidence and an admission that the team had been swamped by a wave of injuries that would have been difficult for any coach to overcome. Positive news also came with the announcement that Don Maynard would become the second player in Jets history to be inducted into the Pro Football Hall of Fame. There were big questions, though, as the Jets went into their offseason. Numerous players would be needing surgical interventions to continue their careers. Not going under the knife, but under more scrutiny than anyone else, was O'Brien, and the biggest question was which version of the Jets quarterback would show up for the 1987 season. Walton remained committed to his signal-caller: 'Kenny has proved he can win in this league,' the coach said as preparations of the 1987 season got underway, 'and when all the offensive parts are running the way they should, he's as good as any in the NFL. He's dedicated, hard working, the team believes in him and so do I.'[1]

Indeed, the team had some flattering things to say about No. 7.

'Hey, he's Irish,' said Jim Sweeney, 'which means he's a little tough and a little crazy. I call him Kenny Timex, because he takes a lickin' and keeps on tickin'.'

'You cannot believe how tough that guy is,' Walton said in agreement with Sweeney's comment. 'He's fearless. He stands in the pocket trying to make something happen. He appears to be oblivious to all the noise going on around him. The big thing with Kenny is his tremendous confidence. He just doesn't expect to lose, he expects to win, to make the big play.'

And it wasn't just O'Brien's toughness that stood out to his teammates.

'In the past we've had some success, but we've never had anyone who could throw like O'Brien,' said Wesley Walker. 'He hangs in there, looks off defenders, he never takes chances. I've been here 10 years and we've never had a QB of that caliber chucking the rock.'

After the playoff loss to Cleveland, quarterbacks coach Zeke

Bratkowski revealed that O'Brien had admitted his pinky finger was stopping him from gripping the ball in his normal manner. The finger had been trodden on in the Pittsburgh game, which did nothing to explain the three sub-par performances against Miami, San Francisco and the LA Rams, but the news did give some hope. Pinky fingers heal, and a healthy O'Brien might start tearing up the league again.

Knees and shoulders tend to take longer to heal. Klecko was not expected back until November, while Mehl and McElroy were both out until mid-October. All three were rehabilitating reconstructed knees, while Marty Lyons had undergone surgery on both shoulders. Offensive linemen Jim Sweeney and Ted Banker has also undergone shoulder surgeries.

The draft was about to offer its annual serving of hope, perhaps with a side order of bemusement. The eccentric Jets drafting was becoming something of a talking point, and a repeat of the disastrous 1986 class could see the team tread water when it badly needed an injection of talent. If drafting purely for need, the Jets might look to the defensive line and linebacker. The offensive line had done better in 1986, but O'Brien and Ryan had still gone down under a combined 45 sacks, and the line had looked shaky again at the end of the year. Even considering the injury status of McElroy, drafting an offensive tackle would require a swallowing of pride, given that two had been taken in the first two rounds in the '86 draft. Most draft experts had the Jets selecting Harris Barton, the offensive tackle out of North Carolina.

Mike Hickey was adamant that he would ditch the philosophy that had marked his 1986 draft, where he had drafted for need, and would return to a 'best player available' ethos. When draft day came, instead of solidifying the line in front of O'Brien by adding Barton (who started 134 games for the 49ers) or even Bruce Armstrong (who suited up 212 times for the Patriots) they selected Texas A&M fullback Roger Vick. The agonised response of one fan in attendance at the draft (crying out 'Oh no!' when Rozelle revealed that the Jets had selected a fullback) summed up the feeling of Jets fans everywhere. Fullback was still an important position in the 1980s, but the Jets already had the versatile Tony Paige. Alex Gordon offered some hope as a second-round linebacker, but both players would last just three seasons with the Jets. It was another swing from Kensil, and another miss.

The draft was a slight improvement over the 1986 version (the Jets got 81 starts out of the 12 players selected) but it still left the team with bare cupboards when veterans began to slow down and drop out of the starting line-up. If the 1987 season was going to be a good one, the Jets were relying on a return to health for their key defenders and a return to form for their key man on offense.

The timing of O'Brien's slump had not only been bad for the Jets, it must also have impacted on sales of an instructional video, *Ken O'Brien's Quarterback Clinic*, which came out in 1987. 'O'Brien concentrates on psychological preparation, knowledge of the fundamentals and lots of drilling,' [2] read a review. There was no mention of whether or not the video gave advice on coping with 62 sacks in a season.

More seriously, the slump came just when O'Brien was looking for an extension on his rookie contract. After four seasons of professional football, two as the full-time starter, he had established himself as an NFL-caliber quarterback, but would the Jets want to pay him as the destroyer he was in that three-game span in the middle of the 1986 season, or the tentative player he became in the losing streak? The opening shot was fired by O'Brien when he failed to turn up for the start of training camp. The ball was in the Jets' court – the fifth-year pro was reportedly looking for a deal averaging around $900,000 a year and would be fined a thousand dollars for each day of camp he missed.

While he waited for a new deal, O'Brien had time to offer a little advice for collegians about to head out into the world for the first time: 'Set your goals and go ahead and achieve them,' was his advice to UC Davis seniors. 'Do what you enjoy,' he added, saying that he was 'having a great time every day. This is something I've been working for since high school.' [3]

Training camp opened with an avalanche of players as the Jets tried to see if quantity could translate into quality. Around 130 players were at camp, 40 more than the previous year, with many jobs up for grabs while established veterans recovered from surgery. Top draft pick Roger Vick was looking exceptional, and the Jets were high on what he would bring to their offense – a ball-control element and a level of physicality that would take pressure off O'Brien and the passing game, as well as limiting the amount of time the defense would need to spend on the field.

O'Brien's absence was a concern, especially considering Ryan had another groin pull when camp opened and was not expected to be able to play for a few days. Walton reached out to Richard Todd again, but the veteran was not interested this time around. A crisis was averted when O'Brien and the Jets came to terms less than a week into camp, both sides agreeing not to go public with the actual numbers. The deal was widely reported as being in the region of $800–850,000 per year and was for just two years. Clearly there had been a little compromise on both sides, with the Jets unwilling to commit bigger money to a player with a question mark hanging over him and O'Brien unwilling to sign for longer at a lower rate. More details emerged later, putting O'Brien at $850,000 for the first year of the contract with incentives that could add another $150,000.

The salary bump would have nudged the Jets' already league-leading average salary a few dollars upwards. Jet players had received an average of $233,700 in 1986. The crosstown-rival Giants pocketed just $186,274 per man – but they could console themselves with a Vince Lombardi Trophy. The Jets topped another chart as well, attracting 608,044 paying customers to Giants Stadium, the best mark in the entire league.

Defusing the contract impasse with O'Brien was a relief, but as the preseason approached, another potentially explosive situation was developing. The collective bargaining agreement between owners and the NFL Players Association was due to expire at the end of August. The players were looking for some big changes in the game – most notably free agency and guaranteed contracts – but insisted that a strike (like the one that had blighted the 1982 season) was the last thing they wanted.

O'Brien gets to work in training camp in 1987, as Pat Ryan watches (AP Photo/Cyrena Chang)

Maybe the Jets should have thought differently. Late season swoons were becoming a hallmark of the Joe Walton era, and a shorter season might have helped. A former Jet, Marvin Powell, was the president of the players' union, while former Oakland Raider Gene Upshaw was the executive director. They would be leading the fight for the players.

With O'Brien back in the fold, the Jets could get down to the serious work of two-a-day practices. In an effort to stop themselves from leading the league in yet another category, they were paying two NFL officials to attend camp for a week. The Jets had been the most penalized team in the NFL in 1986 and the hope was to instil some better habits at the start of the new year. The impact was not exactly instant, as the Jets committed 12 penalties in a messy preseason win over the Eagles. More worrying still, O'Brien was ineffective, as the walking wounded on the offensive line failed to protect him. He completed just five of 12 attempts, for 49 yards.

The second preseason game (against the Bucs and their shiny new quarterback, Vinny Testaverde) was a little better. O'Brien passed for two touchdowns, but overthrew rookie Tracy Martin on what would have been a deep strike. It was a worrying trend for the Jets, as O'Brien's long-range radar had been off for a while now. Still, the steady improvement continued as the regular season approached. Touchdown passes of 40 yards to Shuler and 32 yards to Sohn keyed a victory over the Giants, but O'Brien was still taking too many hits. He was sacked four times and two more sacks were wiped off due to penalties – but they hurt all the same.

Walton was quietly supportive of his team, insisting they were moving in the right direction, but the preseason finale, against San Diego, was a horror show in which O'Brien failed to generate a touchdown drive in three quarters, completing just 11 of 23 passes. The game demonstrated in stark detail how different the NFL was in the 1980s. In the modern game, starters rarely play in the final preseason game, some don't play in any, yet O'Brien was left in despite his best offensive lineman, Dan Alexander, being out with a sore knee.

Putting the franchise quarterback in harm's way for such an extended period of time, behind a weakened line, in an exhibition game, would seem almost criminally negligent today, but O'Brien needed to fine-tune his game. There were encouraging signs that he was making the necessary changes. Even though the Chargers battered him as much as everyone else had, he made one spectacular play under heavy pressure, scrambling to buy himself time and then hitting a long pass on the run. O'Brien was never going to be mistaken for Randall Cunningham, but his running attempts were gradually getting better, albeit at a snail's pace

– he had averaged 1.8 yards per rush in 1984, 2.3 in 1985 and 2.7 in 1986.

Reporters were often frustrated by a player who remained upbeat at all times, one who was unwilling to discuss difficulties and always deflected praise onto his teammates when things went well. His thinking on the five-game slump at the end of 1986 was still unclear. One moment he was admitting he had a problem with his pinky finger, the next he was denying it had been a factor. One worrying sign that the troubles of 1986 were not yet fully resolved was the fact that O'Brien was still wearing padding on his right elbow. Whether or not it was merely preventative remained to be seen. As the regular season approached, however, he did address the issue of his slump, if only in an attempt to put it firmly in the rear-view mirror.

'I have come to grips with it,' he said in the run-up to the opening game against Buffalo, 'and I don't think you'll see any of it again.'[4]

His confidence was a good sign, but there were clouds gathering over the offensive line. Gordon King, the man who had stepped in well for McElroy at right tackle, was ruled out of the Bills' game with a hip injury. Alexander, a guard for his entire NFL career, was asked to make his first start at tackle, with center Joe Fields sliding to right guard and Guy Bingham coming in as center. The Jets were delighted with the play of their rookie fullback, but it was impossible not to wonder how much better things would look if Harris Barton was available to step in at right tackle. Instead, he would be making his debut for the 49ers in a career that would include two All-Pro nods.

The Jets clearly saw their linemen as interchangeable pieces, able to slot in anywhere, but that philosophy was stressed to breaking point on the very first offensive play against Buffalo in the regular season opener. Defensive end Sean McNanie overpowered Alexander and sacked O'Brien, the first of three sacks registered by the Bills in the first half. With the Jets also committing 15 penalties during the game, it looked like the biggest concerns of the offseason had not been successfully addressed.

And then everything snapped back into focus. O'Brien launched a deep pass with deadly accuracy, Walker tracked it coming in directly overhead and caught it on his knees, his momentum carrying him into the end zone for a 55-yard score that brought back the memory of the Jets offense at its explosive best. With Jim Kelly growing, the game was a shootout, but the Jets had rediscovered their swagger to match the potent Bills offense blow for blow and they emerged with a 31-28 victory.

Lightning struck again the following week, on Monday Night Football against the Patriots. Facing a third-and-23, O'Brien zipped a 20-yard pass over the middle to Toon, who sprinted to the end zone after the catch for one of his trademark catch-and-run scores. Commentator Dan Dierdorf made a telling observation when he said the Jets' offensive line was 'almost like an entire offensive line of guards', but for now at least, it appeared to have come together. A streak of 13 straight completions made it easy for Jets fans to hope that O'Brien was getting back to his best, but a new opponent was about to shut him down. The fears over a players' strike had proved justified and the Jets-Patriots game was to be the last for some time. O'Brien would not play again for five weeks.

The 1987 players' strike was traumatic for the entire league, but it was the veteran players who suffered the most. With their union demanding something that owners were steadfastly set against (free agency), there was little chance of success, but added to that was the manner in which the owners chose to proceed. Rather than simply locking the players out, they staged replacement games with whatever teams they could scrape together.

It was inferior football in every sense – but the records of the replacement teams would still count in the final standings. In this way, the Jets went from a 2-0 team feeling pretty good about themselves, to a 3-2 team when the strike was over. And they were riven by dissent, because several big-name players, including Gastineau and Ryan, had chosen to cross the picket lines and play.

'I know the way that it was handled fractured the team for the rest of the year,' O'Brien would later recount. 'That could have been a real good situation for us. My take on it all along was the Players Association was outmanned, and that the owners had better people around them – smarter people around them.'[5]

Gastineau was the only Jet to break the strike on day one, claiming that he had too many financial obligations to pass up pay checks. His actions were considered another example of him putting himself before his team, but this cut a little deeper, as every striking player was paying a financial price. Dave Anderson of *The New York Times* went as far as to suggest Gastineau should be traded when the strike was over if the Jets wanted a shot at coming back together as a team.

Ryan's return to action could also have been divisive, but he ended his strike just one day before the entire thing collapsed, which softened the blow. Also crossing the picket line with Ryan was offensive leader Joe Fields. The owners, in a last display of vindictiveness that did not reflect well on them, refused to allow the mass of players to return and play in the next slate of games, meaning rosters were dotted with a few early-returning veterans (a Pat Ryan here, a Joe Montana there) but were still largely made up of replacement-level talent. Ryan's return proved timely, as he made the difference in an overtime win over Miami that prevented the Jets from losing all three replacement games. O'Brien once more displayed his generous nature when he commented of Ryan's game: 'That shows what happens when you get professional football players involved in these kind of games – the cream always rises to the top.'[6]

When regular games restarted, a week later, it was clear the Jets had lost their edge. More than that, their closeness as a team had been damaged, perhaps beyond repair.

'Some teams didn't let guys cross the line,' O'Brien recalled nearly 25 years later. 'And I think teams that stayed together were the teams that benefited the most. By crossing the line, it was not only that year, but it went longer – there are still guys that I meet that talk derogatorily about guys that came on and played during that time – which I think is ridiculous.'[7]

Ridiculous or not, the bad feeling was real, and the Jets were flat when they started to play again. O'Brien in particular was off his game during losses to Washington and Indianapolis. He passed for just 174 yards and was sacked seven times in each game, while throwing a single touchdown and two interceptions. In the build-up to the Washington game, NBC's Marv Albert had asked Joe Namath if he thought the strike would have any impact on the game, especially considering the Redskins had stayed united while 10 Jet veterans had crossed the picket line. Namath had an interesting take on the situation.

'Well it won't have any effect on the veterans, I know that,' he said. 'The work is the game in hand and so the strike feelings will be forgotten, but what it will affect are the rookies, linebacker Alex Gordon from the Jets, nose tackle Gerald Nichols and Roger Vick. Their learning process has been slowed, so the rookies are going to be more apprehensive today.'

Namath's words proved to be wishful thinking as the Jets came out looking uninspired. The offensive line was once more makeshift. Replacement player Ken Jones (a former Buffalo Bill with 141 starts in 12 seasons) started, because King's hip injury had turned out to be serious. He would not play again. In a typical lack of regard for a player's prior experience, the Jets put Jones at right tackle, whereas he had played left tackle with the Bills. O'Brien took his first sack of the day to end the first drive. He then took sacks on three of his next four passing attempts, two surrendered by Jones, who was unable to handle Washington's Charles Mann. When O'Brien wasn't getting sacked, he completed his first eight passes, but for just 59 yards.

The Redskins offense wasn't doing much either and the atmosphere became surreal as the RFK Stadium fans booed enthusiastically every time Jay Schroeder threw an incomplete pass. Marv Albert commented that it was early for the boo-birds to be out – with five minutes to go in the first quarter and still no score in the game – but the strike had not only been a trial for the players. The fans had suffered as well and were letting the regulars know it.

With O'Brien firmly in the Redskins' sights, Walton attempted to establish the ground game, bringing Vick into the backfield alongside McNeil, having started the game in a one-back, three-tight end formation. Vick enjoyed some success, but McNeil looked sluggish and the offense followed his lead. To Walton's credit, he tried everything – McNeil was substituted for Hector, the occasional deep pass was attempted – but nothing worked. Walker was all but invisible. With five minutes left in the third period, a deep shot to him down the right sideline was well overthrown and two plays later Charles Mann collected his third sack to kill another drive.

Out of nowhere, the offense then clicked. Harry Hamilton came up with a fumble recovery to set the Jets up, and O'Brien delivered three crisp passes – to Toon for 13 yards, then to Shuler for 12 and finally to Shuler again for 15 yards and the go-ahead score. With O'Brien seemingly finding his groove, Walton then called five straight running plays on the Jets' next drive, finally allowing O'Brien to toss a short swing pass to McNeil, who slipped and came up short of the first down. A touchdown might have finished the game, but a Leahy field goal still gave the Jets a nine-point lead with less than 11 minutes to play, and a win looked assured after a Rich Miano interception on the Redskins' next drive.

O'Brien went back to work with cries of 'we want the scabs' raining down from the stands as the Redskins' fans made their disapproval clear. He missed an open Shuler on third down to give the ball back, and it was noticeable that the majority of his successful plays were again coming when he was firing the ball at a stationary target – the timing with his receivers was off and any time he had to lead his man down or across the field, he was struggling. Washington closed to within two points with a touchdown, but the Jets had another chance to kill the game after a 57-yard kickoff return from Jo-Jo Townsell. The ensuing drive went nowhere except backwards – the seventh sack of the day put the Jets in a second-and-19 hole, O'Brien missed an open Kurt Sohn on an out pattern and then a short pass to Hector lost one yard.

After Ali Haji-Sheikh kicked Washington into the lead to cap the Redskins' next possession, O'Brien had 46 seconds to orchestrate a scoring drive to snatch the win, with no timeouts left. An 18-yard pass to Toon and a 12-yarder to Klever followed the familiar pattern – both receivers found open spots in the defense and sat down, allowing O'Brien to drill the ball to a stationary target. On the next play he overthrew his receivers on a deep pass (it was unclear which of Toon or Sohn he was aiming for) and the game was down to three seconds. Rather than allow O'Brien to heave another pass into the end zone, Walton called for a 62-yard field goal attempt from Pat Leahy, which barely reached the end zone.

Things were unlikely to get much better the following week – O'Brien always seemed to struggle against the Colts. Leading up to their week seven encounter, he spoke about them as an opponent.

'They're well-coached, they try to stay basic and beat you up,' he said. 'They've had the same philosophy as long as I've been here – they make you make mistakes.'[8]

Dan Alexander was back at right tackle after the Ken Jones experiment was deemed a failure, but the results were identical to the Redskins game – Passing yardage: 174. Sacks: seven. Constant pressure on O'Brien helped force him into mistakes. He completed just over half of his passes, lost a fumble on a sack and tossed up an interception in a 14-19 loss that dropped the Jets to 3-4 and out of a four-team tie for the AFC East lead. O'Brien's passer rating for the game was a miserable 55.8. He was not helped by several drops, but again his long-range radar was off. One deep pass in the third quarter was so far overthrown that even the speedy Wesley Walker gave up on it and was jogging when it finally hit the turf. When McNeil dropped a simple pass on the next play the Giants Stadium fans started to boo, and even when things went well, something went wrong – Hector made a beautiful pirouette to escape a defender after catching a short pass and made good yardage before fumbling the ball away to set up a Colts field goal.

Hope flared briefly when some accurate passes to Toon set up a 20-yard Hector touchdown run (his sixth of the season) and the defense then held to give the Jets a chance to drive for the winning score. Consecutive sacks set up a third-and-30 and O'Brien's deep pass was nowhere near anyone except the Colts' Freddie Robinson, who easily picked it off.

The slump (four losses in five outings, including strike games) was souring Joe Walton on his team. The upbeat, supportive coach from the offseason, the one who had praised his players for regaining respect at the end of the difficult 1986 season, was turning back into the grim-faced critic. He questioned their work ethic, their commitment and their leadership. In fact, he claimed to not know who the leaders on the team were any more.

It was a valid criticism. Many of the men who had crossed the picket line, for whatever reason, had been leaders. Whether they now felt awkward in picking up their mantle again, or whether there was resistance from the other players to them doing that, there was a void at the top of the Jets. The slump was different to the one that ended the 1986 season, however. The defense was not the problem – they were hanging tough and keeping the games manageable, but the offense was playing error-riddled football and the season was beginning to spiral downwards. Walton hinted at bringing in new players and even benched McNeil for the upcoming game against Seattle.

Perhaps most worrying of all, O'Brien had suffered 23 sacks in the four games he had played. That was on pace for 92 over a full season and could not be sustained. O'Brien also acknowledged that the team was flat, and with their next opponent being a Seahawks team out for vengeance after their humiliation the previous season, that needed to change.

'We haven't been as emotional as in the past,' O'Brien admitted, 'but that's not an excuse. The reason we lost is too many mistakes. If we cut down on them, we'll be fine.'[9]

O'Brien was always optimistic, but Walton saw the mistakes as a by-product of the listless effort of his team.

'You have to play hard to win in this league,' he said. 'All of those things that go wrong stem from not playing hard. If we line up like we're going to work at Madison Avenue, nine-to-five, we aren't going to win a lot of games.'

Walton called each of his players into his office for one-to-one meetings after the Colts game, taking five hours to stress the importance of playing with emotion. Some meetings apparently lasted 30 seconds, others 30 minutes. A little lost in the turmoil was the fact that one of O'Brien's top weapons, Wesley Walker, was slumping. After excelling in the first two weeks of the season, he had caught just one pass in two games following the strike and was injured on the first drive in their next game, against the Seahawks. Diagnosed with a separated shoulder, he was initially expected to miss at least four weeks, but he did not suit up again all year.

The injury took the shine off a strong performance against Seattle. Walton's pep talks appeared to have been effective. O'Brien had flashed his old form and had even shown some good mobility on a couple of plays. At the end of the first half, he moved in the pocket to escape pressure, then stumbled, regained his balance and found Toon over the middle to help set up a field goal. On a third quarter play he was flushed from the pocket, eluded nose tackle Joe Nash and showed decent speed to gain six yards before reaching the sideline, even putting a move on linebacker Greg Gaines to avoid taking a hit.

'Kenny O'Brien's getting absolutely slick out here,' Frank Gifford commented, with a smile in his voice.

The deep pass was still missing from the armory, and the majority of O'Brien's completions were either short check-downs to his backs (eight completions went to McNeil, Hector and Vick), or medium-range connections with receivers sitting in seams. One of his biggest gains, a 26-yard catch-and-run by McNeil, was again set up by good mobility and vision. A flea-flicker toss back from Vick was clearly designed to be a home-run play, but when O'Brien could not find his deep target, he moved around in the pocket to buy time and improvised a dump-off to McNeil, who caught the ball at the original line of scrimmage and did the rest himself.

'Not the way it was drawn up, but it did the job,' was Al Michael's verdict.

'It did not remotely set up,' Gifford added, 'and O'Brien made it happen by dancing around back there.'

Dancing around back there was not O'Brien's most obvious skill, but the offense was having to adapt. The Jets were functioning as a ball-control offense now, mixing the run with short passes. This was far more in tune with the balanced approach favored by Walton, a conservative play-caller at heart.

The loss of Walker, though, was a hammer blow. The Jets did not adequately replace him (he was not easy to replace, to be fair, but Kurt Sohn's 23 catches at an 11.3-yard average was the best the wide receiver corps could offer outside of Toon) and the offense suffered. The combination of Hector and McNeil, a backfield dubbed 'McHector' by *The New York Times*, offered hope. McNeil had responded well to losing his starting job for the first time in his career, and had combined with Hector for more than 100 yards on the ground and another 59 through the air. If Vick had lived up to expectations the Jets could have unleashed a three-headed monster on the rest of the NFL, but after impressing in the preseason, he offered little but a few tantalising glimpses of speed and power, gaining only 257 yards all year.

As well as Walker's dislocated shoulder, Hector and Shuler suffered ankle sprains on the last drive of the Seattle game and would both miss a week, taking a little more luster off the 30-14 win. The McHector backfield would have to be temporarily shelved, but that mattered little as McNeil was back to his explosive best the following week, against Kansas City.

'It was a great day for him to be back in control again,'[10] O'Brien commented, relieved that McNeil chose to have one of his best ever days when three big weapons were missing from the offense. Rain meant the ground attack would be paramount, and McNeil rushed for 184 yards on 26 carries, with Vick chipping in 40 more. It was a quiet day for O'Brien. Sacked four times, he could muster only 132 passing yards. His 18-yard pass to Toon was the only touchdown of the day for either team, but that was enough in a game where the Jets defense was lifted by the return of

Klecko. O'Brien went downfield just once, overthrowing Toon (who was double covered anyway). Short passes and good runs after the reception were the most productive plays through the air.

The deep ball was still on the Jets' minds, even if it wasn't clicking. On many plays it was possible to see O'Brien setting up and looking deep, sometimes twitching a little in anticipation of throwing the bomb. Sometimes, when his receivers were covered, he would not have time to find an outlet receiver before the pass rush got home. Other times, he had time but chose to hold onto the ball in case a player came open late.

'He had time but no receiver,' said Don Criqui in the commentary booth after a second-quarter sack. 'The Jets pass-blocked very well, but O'Brien will take the sack rather than put it up unless he's certain, and we pointed out, he gets sacked the most, but he also has thrown the fewest interceptions this year.'

In the booth with Criqui was Paul Maguire, who was less willing to be charitable.

'You know, you take a look at O'Brien now,' he said. 'You say, alright, that's good that he takes the sack, but Don, you could throw that ball away, out of bounds, as long as there is a receiver somewhere in the area, and O'Brien had a chance… there is a time when you throw that ball out. You put yourself in such a bad problem, now you're looking at second-and-16. That's tough.'

O'Brien made light work of the situation, completing passes to Klever and Toon to gain a first down, but then took another sack, his third of the game, as a blitzing Dino Hackett came through totally unblocked. The next sack, after O'Brien had been given six seconds by his offensive line and still did not pull the trigger, forced him to the sideline for one play.

'He's tougher than a boot, O'Brien,' Criqui commented. 'I mean that's another thing about him. He'll stand in and let anybody whack him.'

O'Brien showed one of his rare flashes of mobility on the Jets' first drive of the second half. Finding nobody open downfield, he stepped up and looked set for a gain of one or two yards before he alertly lateralled to McNeil who gathered another 25, although the yardage padded McNeil's stats rather than O'Brien's. The play underlined recent comments from Zeke Bratkowski, who insisted that O'Brien was a good athlete, citing his excellent basketball skills. He had awareness, and looked good on designed roll-outs, but he lacked the kind of fast-twitch reactions that could get him out of danger quickly. O'Brien was still hitting on a high percentage of his passes (he had completed a league-leading 66.9 percent of his throws after the Chiefs game) but with the deep ball absent from his arsenal, his overall numbers were suffering and the Jets were looking predictable and plodding.

Nevertheless, two wins had them back in a share of first-place in the AFC East, but they blew a chance to grab the lead for themselves by losing for the first time to Jim Kelly's Bills. It was the first of a nine-game-winning streak for the Bills against the Jets, as they took a stranglehold on the division that would ultimately see them win six titles in eight seasons and represent the AFC in four straight Super Bowls. O'Brien would never beat Buffalo again. Five more sacks came at the hands of an emerging Bills' pass-rush and once the dust had settled, the entire AFC East was tied up at 5-5 – equally good or equally bad, depending on your viewpoint.

On a blustery day, McNeil had got off to another blistering start, piling up 89 yards in the first half before leaving the game with a concussion. He touched the ball just four times after the break and the passing game was undermined by seven dropped passes. A small ray of sunshine on a gloomy day was the return of Lance Mehl, seeing his first action since reconstructive knee surgery.

'We didn't play well today,' was Walton's verdict, 'offensively, defensively and special teams. I think the leadership on the field has to step forward.'[11]

The trouble was, the Jets were a fractured team. The three veteran leaders, Klecko, Lyons and Fields, had all crossed the picket line during the strike for one reason or another. The rest of the team's top players, including O'Brien, McNeil and Toon, were not vocal leaders (Rocky Klever would later comment that, 'as far as being a leader, Kenny is more like Ghandi than Patton.'[12] Walton's attitude to the team was also creating friction, as he veered between caring and caustic. Following the Bills loss, he told his players he couldn't bear to look at them and sent them home instead of holding the usual team meeting.

One constant was his insistence that effort was the x-factor. In Walton's eyes, when the Jets lost, it was because they weren't playing hard enough. In the next game, against the Bengals, the Jets kept biting and scratching to the end, pulling out a win after throwing away a 17-0 lead. A blocked field goal, returned 67 yards by Rich Miano for a touchdown, was the winning score, and Miano also sealed the deal with an interception on his best day as a pro.

'Coach always says to play hard for 60 minutes, that it could take until the 59th minute for something to happen,' O'Brien commented after the game. 'Today it did.'[13]

The wild finish rescued a victory for a Jets team that seemed on the verge of rediscovering itself. Vick ran with authority, the defense applied heat to Boomer Esiason with exotic blitzes and, most important of all, O'Brien found his deep touch, connecting with Toon on a beautiful 50-yard strike to the Cincinnati one. O'Brien sprinted downfield after the connection, pointing to Toon as if to say, 'there it is, that's what we've been looking for.' The reaction of the Giants Stadium fans showed exactly how much everyone had been missing the bomb.

Luck even seemed to be on the New Yorkers' side, as an apparent touchdown pass from Esiason to Eddie Brown was instead ruled a sack, as the Bengals quarterback was considered to be 'in the grasp and control' of Gastineau. It was a play that could have been called either way and the Bengals argued to no avail.

The maddeningly inconsistent Jets were consistent in one area, though – the pressure their quarterback was put under. It was hardly surprising, because for most of the season, they had been playing without offensive tackles. Sweeney and Alexander had done the best they could, but were undersized for the wing positions on the line. In fact, the entire offensive line had been made up of guards and centers, backing up Dan Dierdorf's observation from earlier in the season. Sweeney had bulked up to 275 pounds in an attempt to compete at left tackle, the most critical position on the line, but he felt uncomfortable at the weight, which was around 15 pounds higher than he would have preferred.

McElroy had returned against the Bengals, the latest in the reconstructed-knee brigade to make it back onto the field, following Klecko and Mehl. His return to right tackle meant Alexander could slide back inside to his favoured guard spot, but it was another rearrangement, which was playing havoc with the line's chemistry (Fields played left guard against the Bengals – the first time he had lined up there since the 1982 season). Perhaps the Jets would address the line in the next draft…

For now, with some trepidation, eyes turned to December. Under Walton, December was the month where Jets teams went to die. Walton was 4-8 in December as head coach of the Jets, and end-of-year swoons had cost them potential playoff spots in 1983 and 1984, while coming perilously close to doing so in 1986. It was even more of an issue in 1987. In Walton's previous four seasons there had been three December games each year – this time there would be four. With only the division winner likely to make the playoffs, a reversal of fortunes was essential.

But the omens were piling up. The 1986 end-of-season skid had started in Miami on Monday night and next up were the Dolphins, on Monday night. The Jets once more had problems in the defensive secondary – Kerry Glenn had pulled a hamstring against the Bengals and then a revaluation revealed a change of diagnosis. He had ligament and cartilage damage and would require reconstructive surgery. His season was over and he would never start again for the Jets.

It looked like a Marino-O'Brien barnstormer was the only hope for the Jets. What the Jets got was a 27-0 halftime deficit that proved too much to overcome. Marino and O'Brien each threw just one touchdown and the Dolphins eased their way to a 37-28 victory. Mehl injured his other knee and was lost for the year (in fact, his career was over). Left corner Russell Carter dislocated a shoulder. McNeil pulled a hamstring after just one carry. Klecko was flagged for four offsides penalties, one of which negated a Kyle Clifton interception.

There were signs that the Jets were falling apart as a team. Lining up with just 10 men on the field happens from time to time. So does fielding a 12th man. The Jets went one better (or worse) in both instances, once forced into a timeout because only nine players had answered the call for the next play, and once being penalised for having 13 on the field. They gained two yards in the entire first quarter, 42 in the second.

The third quarter started more positively, with O'Brien floating out of the pocket to buy time before hitting Toon with a deep pass to the Miami 14. A stiff-arm on Glenn Blackwood then sprung the receiver into the end zone. On their next drive, Pat Ryan set up to hold for a field goal but instead took off for his first rushing touchdown as a pro, and when Johnny Hector scored on the first play of the final period, hope was rekindled. A rare Marino rushing score pushed the Dolphins' lead out to 37-21, and a final Jets touchdown (a 46-yard return of a fumble by Bobby Humphery) was too little, too late.

The rejigged offensive line was again a problem, and veteran Joe Fields would later talk of how difficult it is to change position. A center cannot simply be plugged in at guard, nor a guard at tackle, and expect to play instinctively. Fields was playing left guard after a long career at center and commented on the difficulties.

'I was playing a new position and I was thinking too much,' he said, looking back on the game a few years later. 'So many things were going wrong that every play was a struggle, whether I blocked the right guy or not.'[14]

The Jets had shown spirit, and had certainly dealt with more than their share of adversity as one key contributor after another had been removed from the playing field. For Walton, however, this was a snapping point. After the game he began to speak about big changes coming up in the offseason. His early years in charge had been marked by significant overhauls in both player and coaching personnel, and it looked like he

O'Brien takes one of four sacks in a loss to the Patriots in week 14 (AP Photo/Mark Lennihan)

would be returning to that blueprint as the season spiralled down the drain. Walton had harangued his players at halftime, which at least jolted them out of the torpor that had seen them gain a total of two first downs, while giving up 18.

The game ended in ugly fashion, when a Marty Lyons block on Humphrey's fumble return left Miami's four-time All-Pro center Dwight Stephenson on the ground, his left knee badly damaged and his career over. Lyons was accused of a cheap shot, a charge he robustly denied, pointing out that he and Stephenson were friends who had played together at Alabama.

The following week, against New England, Steve Grogan put together one of the more bizarre stat lines you will ever see. He completed just 11 passes, but four of them went for touchdowns as New England blazed out to a 35-6 halftime lead on their way to an easy 42-20 victory. The Jets appeared to be in freefall now, inventing creative ways to shoot themselves in the foot. They committed 14 penalties, including another three offside penalties from Klecko. O'Brien was sacked four times and lost the ball on both a fumble and an interception (as he had against Miami). He was so shaken up after one hit, he had to leave the game for a play. Part of the reason, once more, was instability on the line. Fields was forced out with a concussion and Mike Haight, the forgotten No.1 draft pick from a year ago, replaced him, making his first appearance on the line for 1987. He was promptly injured as well.

Perhaps aware that he was losing the team, Walton attempted to build bridges after their second straight woeful performance, but his conciliatory gestures were simply an extension of the near-schizophrenic approach he had taken over the season – haranguing players after one defeat, putting the blame on his own shoulders after another. As John Madden prepared to commentate on the Eagles game, he reported that Joe Walton had said, 'If we can't respond when we're playing the Miami Dolphins and the New England Patriots, we really aren't a playoff team anyway.' It was a downbeat statement, hardly one to inspire his troops, who lost the last two games of the season to make it an 0-4 December. The coach's mood was not improved when an article appeared in *Newsday* in which several unnamed players criticized his coaching style.

The slump left Walton with a 4-12 record in December, as well as leaving the Jets out in the cold with an awkward-looking 6-9 record, the final legacy of the strike-marred, 15-game season. During the Eagles game, 'Joe Must Go' chants had rained down from the stands and there was a smattering of boos after the team went three-and-out on its opening drive, with O'Brien missing on two passes, as well as taking a hit on the second one. Madden summed the start up in his inimitable style: 'That wasn't the type of start that Joe Walton and Ken O'Brien were talking about… They really don't have confidence. They wanted some confidence. The first pass was almost picked off. The second time he throws, he gets up looking out his earhole.'

The boo birds were warming to their task after another three-and-out and another two incompletions. A fumbled snap on their next drive led Madden to declare that, offensively, the Jets were close to rock bottom. O'Brien was battered, hitting the ground three times on sacks and multiple other times after releasing the ball. He compiled good numbers – eclipsing the 300-yard mark for only the second time all year and throwing for two scores – but he also fumbled twice. The numbers also disguised a poor start, in which he hit Eagles defenders in the hands three times in the first four drives, without any of them sticking.

Madden lamented the number of pressures (10) and hits (four) he had taken in the first half.

'But that's just one half,' he pointed out.

Pat Summerall commented, in the inimitable style that was such a perfect foil for Madden's verbosity, 'I wonder if he's had fun.'

Madden then invented a new term. After getting hammered to the turf after attempting a short pass to Vick, Summerall called it a dump-off. Madden corrected him: 'That's even more than a dump-off,' he said. 'I mean, that was more like a slam-dunk-off. O'Brien's back here, now he starts to feel the pressure from the back side *and* the front side. So all he's doing, he wants to get rid of that ball before the impending doom. But you get the doom anyway.'

'It's been a tough year for Joe Walton,' Madden mused as the game wound down. 'It seems like since the strike they've never gotten back to it, because remember the game, the last game before the strike, they played on Monday night and they looked like one of the best teams in football. Then they came back after the strike and they just struggled.'

With O'Brien tasting the AstroTurf after almost every throw in the second half, he began to look visibly beaten down. On his best play of the game, a signature deep strike to Toon for a 51-yard touchdown (although it came in garbage time) he took one of the hardest hits of the day, from rookie middle linebacker Byron Evans. O'Brien landed heavily on his right elbow and got to his feet with his arm hanging limply.

Before the final game of the season, Walton called a meeting in an attempt to clear the air with his players. The meeting did not go well, as he responded testily when the players spoke up. Fields said how much it had hurt when Walton had called them 'pea brains', and Rocky Klever picked up the theme, telling Walton how insulting it was to be told you would be nothing without football. If anything, the meeting had made things worse.

In the season finale, against the Giants, O'Brien was again seen holding his right forearm in severe pain after a hit, raising questions once more about the health and durability of the Jets' quarterback. After another late-season collapse, the durability of the head coach was also in question.

O'Brien celebrates the game-winning touchdown against Miami in week 13 of 1988 (AP Photo/Ray Stubblebine)

Chapter Seven
The End of the Walton Era

Could Walton survive another end-of-season collapse? On his watch the Jets had lost their last two games in 1983, seven of their last eight in '84, two of their last four in '85, five straight in '86, and now four straight in '87. In 1985 and 1986, the team had ridden out rough finishes to still make the postseason, but in the other three years, the losses had thrown away promising positions.

Talk began that the evaluations at the end of the season might start with the man in charge, but Jim Kensil moved quickly to put that talk to rest, insisting that it was up to the players to do better. Among the team's big names, it was widely assumed that Gastineau was as good as gone, as well as Klecko and possibly Lyons. McNeil was considered tradeable. Kensil might have looked to Mike Hickey's shortcomings in the draft – as the team got older and succumbed to mileage and injury, there was no production line of young talent waiting to step in. Mike Haight made the first start of his career in the 1987 season finale against the Giants, the first start by any player from Hickey's 1986 draft class. Nuu Faaola was the only other player from that draft still on the team.

Walton was not left to dangle in uncertainty. Team owner Leon Hess made the call that he would return in 1988, but many of the Jets' biggest names would not. Klecko, a legend who would have to wait more than three decades to be voted into the Hall of Fame, was told it was time to hang up his cleats. He disagreed and went off in search of a new team, eventually landing with the Colts for one more season. Fields was also done with the Jets, but not quite done in New York. He suited up for the Giants in 13 games in 1988, but did not make any starts.

Other ageing players to be ushered out were punter Dave Jennings, defensive lineman Barry Bennett and offensive tackle Gordon King (who had missed all but the first two games of 1987). Other big names that had been expected to leave did not. Gastineau was staying, but he had become progressively less effective. In 1983 and '84, he had totalled 41 sacks. In 1986 and '87, that total was just 6.5. Lyons was still wanted, as was veteran guard Dan Alexander, at times the only dependable player on the embattled offensive line. Coaching changes were minor – Wally Chambers came in as defensive line coach (displacing Ray Callahan, who was bumped up to special assistant to Walton) and Mike Faulkiner took over the defensive backs.

The moves were hardly radical – none of the released players would have significant impacts on other teams – but the 1987 season, and especially the strike, had left a bitter taste in some mouths. Kurt Sohn was uncertain that he wanted to go through another season with Walton at the helm, while linebacker Bob Crable suggested an outside consultant might be needed to identify the team's problems and help put together a plan to overcome them. Nothing as radical as that was implemented, possibly because the front office had a pretty good idea of where the problems lay – it was in the trenches that the Jets had become old and toothless, and that had only been exacerbated by the decline and subsequent release of four players, two on each side of the ball. As the college draft came around, the team was (once more) looking to beef up the offensive line and add some predators on the defensive side.

The offensive line situation was especially galling. Lulled into complacency by an improved showing in 1986, the team had looked elsewhere in the '87 draft, but the selection of Roger Vick was looking like an indulgence of monumental proportions now. He had been decent as a rookie, but a decent offensive tackle would have made so much more of a difference. The incumbents were adding weight in the offseason – Haight had packed on 10 pounds and McElroy 12 – but new blood was needed. The position was therefore a top priority again as scouting reports were analysed and a list of potential selections put together. Frustratingly, there were few solid offensive tackle prospects. Wisconsin's Paul Gruber was the consensus best lineman available, but he was unlikely to fall to the Jets, who were picking eighth. That might lead to a slight reach for a player like USC's Dave Cadigan.

One other change in the air seemed almost reluctant. Walton admitted he would be tempering his fearsome training camp for the coming season. He was far from wholehearted in this decision, revealing to journalists that he had a scrap of paper on his desk with the phrase 'To thine own self be true' written on it. It was a noble sentiment, and if a coach was going to go down, he might as well go down doing things his way, but the late-season collapses could be ignored no more. The 1988 season would be one where Walton made a serious effort to build a better relationship with his players, but his last two years in charge would be mixed. While a revamping of the roster brought in youth, prompting a brief return to competitiveness in 1988, the 1989 season was nothing but a complete tailspin. For O'Brien, the last two gasps of the Walton era saw him seriously questioned as the Jets' long-term quarterback for the first time in his career. He would be benched towards the end of both seasons, as his passer rating ticked steadily downwards.

But there was hope in the air as the team got down to preparations for the 1988 season. The feeling was that the draft had been an improvement, and this would be borne out over the coming years. After the miserable 1986 and 1987 efforts (43 and 81 combined starts, respectively), Hickey at least found some serviceable players. Although none of them would become stars, they did combine for 470 appearances and 274 starts for the Jets. There were the usual (and inevitable) strike-outs, but they are a factor of every team's draft, every year. Second-round pick Terry Williams saw playing time in only 11 games and never started, while seventh-round running back Gary Patton was even more of a miss, never suiting up in the NFL. The team had been serious about wanting to get bigger. Their final pick, 12th-round defensive tackle Albert Goss, was 6'7" and weighted 355 pounds, making him (at the time) the biggest player ever selected by the Jets). His size didn't help, as he never played a down.

Right at the top of the draft, the Jets had been given another lesson about the perils of picking for need. No fewer than 11 of the first 15 selected players would go on to appear in at least one Pro Bowl (two made it all the way to the Hall of Fame) but almost inevitably, the Jets found one of the other four. Dave Cadigan was indeed the choice, but almost as soon as he was taken the rumor mill began to report that his physical attributes were at least partially due to steroid usage. Cadigan would refute the claims, admitting to having used steroids but denying that it had been for any length of time. O'Brien was pleased with the choice, calling up his new teammate to tell him how much he liked offensive linemen, but the search for a starting left tackle was not over – after just four starts at tackle in his rookie year, Cadigan would switch to guard. Somehow, on a line famously made up of guards and centers, the Jets had managed to find another one.

There was also hope that the team was coming back together after fracturing in 1987. The efforts Walton made to rebuild personal relationships were appreciated by the players, and O'Brien commented that the coach was handling things well, allowing the players to talk to him about past grievances in an effort to clear the air moving forward. In an era before email or WhatsApp, Walton instead kept his team up to date with his thinking through (rather quaintly) regular letters. The coach was upbeat in the build-up to the new season, refusing to look at his team as being in rebuilding mode.

'Rebuilding?' he asked, rhetorically. 'No, I'd say refurbishing with a look to the future. We must have the patience to work with young people this season. There will be a new blend that will develop. As a football coach I hate to think of 'rebuilding', and I don't. I don't think that's what we have to do. But make no mistake, we have to recharge ourselves. I think we need that young spirit to add to our corps of veterans who have proved they can win.'[1]

Walton went on to touch on the two most important elements needed for a successful season: 'We have to get healthy, a problem that has concerned us for all the years that I've been here. But more important maybe is that we have to regroup and get back to being one. We have to get back to caring about each other. Caring about our teammates, being New York Jets, and our fans.'

The Jets were younger, nowhere more so than in the defensive secondary, where three rookies made an impact in training camp, while former first-round draft pick Russell Carter was traded for a conditional sixth-rounder. Out of 148 players as training camp opened, more than a hundred were rookies, first-year players or injured veterans making their return. It would be some feat to pull a team together out of such a mix, especially with established veterans continuing to fall by the wayside – Lance Mehl announced his retirement in July, having failed to recover from his second major knee injury in as many seasons. Still, the mood was buoyant when the veterans reported to training camp on Sunday, July 25, perhaps partly because they were anticipating an easier Camp Walton than usual. After a short holdout, Cadigan signed a four-year deal worth more than $2 million and was pencilled in at left tackle. O'Brien, who had gone down under 152 sacks in his three seasons as full-time starter, finally had something to smile about. Overall, he saw an improved line, with Sweeney returning to his natural position of center, bringing more bulk to the position than long-time starter Joe Fields.

The early results were not encouraging, as O'Brien was sacked three times in the preseason opener against the Eagles. With the offense failing to do much of anything, Walton took the decision to keep O'Brien in the game into the fourth quarter, despite the beating he was taking. He completed just five of his 14 passing attempts. Walton would later claim that O'Brien needed to get used to working behind his new line, but letting the line make its mistakes with a back-up in the game might have made more sense.

And still the team continued to be reshaped. Two more veterans in the secondary, cornerback Jerry Holmes and safety Harry Hamilton, were released. Most of the veterans let go by the Jets did not do much elsewhere, but this pair clearly had plenty of football left in them. Holmes started 60 games for the Lions and Packers over the next four seasons, intercepting 11 passes. Hamilton started 50 games for the Bucs over the same time-frame and made 17 picks.

Against the Giants, in the second preseason game, Jets quarterbacks went down under a combined seven sacks, although O'Brien was only nabbed twice in the two quarters he played. Reggie McElroy played so badly at right tackle that free agent Jeff Criswell was elevated in the depth chart. He would alternate drives with McElroy in the third preseason contest, against the Browns in Montreal. Criswell would not stick at right tackle, but after Cadigan failed to nail down the left tackle spot, the rangy Criswell would start 104 games for the Jets at that position, and then another 39 for the Chiefs. Having twice failed to find a left tackle in the first-round of the draft, the Jets were about to find one they had signed off the street.

McElroy responded well to the challenge. In the week before the game he ditched the knee brace he had been wearing since coming back from reconstructive surgery, claiming it was sapping his confidence. He went on to start all 16 games for the Jets in 1988, and his good play helped O'Brien snap an unpleasant streak – he had suffered at least one sack in 27 straight games, including exhibition and playoff contests, but against the Browns the sack column remained empty. O'Brien cited a new-found willingness to throw the ball away when no target was open (something he did twice against the Browns to avoid would-be sacks). Less encouraging was the return of the injury bug – seven-year veteran linebacker Bob Crable suffered a knee injury that was at first thought to be minor, but was actually career-ending.

The final preseason game, against the Packers, suggested it was going to be a long season for the Jets, and for O'Brien in particular. With Cadigan and Haight still getting used to playing alongside each other, the left side of the line was a source of constant pressure as O'Brien took three sacks and was knocked down many more times. The first three drives yielded zero first downs and even a return to some sort of form by Gastineau (he had two sacks against the Packers' starting o-line) was scant consolation. O'Brien did throw his first touchdown pass of the preseason, but his completion rate of less than 52 percent over the four games was uncharacteristic. He also suffered an injury to his left shoulder against Green Bay, but was declared fit to start the season-opener. The Jets offense was stuck in neutral and their quarterback was already banged up, but there was no pause button. The season was about to start.

The 1988 season was one of the strangest for the Jets. At times competitive, at times ineffective, they answered some questions and posed a raft of new ones. O'Brien got better protection than feared, but it wasn't as if he was playing behind the Great Wall of China. He was sacked 37 times in 14 starts, and there was still the feeling that some of them were his fault. Pat Ryan took just five sacks during his playing time, at a significantly lower rate per attempt than O'Brien.

The Jets kicked their addiction to late-season swoons, winning three of their last four games, but they had dug themselves into a 5-6-1 hole before that and they narrowly missed out on the postseason. Gastineau was back (he collected seven sacks in the first five games) and then he was gone again, this time for good, as he quit the team and the game in bizarre fashion at the midseason point.

The season started sloppily, with a rain-soaked defeat in Foxboro. O'Brien took five sacks, four of them in the second half, as the line struggled. Cadigan was taken back to school by Patriots linebacker

Andre Tippett, and the line didn't even make it through one game intact, Jeff Criswell coming in to replace an injured McElroy.

The miserable opening made what happened next all the more surprising. Out of nowhere, the Jets caught fire and went on a three-game winning streak. It started in Cleveland, the site of one of the most painful losses in franchise history two seasons earlier. Walton juggled his linemen, bringing in Ted Banker to replace Haight at left guard, feeling that Cadigan at left tackle, and Sweeney at center needed a steadier veteran presence between them.

With Al Toon making his first start after missing the Patriots game, and a slimmed-down Roger Vick seeing plenty of the ball, the offense looked balanced as they drove to a 22-yard field goal from Pat Leahy, who had moved into the NFL's all-time top 10 in scoring the previous week. Later in the quarter, O'Brien hit Walker on a beautiful 49-yard pass from his own 14-yard line. It was only the second catch Walker had made in the young season so far, but it was a sign that he still had what it took to torment a secondary, as he withstood solid contact from Frank Minnifield to stay upright and haul in the pinpoint bomb. Leahy then almost added another six points after scampering into the end zone for his first touchdown on a fake field goal, but the play was called back for holding and he had to settle for adding the six points by a more conventional route, with two more field goals. Another touchdown was cancelled by penalty, O'Brien's perfectly lofted ball for Johnny Hector being ruled out by a pass interference call on Toon.

The modified offensive line was doing a good job, drawing praise from commentator's Mel Proctor and Al DeRogatis (who had worked as an analyst on NBC's broadcast of the Jets' Super Bowl victory back in January 1969), and there was a sense that everything was oh-so-nearly slotting into place. Then, just before halftime, O'Brien took one of the most brutal sacks of his career. Reminiscent in some ways of the devastating collision served up by Andre Tippett in the 1985 wild card game, this one saw Browns linebacker David Grayson deliver a hit that would have drawn a flag in the modern game. Grayson lowered his head to spear O'Brien in the side of the helmet, lifting both of the quarterback's feet off the ground and dumping him on his back on the infield dirt of the dual-sport Municipal Stadium. O'Brien stayed on the ground for a few moments and then got to his feet, pointing at Grayson with a good-natured smile, congratulating him on the play.

'O'Brien appears to be alright,' commented Proctor. 'He was sacked 50 times last year. In the last couple of years he spent more time looking at the sky than Doctor Carl Sagan.'

The play was an anomaly, however, in a game where O'Brien was mostly given time to throw, sitting back in the pocket while his linemen kept a powerful Browns defense at bay. For the first time in his six years as head coach, Walton awarded a game ball to the offensive line and it was well deserved. It also demonstrated how efficient O'Brien could still be when given time, as he completed 19 of 30 passes for 256 yards and a 90.4 passer rating. Some downplayed the win, pointing out that the Browns were without their star quarterback, Bernie Kosar, and lost replacement Gary Danielson in the third quarter.

'We still had to come out and make our plays,' O'Brien pointed out. 'That's just a part of football.'[2]

After two games, O'Brien had yet to throw a touchdown. He put that right against the Oilers the following week. Houston had taken over the mantle as the league's dirtiest team under head coach Jerry Glanville, and the Jets geared themselves up for a physical encounter.

'They seem to have that reputation,' O'Brien commented in the build-up to the game, 'but I don't know. I haven't watched them, but we can't be too concerned about how they play. We have to take care of our own business.'[3]

The game was prickly from the start. Taunting from rookie corner James Hasty on Oilers receiver Ernest Givins prompted a shoving match and the first of five personal foul penalties called against the Jets, as they set out to fight fire with fire. There was another helmet-to-helmet hit on O'Brien, this one from defensive end Robert Banks, but despite the rough treatment, there were signs that the passing game was coming back into focus. A deep pass down the right sidelines was accurate but misjudged by Sohn, who just failed to make the catch. Then Toon failed to bring in an easy catch that would have been a 15-yard score. Two plays later, O'Brien had his first touchdown of the season, an eight-yarder to Kurt Sohn. In an uncharacteristic show of emotion, O'Brien ran into the end zone, grabbed Sohn, and butted heads with his good friend four times.

On the Jets' next offensive play, after an interception by another rookie, safety Erik McMillan, O'Brien lofted a 44-yard bomb to Walker to set up an eight-yard scoring run from McNeil. A 24-yard catch-and-run from Hector (with a 15-yard personal foul tacked on), set the Jets up at midfield on their next possession, from where O'Brien found Walker on his second bomb of the day, this one good for a 50-yard touchdown. It was looking an awful lot like 1986, and after the Oilers missed a short field goal the Jets started driving again, with Al Toon threatening to take over the game. He made two catches on the drive before he was levelled attempting to make a third, Jeff Donaldson hitting him square in the jaw and knocking the receiver out of the game. Toon was helped off the field, clearly woozy. Unknown at the time was the fact that this was just the start of a string of concussions that would ultimately cut Toon's career short. The drive ended with O'Brien's third touchdown of the half, a perfectly lobbed four-yarder to Walker.

'Beautifully laid out there,' said Al DeRogatis. '[Walker] beats his man, and Kenny O'Brien just lays it in. You just don't do it much better.'

It capped a brilliant half from O'Brien, who had completed 13 of 18 passes for 226 yards and the three scores, setting the stage for the largest winning margin in team history, 45-3, to that point. After adding another 34 yards to his total, he gave way to Ryan, who was just as effective, hitting on all five of his passes, including a perfect 23-yard scoring toss to Walker for the receiver's third of the game. The Jets offense had not looked this good, this able to strike from any range, since the Atlanta game in 1986, and it wasn't just the delighted fans in Giants Stadium who saw this as a return to those glory days.

'It's great to show we can still make the big plays,' Walker commented after his huge day (six catches for 129 yards and three touchdowns). 'We weren't sure if we could get the coverages we were looking for. But we did, and we took advantage.'[4]

'We just pick up and go with what is hot for us,' O'Brien said of the Jets' offensive philosophy, 'and Wes was as hot as a pistol for us.'

After the emphatic victory, talk started of this new-look Jets team, with a revamped offensive line that had suddenly clicked, a group of upstart youngsters in the defensive backfield and a return to form for Gastineau, who notched two sacks against the Oilers. The league's newest bad boys had been sent home thoroughly chastened, and just about the only contribution made by their flamboyant head coach was to leave a ticket at the stadium for the phantom of the opera. Around a hundred people turned up at the ticket office to try and claim it, but none of them bothered to dress in costume to reinforce their bid.

As quickly as things had come together for the Jets, they began to unravel. Health, that critical and elusive ingredient that Walton had spoken about before the season, became an issue once more as the suddenly effective offensive line was undermined before the next game. Cadigan, who had been performing well at left tackle, missed the Detroit game after picking up an ankle injury in the third quarter against Houston, forcing Criswell to step in. Although Criswell would become a decent player, he would commit four penalties and give up a sack in a shaky performance against the Lions. Then, in the second quarter of that game, Dan Alexander injured a calf muscle, bringing in Haight. He could not play on the right side of the line, so he took over the left guard spot, forcing Ted Banker to slide over to right guard. Just like that, three-fifths of the line had changed and O'Brien was harried all day. He took four sacks and was also forced to attack underneath the coverage for most of the game as pressure from Lions pass-rushers made it impossible to look downfield.

In a mausoleum-like atmosphere (less than 30,000 fans showed up and the Silverdome was like an echo chamber) the Jets were being held at 10-10 in the fourth quarter when they finally found a way to break through, taking a risk with a slow-developing play that was aimed to free Walker behind the coverage. The play, called 'Waggle Left, X Stop, Spread Special' worked perfectly and Walker caught the game-winning touchdown backing into the end zone uncovered.

'We put that in especially for this game,' O'Brien said after guiding his team to a 3-1 record with an efficient but unspectacular passing performance that saw him complete 71 percent of his passes for 253 yards. 'It's just slow developing. You can't rush it. It's almost like a broken play. If they [the offensive line] give you that much protection, it's tough for the DB to cover that long.'[5]

There had been few fireworks, but a young team had shown resilience in winning a scrappy game when far from its best. O'Brien had seen his interception-free streak end at 211, the second-longest streak in NFL history, but the mood remained positive – O'Brien always stressed that statistics were not important to him and claimed not to have been aware of how lengthy his streak had become.

Quietly, the Jets had found their way back to the top of the AFC. Going into their game against the Chiefs, they ranked first in time of possession (33:11 per game), first in third-down conversions (34 of 64) and were tied for the lead in turnovers at plus-five. Everything appeared to be set up for the winning streak to continue when the offense was boosted by the return of Alexander at right guard. His return allowed Banker to go back to the left, and against Kansas City the early signs were good.

O'Brien looked sharp and the running game sparked for the first time. With Vick enjoying a career day (15 carries for 95 yards) and McNeil at his slippery best (22 carries for 154 yards), Walton had the luxury of calling a balanced game that piled up 542 total net yards. Scoring was not so easy, though. Hector dropped a short pass in the third quarter that would either have been a touchdown or a first-and-goal inside the one, and the Jets were limited to a 3-0 lead after the first quarter having dominated on both sides of the ball.

On the Jets' second play of the second quarter, O'Brien found McNeil on a short pass and he turned it into a 19-yard gain. Just as the camera panned away from O'Brien, two Chiefs hit him, and replays showed that he landed heavily on his right elbow, getting up slowly and looking a little shaken. There seemed to be no ill effects, as he zipped a pinpoint 17-yard pass to Sohn a few plays later to convert a third down and set up a four-yard touchdown run from Hector, who scored behind a superb block from Banker, pulling from his left guard position.

A pair of turnovers kept the Jets from adding to their score until they were given a short field by a 33-yard punt return from Jo-Jo Townsell late in the third quarter. A balanced drive was capped by a one-yard Hector run, his second score of the day, giving the Jets a 17-3 lead. It was to prove the highpoint of their season. A Chiefs offense that had managed just 146 yards up to that point, against the league's best defense in terms of points allowed, was about to wake up. An 80-yard catch-and-run by Carlos Carson made it 17-10, and with the Jets driving towards another score, Vick fumbled at the Chiefs' 23-yard line. After getting the ball back, the Jets were driving again... but they were increasingly relying on the run. When they did attempt to pass, O'Brien was either sacked or forced to check down, with the Chiefs guarding against the deep pass. A second Steve DeBerg touchdown pass in the last minute tied the game, but there were more opportunities for the Jets to win. A flurry of O'Brien passes in the last few seconds almost put them into field goal range, and then the first drive in overtime led to a field goal attempt. The rain had started to fall, and it fell hard, joined by a strong wind. O'Brien bobbled a snap, losing a couple of yards that may have forced Leahy to put a little extra leg into his kick. It sailed wide right.

O'Brien then set the Jets up for another field goal attempt at the Chiefs' 15, but Walton called for another running play, hoping to center the ball to make things easier for Leahy. McNeil ran into a crowd, fumbled the ball, and the Chiefs recovered. Incredibly, there was one more chance after Bobby Humphery intercepted DeBerg at the Jets 49 with just 25 seconds to play in overtime. Two more completed passes put the Jets at the Chief's 34, but they were unable to stop the clock and the game ended in confusion and acrimony as the officials took an age to work out how to handle an illegal procedure penalty against the Jets. Walton argued with the officials to no avail, and the Jets had somehow failed to win a game where they had rushed for 272 yards and held the ball for 14 minutes more than their opponent.

The 'Joe must go' chants that followed Walton off the field were uncalled for, as the Jets were still one of the surprise teams of the season. It was impossible to criticise Walton for running the ball so often – McNeil and Vick had been at the top of their game – but that one last running play, when they were already in position for a 32-yard attempt, would haunt the team for the reast of the season. Walton admitted to thinking long and hard about the play, but finally said he would do the same thing again, and was even planning another running play to try to get down near the 10. In Walton's favor was the fact that McNeil hadn't fumbled since 1986.

The tie prevented the Jets from joining Buffalo at the top of the AFC East, but there was no sign of a let-down when they travelled to Cincinnati to face an up-and-coming Bengals team. O'Brien came out looking to throw deep, overshooting Walker on one play and checking down to Freeman McNeil on another. The defense, however, was on target. On their first play they sacked Boomer Esiason for a safety and on their second they forced a fumble by Stanley Wilson, setting the Jets up at the six, from where Roger Vick scored two plays later. Special teams had also answered the bell, downing a punt inside the five to set up the safety and blocking a field goal the first time the Bengals threatened. The Jets were 9-0 up against one of the hottest teams in the league.

Everything went wrong from that point, as Eddie Brown scored on a 60-yard bomb from Esiason on the Bengals' next drive. O'Brien took two sacks to kill the Jets' next drive, fumbling both times, although the Jets recovered the ball on each occasion. A second Esiason pass to Brown, this time from just eight yards out, gave Cincinnati a three-point lead (Jim Breech had managed to miss both extra point attempts).

The Jets tied the game at 12 with a 30-yard field goal, but O'Brien was under siege, generating just 54 passing yards in the half as he was repeatedly hit. Esiason put Cincinnati in front at halftime with his third touchdown pass.

The second half started in much the same way as the first. Troy Benson recovered an Ickey Woods fumble on the Bengals' first play to give the Jets great field position and O'Brien went short to Toon from the 11. Toon jinked his way into the end zone for his first touchdown of the year to tie the game once more. Woods then earned redemption with two scores to take the game away from the Jets, performing his awkward little touchdown dance, the 'Ickey Shuffle' to the delight of the Bengals home crowd. O'Brien fumbled again after another sack, killing a promising drive, and just missed on a deep bomb to Toon, David Fulcher making a great play to knock the ball away at the last moment, saving what would have been a 42-yard score.

There isn't always an obvious moment in a game that turns it, or an obvious reason for a defeat. The Jets' ground game was okay but not dominating, and O'Brien's passing was sharp and accurate, despite the punishment he took from the Bengals. What was apparent, however, was that the deep ball had been removed from the Jets' offense once more. Following that barnstorming show against the Oilers, teams had guarded against the bomb and although O'Brien frequently looked deep, and occasionally uncorked a bomb, his targets were not running free through the secondary and he often had to overthrow to avoid the risk of an interception. On the times when he hung in the pocket looking for a man to break free, he was repeatedly caught for sacks, and his three fumbles against the Bengals were a career high.

It was symptomatic of a league where tendencies were studied more and more, and film study had moved on to the more accessible videotape (the league had made the switch from old-fashioned film in 1986). It was far easier to give a player a VHS tape of an upcoming opponent rather than gathering them in a darkened room with a projector. The coverage offered by the NFL in its game film was extensive, including shots from the end zone and the use of wide-angle lenses (similar to the all-22, full-field view used by today's analysts). Defensive players could see exactly how the Jets' deep passing game worked, and they were set on taking it away.

There were other revolutions in play. The Bengals made use of their no-huddle offense, keeping the Jets from substituting defenders and three times drawing penalties for having too many men on the field. Esiason had the authority to change plays at the line of scrimmage, depending on what he saw, while Walton's system was less flexible. The chaos caused by the Bengals' approach masked the fact that Esisason only completed 10 of his passes against the Jets, but they went for 230 yards and three touchdowns.

The problems with pass protection had returned, as Cadigan looked shaky in his first start after being benched. He was benched again for Criswell during the Bengals game and with the Bills' Bruce Smith on the horizon, the Jets allowed Gastineau to practice against the rookie, hoping it would sharpen his game. It was all for nought, as Cadigan suffered a sprained left foot after getting kicked during practice and was ruled out for at least four weeks. He would not play at tackle for the Jets again. O'Brien also went into the Bills game missing his top target, as Shuler was ruled out with a pinched nerve in his neck, and the defense would have to manage without emerging pass-rusher Alex Gordon.

If the Bengals game only got away from the Jets at the end, the Monday Night Football match-up with Buffalo was an entirely different story. O'Brien had insisted that being on primetime TV was nothing to get worked up about.

'It's just another game,' he said in the days before the contest. 'An important game, but it would be just as important if it was on a Sunday. They're in first place in the division. We need to close in on them, so it's a big game, but not because it's on Monday night television. There's a lot of enthusiasm and everyone in the league is watching. But we can't lose sight of it as another game, a game you have to take in stride. The only hard part is waiting around for 9 o'clock. That's a late start.'[6]

It turned out there was another hard part to the game – Bruce Smith. The second-year defensive end terrorized the Jets offensive line. On a string of three plays, after the Bills had already staked a 17-0 lead, he beat Criswell inside to dump McNeil in the backfield on a running play, drew a holding penalty on Ted Banker and then beat Criswell with a spin move to sack O'Brien. After the sack, Smith's second of the first quarter, ABC put up a telling graphic. In 140 games and 3,762 passes, Joe Namath was sacked 175 times. In 60 games, O'Brien had thrown 1,781 passes and had been sacked 196 times.

The Jets generated four net passing yards in the first quarter and O'Brien was taking a beating. After falling further behind, Walton changed up his game plan in an attempt to neutralize the devastating pass-rush. O'Brien hit Hector on a screen that gained 11. Then, with the Bills playing the run on third-and one, he found tight end Billy Griggs with an accurate mid-range pass that went for 21 yards. On the next play Walton got even more creative, calling a flea-flicker that gave O'Brien enough time to look deeper, and he found Toon for a 26-yard pass to the Bills' nine. A conventional drop-back pass then resulted in a six-yard gain to Toon, but O'Brien was flattened by Smith after he released the ball. It was clear that anything other than quick-hitting passes or some form of misdirection was going to result in the quarterback getting killed. The drive ended in a Hector touchdown, but any hopes were quickly snuffed out when the Bills scored again.

The next time O'Brien got the ball he was drilled on a safety blitz. The play was intended to get the ball out of O'Brien's hands quickly, but Leonard Smith was quicker, charging up the middle totally unchecked. O'Brien was hit directly under the chin by the crown of Smith's helmet as he let go of the ball, before landing hard on his right elbow and shoulder. Clearly shaken, he took a while to get to his feet.

Kenny Timex was taking a lickin', but for now at least he was still tickin'. The same could not be said for Ted Banker. A couple of plays after his huge hit on O'Brien, Leonard Smith was part of a jailbreak blitz that buried the quarterback on a third-and-five passing attempt. O'Brien was fine, but Banker, who had been bull-rushed to the ground by Fred Smerlas, had twisted his left ankle, suffering a foot sprain that knocked him out of the game and would keep him out for the next four weeks. The left side of the Jets line was out of action and the replacements were struggling. It was open season on Jets quarterbacks.

After the half, trailing 31-7, the Jets came out swinging, but a deep pass from O'Brien was so far off target, as well as being underthrown, that it looked like it had been aimed at Bills safety Mark Kelso, who duly intercepted it.

'That's about as bad a pass as you're going to see Ken O'Brien throw,' said Frank Gifford. 'He just hung that up.'

The mood at Giants Stadium was getting ugly. As well as numerous brawls between fans, there were at least two fires in the upper deck and an enthusiastic rendition of 'Joe Must Go'. Amid the chaos, Erik McMillan returned an interception for a touchdown and O'Brien treated the fans to a display of prestidigitation that a magician would have been proud of. Having just shrugged off another sack, he dropped back to pass, cocked his arm, lost grip of the ball, turned to catch it out of the air and shovelled it to tight end Billy Griggs, who made some nice yardage and then fumbled the ball himself.

It was that kind of night, and it turned out to be that kind of week. Having been featured in a TV spot at halftime during the Monday night demolition, Gastineau shocked his teammates by retiring from football in the middle of the following week. Gastineau's resurgence (he had seven sacks in as many games) made the decision all the more painful, especially for the team's younger generation of defenders, who had struck up a rapport with the controversial defensive end. The only consolation was that the next opponent was Miami.

O'Brien typically had his best games against the Dolphins, but something was wrong. Although he threw three touchdowns, and the Jets won an entertaining game they desperately needed by a score of

44-30, this was not one of the trademark shootouts between him and Dan Marino. The deep pass was malfunctioning – Walker was open three times for what would have been long scoring passes, but O'Brien over-, under- and then overthrew him again. O'Brien finished with just 174 passing yards, having completed less than half of his attempts, while Marino had exploded for 521 yards. The difference in the game had been a solid ground attack (159 yards on 36 carries), five interceptions (three of them from McMillan, who returned one for his second touchdown of the season) and two fumble recoveries.

It was the same story the following week, as O'Brien missed Toon from the Steelers' 30-yard line, underthrowing his receiver, who was heading into the end zone wide open. Two plays later a short pass to Griggs that the tight end took into the end zone was wiped off on for an 'in the grasp' sack, but O'Brien's other passes were sailing high or wide. Toon made a leaping one-handed grab of one pass but was unable to clearly establish control before stepping out of bounds. Walker jumped helplessly for another ball, then Toon saw a high pass go off his fingertips. O'Brien had opened one for eight. In the commentary booth, Marv Albert and Paul Maguire speculated that the tinted mask O'Brien was wearing might have been affecting his vision.

Walton did not lose faith in his quarterback, calling a steady stream of passing plays, and O'Brien responded with a sequence of eight completions in 10 attempts, including a two-yard touchdown to Mickey Shuler, but it proved to be just a brief flurry, as he would complete just four more passes all day, ending with a miserable 24.4 percent completion rate.

The 24-20 win masked the difficulties, lifting the Jets to a 5-3-1 record. The fans were pleased, having finally beaten the Steelers at the tenth time of asking, and they were less raucous than usual following a ban on beer sales at Giants Stadium in the second half of games, but there was clearly a problem. O'Brien would throw no touchdowns and three interceptions over the next two games, both losses as the Jets faded from playoff contention, and his week 11 game against the Patriots was one of the worst of his entire career. He completed just 11 of 30 passes for 134 yards.

Once more, trouble on the offensive line was playing its part. Against Indianapolis, in week 10, Mike Withycombe saw his first ever game action after right guard Guy Bingham injured his knee. Bingham himself had been subbing for Dan Alexander, whose playing streak (not counting the strike games in 1987) had come to an end at 172 as he dealt with a bruise to his calf. O'Brien was streaky again, once completing 12 straight passes, but connecting on just eight of his other 19 attempts. Scrambling for men to man the trenches, the Jets signed guard Ron Tilton, who had not played since 1986 and would not play a down for the Jets. Finding quality replacements was not easy and it just continued to get worse as Jeff Criswell left the Patriots game with a knee injury, although he was able to return the following week.

As had happened in 1986, O'Brien insisted there was nothing physically wrong with him, but his sudden inaccuracy told a different story, and was the major factor in the Jets' slumping offense. Walker had all but disappeared – over a four-week mid-season period, rookie safety Erik McMillan caught more passes than the star wideout. Toon was morphing into a possession receiver, piling up receptions but averaging barely over 10 yards per catch. O'Brien's per-attempt average had dipped to a league-low (among starters) 5.92 yards.

Over a six-game period, the Jets had gone 2-4 and O'Brien had completed less than half of his passes. He had failed to reach 200 yards in any of those games, and the result was inevitable. For the second time in his career, and in similar circumstances, O'Brien was benched. He just wasn't playing like himself.

Back in 1986, there had been the injured pinky, which may or may not have been a factor in how he was able to grip the ball at the end of the year. There were the repeated blows to his padded right elbow, and there was speculation that his arm had simply grown tired after all the bombs he had heaved up into the air. This time, O'Brien insisted that his arm strength was still good, pointing out that the team had analysed his throwing motion during practice in light of his slump. Whether or not anything was being kept from the media (and teams would often be tight-lipped over minor things that could be kept off an injury report), that remained the company line as Ryan took the reins, but his tenure was once more brief. Following a close defeat to the Bills, he was enjoying his best game as a pro against Miami before being forced out with a concussion. Passing for 341 yards, he had led the Jets to a 24-14 lead before things unravelled after his injury. Three third-quarter touchdowns from Marino gave the Dolphins the lead until O'Brien came off the bench, to an enthusiastic welcome from the Giants Stadium crowd.

O'Brien hadn't been out of action for long, but he looked refreshed as he hit Shuler on a 12-yard pass, then floated out of the pocket to buy time before finding Hector on a 30-yard catch-and-run right down the middle of the field. Quickly getting into the flow of the game, O'Brien had a rare run up the middle for five yards to open the fourth quarter, laughing about it in the huddle afterwards, and then lofted a perfect pass to Shuler in the corner of the end zone for a seven-yard touchdown. On the Jets' next possession he ripped a 13-yarder to Toon, and then overthrew Walker on a deep ball.

'You've got to hand it to Ken O'Brien,' said Bom Trumpy in the commentary booth. 'When you have a starting quarterback, and this week it was Pat Ryan, he takes about 95 percent of the snaps in practice. Ken O'Brien was also not the starter two weeks ago against Buffalo... so for Ken O'Brien to come out and throw the ball the way he's thrown, he's obviously said, "wait a minute, you know. I got two ways to take this. I can be upset that I'm not starting, or I can stay ready." He's obviously stayed ready.'

A few players later, Walker broke free in the end zone and O'Brien found him from 18 yards out to put the Jets into the lead. After the defense held, O'Brien ran out the clock, the highlight of the final drive being a 13-yard pass to Toon, his 14th reception of the day, to convert on third-and-eight. 'Tooooоon,' called the crowd, as they enjoyed the familiar emotions of a victory over their divisional rivals.

It had been a stunning turnaround. From no offense at all, to the highest yardage total (597) in team history, and while O'Brien would rightly be praised for being ready to come in off the bench, thoughts went out to Ryan, who once again had been given his chance only to see injury take it away. He had passed for 269 yards in the first half alone, and it had taken a cheap shot from the Dolphins' Mark Brown (who was ejected and later suspended for one week) to slow him down and, ultimately, take him out of the game. Ryan was a tough player, but he was an object lesson in the fact that O'Brien's resilience was not commonplace, nor something to be dismissed lightly. Few quarterbacks could take the punishment dished out behind the Jets' offensive line and keep on getting up.

Walton found himself with a big decision as a second game against the Chiefs drew near... and O'Brien was just about to make things a little more complicated. On the sideline during the Miami game, he had been seen flexing his right shoulder, in a manner that suggested he was in discomfort. Having insisted for weeks that he was fine physically, it now emerged that he was suffering from bicep tendinitis in his throwing arm, and had taken an anti-inflammatory shot after his relief appearance against the Dolphins. There was confusion over the details – the team appeared to think O'Brien had kept the severity of the injury quiet, whereas he said they knew all about it. Whatever the truth of the matter, it would be several days before the anti-inflammatory would work, so the starting job for the following game was up in the air.

O'Brien also revealed that tests done in the week before the Miami game had revealed a significant loss of strength in his throwing shoulder, which would explain his suddenly inaccurate passing. Further analysis would later reveal that he had subconsciously altered his throwing motion in an attempt to alleviate the discomfort. It was even possible that the change in throwing motion had triggered the tendonitis.

Bicep tendonitis (literally inflammation of the bicep tendon) can be a repetitive motion injury, caused by performing the same action repeatedly. Baseball pitchers are more prone to such injury, given the massive stress they place on their throwing elbow, but a quarterback can be susceptible to it as well, and the news brought back memories of Paul Zimmerman's comments about O'Brien's arm two years previously.

'O'Brien had come into camp during the summer and thrown five days a week,' Dr. Z had written in the pages of *Sports Illustrated*. 'When he wasn't practicing on the field during the season, he was throwing on the sideline, always throwing... he was young and strong, and his arm had lightning in it. Then his arm got tired.'[7]

Was this a recurrence of the same problem? Tendinitis could also be caused by an injury to the tendon. O'Brien had taken 185 sacks since 1985. He had been knocked to the ground after releasing the ball many more times than that, and on many of those times he had landed on his right elbow, on hard AstroTurf. The team had admitted to him having bursitis (inflammation of the bursar sac) in his throwing elbow at the end of 1986. Like tendonitis, bursitis could be caused by a repetitive motion or a direct injury, or a combination of both. The only cure for such inflammation is long-term rest, but that is a luxury an NFL player is seldom allowed.

Ryan eventually got the starting nod against the Chiefs and played well again, leading the Jets to a 10-point lead in the final quarter. The defense was unable to hang on, and this time there was no time for late-game heroics from O'Brien. James Saxon, behind a block from Christian Okoye, scored from a yard out on fourth down to win the game (despite a desperate kick return where the Jets lateralled 12 times to no avail) and end the Jets' faint playoff dreams. They had lost eight straight regular season games in December, and O'Brien's slump wasn't the only problem – the pass-rush had disappeared with the retirement of Gastineau (24 sacks in the first seven games of the year had been followed by just eight in the seven games since he had retired) and the rookie-heavy secondary had fallen apart as opposing quarterbacks were given time to dissect it.

The Jets, always a team that marched to the beat of its own drum, responded by giving Walton a contract extension. He was still the only Jets coach in history with a winning record, although it had dipped to 47-45-1. The front office (specifically Steve Gutman, who had taken the position of team president the previous June) expressed satisfaction with the youth movement that had transformed the roster in 1988. Walton would go into 1989 ranked eighth among NFL coaches in terms of longevity with their current team. All of the seven coaches ranked above him had taken their teams to the Super Bowl, but the Jets had different goals. Gutman spoke of their aim being to win the AFC East.

It was true that the Jets had made progress in some areas during an up-and-down year. Notably, they were much younger, and Walton had made great efforts to improve his relationship with the players after the car wreck of the 1987 strike-shortened campaign. The payoff for that was a team that did not give up even when the season had effectively ended. In the last two games of 1988, the Jets showed resilience and grit and scratched out two wins, ending their December jinx and apparently setting themselves up for a step forward in 1989. The games were notable for one other reason as well. They saw O'Brien win back his starting job.

Ryan started against the Colts in week 15, but was out of sorts, possibly suffering lingering effects from the concussion he had suffered in the Miami game. He threw three interceptions in the first half, to go alongside just four completions, and he was seen talking to O'Brien on the sideline, perhaps saying that he was not feeling it. O'Brien started to swing his arm to warm up his shoulder and grabbed his helmet.

After stepping into the fray, it wasn't a stellar performance from O'Brien. He completed barely half of his passes, but he led three touchdown drives, including an accurate 33-yard scoring strike to Toon that beat a Colts' blitz on third down. On the sideline, Walton punched the air with delight and was then seen slapping his players on the shoulder as they came off the field. Shuler even got a hug in a genuine show of affection from the coach.

The 34-16 win gave the Jets something to play for in their final game. At 7-7-1, they could finish with a winning record if they knocked off their crosstown rivals, the Giants. As a bonus, beating the Giants would go a long way to keeping them out of the playoffs. Walton had, of course, once been a tight end for the Giants. In the build-up, he had these words to say on the personal relevance of the game: 'I still have a little blue in me. But I want to kick them where it hurts.'

As it happened, it wasn't a kicker who put the hurt on the Giants, it was O'Brien, who was returned to the starting job after four weeks as the back-up. The official reason cited was that Ryan had a sore shoulder, but his problems were with his left (non-throwing) shoulder, while O'Brien still admitted to having soreness in his more important right shoulder. If the Jets had not been concerned with winning, they would have continued to rest O'Brien for a game that would be the last of their season whatever the outcome – clearly, they were all-in on winning.

Walton's gameplan was clear. Establish the run and catch the Giants by surprise with mid-range passes. It worked perfectly on the Jets' first drive, as a series of runs from McNeil and Hector moved the chains, and then O'Brien lofted a 28-yard pass to Toon. As the drive continued, Vern Lundquist came up with some interesting information when chatting with Terry Bradshaw.

'O'Brien with a shoulder injury,' he said. 'Interesting, Terry, he was telling us that it caused him to alter his throwing motion and Pat Ryan noticed it about five weeks ago.'

'Right,' Bradshaw replied. 'Ryan was the one that noticed O'Brien had changed his motion, by looking at practice tape. He said, "Ken, you're not throwing the same way, look at this", and he pointed it out to O'Brien, and he didn't realise he had a shoulder problem. Then he went to the doctors and they all started looking to find out what the injury was.'

The opening drive led to a field goal and when they got the ball back, O'Brien went deep on the first play to Walker, hitting him for 37 yards. The play would have gone for a touchdown had O'Brien been able to lead his receiver, who had got behind the defense. After four running plays, O'Brien threw a high ball up for Shuler, who grabbed it for a touchdown, and the Jets led 10-0. O'Brien's best pass of the day came on the next drive, a 49-yard bomb that hit Walker on the run to set up another Leahy field goal.

'Kenny O'Brien, shoulder injury and all, is having a big first half,' said Lundquist as O'Brien displayed uncharacteristic emotion on the field, punching the air with delight. On three drives, he had hit passes of 28, 37 and 49 yards, but the Jets only had a 13-0 lead.

As the Giants fought for their playoff spot, the game became tight. Their defense put the clamps on O'Brien, while Phil Simms began to find his rhythm. He threw three touchdown passes and the Jets could only respond on a short drive after Sohn, in his last professional game, recovered a fumbled punt and McNeil scored from six yards out. Simms' third touchdown gave the Giants a 21-20 lead with less than five minutes remaining, and it looked like the Jets' quest for a winning record had fallen short, until they put together their last drive of the season.

It started with another stellar play from a special teams unit that had been special all year. Bobby Humphery set the Jets up at their own 48-yard line and Walton put the game in O'Brien's hands. Vick caught a tipped pass for six yards and then another for 11 more. Toon caught a short pass for four yards before a Hector run set up a third-and-two at the two-minute warning. With the ball at the Giants' 27-yard line, a Leahy field goal would have been a 50-50 shot, especially considering the blustery conditions, so a conversion was critical. O'Brien took a short drop, hit his back foot and fired another high pass at Shuler, who caught the ball at the 17 and trundled to the 11. The 16-yard gain made a field goal a mere chip-shot, and the Jets were able to start bleeding the clock. Two- and four-yard runs from McNeil put the ball at the five-yard line with 41 ticks left in the game.

As O'Brien came up to the line of scrimmage, Bradshaw mused on the possibility of a pass.

'Play action Vern?' he asked. 'Do you take a shot?'

'Don't think so,' was Lundquist's reply, but O'Brien did just that. Although the play sent in by Walton was another carry for McNeil, O'Brien saw that Toon was being covered one-on-one by a safety and called an audible. Toon visibly reacted, reset himself and then ran a pattern into the end zone. O'Brien lofted a perfect pass over Tom Flynn's

O'Brien reacts after throwing the winning TD against the Giants (AP Photo/ Ray Stubblebine)

head and the Jets had their third touchdown of the game. O'Brien had gone five-for-five on the final drive.

'Toon to the left,' Bradshaw commented on the replay. 'Man-for-man coverage. Notice that it's Tom Flynn, No. 28, that has Toon man-for-man. Flynn's not even a cornerback, he's a safety, he's playing out of position. A perfectly thrown ball, a fine route by Toon, but what was really good, what was really good, was the call. You don't complete it, big deal, we're gonna kick a field goal anyway. If they gamble and blitz us to stop our run, we might fumble the football, so why not throw it into the end zone?'

The game was about more than O'Brien, of course. As well as being Sohn's last game, it also marked the first time Freeman McNeil had played in all 16 games of a regular season. The defense, much maligned coming into the game, sacked Simms eight times, two of the sacks by a fired-up Marty Lyons and three by a little-known speed-rusher named Ken Rose. Still, it was the return of O'Brien to the starting role that was the headline.

'You've got to feel happy for Ken O'Brien,' said Marv Albert in the CBS studio after the game. 'Lost his job for a while, here he is back.'

O'Brien then appeared on the screen behind Albert to offer some post-game quotes.

'Special teams have been doing it for us all year long,' he said in response to a comment about Humphrey's kick return that set up the winning drive. 'They don't get the recognition they need, but when they make those kind of plays, it makes it easy for the offense to finally put it in.'

Bradshaw then asked who had called the final pass to Toon and O'Brien, as was his usual style, tried to deflect the credit for the call. 'We kind of audibled that at the line of scrimmage,' he replied. 'They came with their goal-line defense to try to stop us and Al was out there one-on-one so I just said "what the heck, let's give it a shot." Al comes through all the time and he did once again... I think it sent a message to ourselves about how good we can be if we play well and play well every day of the season, so we're excited about our future and today was just the topping for it.'

O'Brien was then asked what the game meant to him. Having first tried to turn it into a question about the team, he admitted it had been important personally.

'For us it's a big plus,' he said, 'and for me especially. I haven't beaten the Giants since I've been here, and there's a lot of people who've always thought of the Jets as second-class citizens. We have a long way to go but today was a step in the right direction.'

In further interviews, O'Brien gave a little more insight into the game's decisive play, and his confidence in Toon.

'I knew if I could get it in there, he'd come down with it,' he said. 'He's all-league, all-everything. [This game] shows we can play with anybody. There were a lot of clouds over us – winning in December, and being able to defeat a team like the Giants... those were some of the things we had to overcome and we did.'[8]

The game ended the season on a high. Although they had missed the playoffs, the Jets had transitioned to a younger team while remaining competitive. An offseason of rest and rehab for O'Brien's shoulder could set him up for another effort, and hopes were high as the Jets packed up their lockers and headed home.

The optimism for 1989 was justified. The team had displayed unity in adversity in 1988, and the image of Walton hugging his players as they came to the sideline in the season finale against the Giants was an encouraging one.

There were still problems. Cadigan had failed at left tackle and would be converted to guard – the Jets were still no nearer to solving their problems on the offensive line, having sunk multiple draft picks into the tackle position over recent years, only to see them all flame out or transmogrify into guards. There was the lingering concern over O'Brien's arm and its ability to stand up to the rigors of a 16-game regular season and (dare they hope) playoff games as well. But overall, the mood was upbeat.

'I told the players that I thought we learned a lot,' said Walton as thoughts turned to a new season. 'And I conveyed to them how much I enjoyed coaching them. If we take all of the things we learned and some of the progress we made, that's really the rewards we had last year. And we did learn a lot and it should hold us in good stead for this year.'[9]

Walton also spoke directly to his own change of approach, which had paid off by repairing his relationship with his team.

'I think I've learned you're never too old to change or try to do things differently,' he said. 'I said last year I thought the team and myself made mistakes. It was up to us to try and correct them. You never stop learning. We still have a lot of teaching left to do. A lot of the young people who progressed last year will need a good off-season program and will need the coaches to work with them again. We still have a long way to go and we've got to get better.'

One player who appreciated the change of tack was O'Brien.

'It's hard to change things,' he conceded, 'but everybody felt that it worked out better last year. Joe was in total control, and it showed in how the team played. He was positive all year and he helped create the attitude everybody has now.'

The postseason went well in one sense for O'Brien, as he signed a new three-year deal worth $4.2 million, a healthy raise on his reported $850,000 salary from 1988. But his battered shoulder was still a problem. In March the team announced that the shoulder was around 90 percent rehabilitated, but two months later that tune changed. Now referred to as 'rotator cuff tendonitis' by the Jets' trainer, Bob Reese, O'Brien was candid about how it was still affecting him: 'It feels tight,' he revealed, 'like there's something sticking in the shoulder.' [10] His workout routine would limit the number of throws made during training camp and emphasise light weightlifting, but for the first time there was talk of possible surgery if the shoulder did not respond. Ryan had already gone down that route, having rotator cuff surgery on his throwing arm.

It was a brave new era for the NFL, as a form of free agency, known as 'Plan B', had been instigated. It was to prove a short-lived experiment, gone by 1992, but while it lasted it gave teams another way of improving, at least a little. Each team could protect 37 players on its roster. The remainder were free to negotiate and sign with another team – so although this did offer to increase player movement, the players involved were usually marginal talents. Still, the Jets took a hit where they could least afford to, losing offensive guard Ted Banker to Cleveland, where he joined departed defensive coordinator Bud Carson, who was now head coach of the Browns. Still looking for help at tackle, Steve Collier was one of the Jets' first signings in Plan B. He had just six starts to his name, all back in 1987, and he never played a down in New York.

The draft was another opportunity to boost the offensive line, but the Jets found themselves in a similar position to the one they had faced during the 1987 draft. The line had shown signs of coming together late in 1988, and Criswell appeared to be a solid enough left tackle, so the team chose to address other needs. In 1987 they had gone for a fullback, Roger Vick, instead of shoring up the offensive line. In 1989, it was linebacker Jeff Lageman.

Lageman was a good player, who would give the Jets six productive seasons, mostly at defensive end. He registered 10 sacks in 1991 and the truth was there were no solid tackle prospects in the 1989 draft anyway, but he was another of the head-scratching draft-day decisions from the Jets' front office. A team desperate for pass-rush help had taken a player with one career sack in college, a player the Raiders had been hopeful of selecting with their first pick of the draft – in the fourth round. That may have been wishful thinking, but there was a feeling around the league that the Jets could have taken him with their second pick, and maybe brought in a receiver, such as Andre Rison of Michigan State, with their first. Rison proved to be a problematic player, suiting up for seven teams over a 12-year career, so who knows how long the Jets would have had him, but as Wesley Walker faded, Rison could have added something. He amassed 10,205 receiving yards and scored 84 touchdowns.

The Jets did draft a couple of receivers, one of them a college quarterback called Tony Martin, whom they hoped to switch to wideout. As a player who had never taken a snap as a receiver, it was obviously going to take time for Martin to transition, but early reports out of training camp were good. He earned praise from Walton after one practice in early August... but less than a month later he was gone.

The team hardly had a crowded receivers room, and with Walker now 34, the Jets were looking ahead to a replacement (they would spend a supplemental draft pick on Rob Moore the following year, costing them their first-round pick in 1991). Martin obviously was not picking up his new role quickly enough for the Jets' liking, and to be fair he did not play a single down for anyone in 1989, but after that he caught 593 passes for 9,065 yards and 56 touchdowns, at an average of 15.3 yards per reception. The numbers would have placed him firmly at No. 2 in the all-time Jets receiving chart, behind Don Maynard. Perhaps they should have shown a little more patience, but instead of holding on to Martin, they kept Titus Dixon, a 152-pounder who appeared in three games for the Jets and never caught a pass.

On the offensive line, they didn't miss on any greats – not one offensive tackle would go on to make a Pro Bowl appearance, not even overall No. 2 pick Tony Mandarich – but they did pass on a couple of solid players. Andy Heck and David Williams were both available when the Jets selected Lageman, and both turned out to be good pros. Heck started 164 games for three different teams and went on to become a highly respected offensive line coach, while Williams started 106 games for two teams. Ironically, Williams' last two seasons would be with the Jets, part of the free agency spending spree that was meant to turn the franchise around after a 3-13 season under Rich Kotite. There were some great guards available, including eight-time Pro Bowler Steve Wisniewski... but the Jets were drowning in guards following the conversions of Dave Cadigan and Mike Haight. The offensive line would therefore be mostly unchanged going into the 1989 season – and O'Brien would be sacked 50 times. It turned out to be a dire year, costing Joe Walton his job regardless of the extension he had so recently signed.

The omens were not good from the start. While O'Brien's shoulder continued to be a problem, limiting the amount of time he could practice, the line had troubles of its own. Against the Giants, in a training camp scrimmage, the Jets surrendered either seven or eight 'sacks' (reports varied) in 48 offensive plays. They were 'sacks' because no tackling was allowed during the scrimmage, but that restriction would soon be lifted.

As preseason games started, Walton was venting his frustration at a lack of urgency from his veterans – at least, the ones who were present. Starting wideouts Toon and Walker were holding out in contract disputes, as was right tackle Reggie McElroy and running back Johnny Hector. There was a rash of injuries to contend with as well. Walton admitted that the offensive line was the team's major area of concern, with their steadiest player, Dan Alexander, going into his 13th season and his heir apparent, Dave Cadigan, unsure over how he would perform after changing position.

O'Brien and Ryan were both on limited duty. O'Brien was held out of the second preseason game, against the Eagles, and Ryan was expected to get just 15 or so plays before third-stringer Kyle Mackey took over. Despite this, the official line was that both quarterbacks were fine physically. It was clearly not the case, and despite the caution, the team's second-worst nightmare played out against the Eagles in North Carolina State's stadium – Ryan sprained a knee and was expected to miss as much as eight weeks.

The injury had a knock-on effect, as O'Brien would have to see increased playing time in the warm-up games, but things got even worse when, three days after Ryan's injury, O'Brien himself went down in practice. Mike Haight, getting up to speed after missing time at left guard, stepped on O'Brien's foot, breaking a toe. Jets' quarterbacks were used to their offensive line getting them hurt, but it wasn't usually as direct as this. The Jets starter would miss the following pre-season game, and former Steeler Mark Malone was signed as a backup to the backup to the backup. The big concern with O'Brien was not so much the toe itself, but the fact that favoring his left foot might cause him to change his throwing motion again, and that could play havoc with his recovering shoulder.

Mackey showed what a more mobile quarterback could do in the preseason game with the Giants. On one play, although Giants rushers were getting through, he used his feet to buy himself six seconds of time, before calmly finding running back A.B. Brown, who made a nice gain.

The Jets were intrigued by Mackey, and he would get a chance to start later in the season.

After a week of rest for his damaged toe, O'Brien was given three quarters of action against the Chiefs in the preseason finale. The extended time was considered critical as the offensive line began to come together following the return of McElroy, and the receiving corps welcomed back Toon. It often seems to be the case that holdouts get hurt when they return to play after missing a considerable amount of training camp, and sure enough Toon suffered a dislocated shoulder trying to catch his first pass against the Chiefs. He was ruled out for the regular season opener. O'Brien took some heavy hits in his time under center, but as the regular season opened, there was still optimism.

Some of this stemmed from knowing that things could be far worse. New England, the Jets' opponents on opening day of the regular season, would be without three defensive starters. Andre Tippett, Garin Veris and Ronnie Lippett had all been injured in the final preseason game and all would miss the entire year – the kind of doomsday scenario that would eventually convince teams to stop playing starters in the final week of preseason games.

The optimism proved unfounded, as the Jets never achieved take-off in 1989. Against the Patriots, on a brutally hot day (it was 115 degrees on the field) the Jets came out cold, allowing touchdowns on the first three Patriots drives. In contrast, the crowd was in midseason form, booing the Jets as early as their second drive of the game, and when O'Brien was shaken up after a big hit, the crowd actually cheered. He left the game for a play and was booed as he walked back onto the field.

'Listen to the greeting as Ken O'Brien makes his return,' said Marv Albert.

'This is sick,' was Bob Trumpy's verdict. 'This is not healthy.'

'Obviously, the fans [are] also reacting to the problems that the Jets are having here in the first half,' Albert went on, 'and they're putting it all on the shoulders of the quarterback, Ken O'Brien, who's had his ups and downs the last two years.'

Something changed at halftime, as the game turned completely on its head. Erik McMillan blocked a punt and intercepted two passes, while O'Brien caught fire, throwing deep with accuracy and touch. After a one-yard scoring lob to Vick, he connected with Michael Harper on a 48-yard rainbow to set up another score and then hit Jo-Jo Townsell on a gorgeous 49-yard bomb for a touchdown. Townsell, enjoying his first touchdown in the NFL having excelled for years as a return man, looked very much like Wesley Walker as he hauled in five passes for 97 yards, but the pass that would haunt O'Brien and the Jets came in the last moments, as they nursed a three-point lead. Harper got behind the defense on what would have been a 96-yard bomb to put the game away. Perhaps O'Brien was simply not used to working with Harper, but the ball was a yard or two overthrown and the chance had gone. The Patriots rallied to retake the lead and win the game. The following week O'Brien was intercepted a career-high four times against the Browns and the Jets were 0-2 for the first time in his career.

The Dolphins provided their usual pick-me-up in week three. As Charlie Jones and Merlin Olsen got ready for the game, they were in hopeful mood.

'When these two teams meet, there seems to always be an explosion,' said Jones.

The game was certainly eventful, but it was the Jets' special teams that provided the biggest explosions. George Radachowsky returned a blocked field goal 78 yards for a score and then the punt return team scored a safety after a wayward snap was fielded by Reggie Roby in his own end zone. Those scores kept the Jets in a game where the offense struggled in the early going.

After passed for just 69 yards in the first half (as opposed to 200 from Marino) O'Brien came to life after the break. Having consistently opted for underneath passes, he opened things up on the Jets' first possession of the third quarter, finding Toon for 19 yards, then bouncing back from a heavy sack to find him 19 yards downfield again – this time Toon cut back after the reception to take it to the end zone for a 37-yard score.

'What a ballgame he is having,' said Jones, referring to Toon, 'and the fireworks that we looked for are beginning to happen in the second half.'

The fireworks continued as Miami scored again and then O'Brien started hitting passes left right and center. Having eluded a near-certain sack, he found Shuler on the sideline, who barely brought both feet down inbounds. Then O'Brien found McNeil and finally a little flip out to Johnny Hector was turned into a 23-yard touchdown thanks to some nifty moves after the catch. Though under heavy pressure, O'Brien displayed mobility, escaping another near-sack on the Jets' next drive before firing a pass on the move that Toon caught for a 23-yard gain. Toon then caught 20- and 14-yarders on his way to a 10-catch, 159-yard day.

'Al Toon has taken over this ballgame,' said Jones in the commentary booth. 'He has actually taken over the whole offense.'

A tiptoeing one-yard score from Hector tied the game and then James Hasty intercepted Marino to get the ball back with 2:48 remaining. An eight-yard pass to McNeil gave O'Brien the 12th 300-yard game of his career and four plays later he hit his third touchdown of the day, this one a perfectly lofted pass to Vick from 11 yards out to give the Jets their first win of the year, 40-33.

It had been a remarkable half for the Jets quarterback. It was not one of his vintage barnstorming days – there were fireworks, but no bombs – but he had been a model of efficiency, completing 19 of 22 passes for 260 yards and three scores after halftime. Marino had outperformed him individually (the Dolphins passer had 427 yards to his credit after the game) but once more the Jets had found a way to win against their old rival.

'We always play games like this against the Jets,' said Marino. 'We let things slip away from us at the end. We've got to find an answer to that.' [11]

It was O'Brien's fifth win in nine games played against Miami, and his third in a row. Since the series had exploded with the week three encounter in 1986, Miami had gone through a mind-numbing experience – they had averaged more than 37 points per game, but had lost four out of six.

Unfortunately for the Jets, they could not play the Dolphins every week, and they came back to earth with losses to the Colts and Raiders. The Monday Night game against Los Angeles was vexing. O'Brien passed for 348 yards but could only get his team in the end zone once.

'I feel I let some people down,' he said, after an 87-yard interception return had won the game for the Raiders. 'I thought the defense played well and our offensive line played well. I tried to force some things and made some mistakes. That's hard to swallow.'[12]

Key players had been in and out of the line-up. Walker, in what would be his last season in the NFL, had appeared in only one game and had no receptions. Shuler had missed the Raiders game and would appear just three more times in a season that would be his last for the Jets, and Toon was about to miss the next four games as the high-octane offense that once terrorized the NFL became a distant memory.

Walton's reaction to the Jets' 1-4 start was stunning. O'Brien was benched again, but not for the sparkplug that was Pat Ryan (he was still out with injury), but for journeyman Kyle Mackey. O'Brien was out of form, there was no doubt about that – he had thrown just six touchdowns in five games, and nine interceptions, but with his top targets missing so much time it was unsurprising that the passing game should falter, and the ground attack was struggling. Behind the patchwork offensive line, McNeil had 202 rushing yards over the first five games, while Hector had 83 and Roger Vick 129. Mackey, whose father, Dee, had played for the Jets back in the sixties, would have almost nothing to work with.

O'Brien was upset about the decision ('What kind of player would I be if I wasn't upset about being sent down?' he told NBC commentator Ahmad Rashad), but there was little else Walton could try in an attempt to spark his team into life. The move did not work. On Mackey's first play he was victimized by the Jets' struggling offensive line, as McElroy was beaten by Rickey Jackson. As Mackey looked for a target, Jackson swatted the ball out of his hands and the Saints recovered. Mackey went seven of 14 in a half of action, good for just 74 yards, and was unceremoniously benched himself after the break. O'Brien sprained his left thumb in the second half and was unable to get the Jets into the end zone – both of their touchdowns came on defensive plays.

The game was symbolic of the strangely listless Jets team, and it dropped Walton's record as head coach to .500. He had won 50 games, lost 50, and tied one. The jokes had started about the Jets' 'prevent offense'. Over the previous three games, their defense had scored three touchdowns. The offense? Just one.

Things were bad, but they were about to take a turn for the bizarre. Mackey had suffered a lacerated elbow in the Saints game, and the cut had become infected. It was hoped that antibiotics would allow him to retain his starting job against Buffalo the following week, until he injured the elbow further – while asleep. The story Mackey told the Jets (and it was just crazy enough to be true) was that he had rolled over in his sleep and cracked his injured elbow on the nightstand by his bed. He was out (in fact his career would stretch to just one more game), and O'Brien was back in, recently diagnosed with a chip fracture of his left thumb.

O'Brien could look forward to passing to Jo-Jo Townsell and two newcomers in Chris Burkett and Phil Epps. It was a wide receiver corps unlikely to strike fear into anyone and the Bills duly rolled to a 34-3 victory, sacking O'Brien five times. He completed less than 38 percent of his passes for just 140 yards. When the Jets lost to San Francisco the following week (with the defense again scoring the team's only touchdown), O'Brien had gone five games without throwing for a score.

In the build-up to the 49ers game, O'Brien had spoken about the problems faced by both the team, and himself personally. On the decision to bench him, he was tight-lipped: 'That was just Joe Walton's decision,' he said, 'and it was just the decision he made.'[13]

Never one to rock the boat, O'Brien had effectively used 14 words in saying absolutely nothing, but venting his frustration, which he must have felt, would not have helped. When pushed to do so, he refused to take the bait: 'That's pretty personal,' he said, 'and leave it at that.' His mantra remained one of personal belief and faith: 'I've been here when it's been good and now it's bad. But you've got to believe in yourself, and you've got to believe that things are going to come around. Otherwise you're not worth your salt. That's kind of what we're facing now.'

As had become standard practice now, he did not throw on the Wednesday before the next game as the sore rotator cuff and bicep tendonitis in his throwing arm ebbed and flowed like the tide. O'Brien downplayed it when talking with reporters, joking that, 'I know how to throw. I don't think I'll forget how to do that.'

Walton also had a dry sense of humor when in the mood, and when asked to explain what had gone wrong with the offense he said: 'I have to get out to practice in a couple of minutes, and to explain that would take quite a long time. So I will just spare the time for some other question.'

There were plenty of other questions, as there always are on 1-6 teams, but as an offensive specialist, it was the stagnant offense that was casting the biggest shadow over Walton's reign as head coach.

'I think we've got a lot to prove now,' O'Brien admitted. 'And that's really what we're going after. We're all going out there to get it done. We've got to go out there and get on the ball and just go. Cutting down on the mistakes, I think, is the main thing. Then we'll be fine.'

The Jets were unable to cut out the mistakes against the Niners and, at 1-7, the season was effectively over, if indeed it had ever actually started. The game was a fitting comment on a lost season. After a terrible first half (90 yards of offense in the first quarter wasn't disastrous, but in the second they netted zero) the offense had not scored a touchdown in 11 quarters.

Walton tried to jolt his team into life at the start of the second half, calling an onside kick, which the Jets recovered. But as the offense trotted out, facing just a 13-point deficit, it became clear that something had changed at halftime As well as failing to move the ball in the first half (the team's lone score had come on a fumble recovery by the defensive scoring machine that was Erik McMillan) the Jets had allowed four sacks

O'Brien fumbles after the first of nine sacks against the 49ers (AP Photo/Bill Kostroun)

and Walton had taken action. It was drastic action, but the commentators did not notice until two plays had been run, and even then, the changes were so wholesale that there was confusion.

'Jim Sweeney has moved to left guard,' said Dick Stockton from the booth. 'Adam Schreiber has taken over at center for the Jets. Injuries continue to mount up for New York.' Stockton was assuming that an injury had led to the rejig on the line, but as the Jets lined up for their next play it became apparent that something bigger was going on. 'And in fact, Dave Cadigan is in the line-up as well,' Stockton said. 'We'll check the entire offensive line.'

After another play, the announcers caught up – almost.

'Dan Alexander is playing right tackle,' said Stockton. 'Dave Cadigan is the right guard. Adam Schreiber is the center. And a shake-up for the Jets' offensive line.'

'An entire shake-up,' added Dan Fouts, 'and whether it's due to their performance or due to injuries… I have to think it's due to that poor, poor performance they put on in that second quarter.'

It took a while for everyone to realise exactly how drastic Walton's moves had been. Sweeney was actually at left tackle rather than guard – Walton had benched both of his starting tackles, and the Jets' offensive line was once again all guards and centers. After an initial flurry of success, leading to a field goal, the game settled back into its old pattern as O'Brien was sacked a further five times, giving him a total of nine, the second-highest mark of his career. After one of the sacks, in the fourth quarter, chants of 'Joe must go' rained down from the stands, and many fans had brought signs along, bearing the same slogan, clearly anticipating another disappointing game. The line was completely falling apart by this stage and on one drive in the final quarter O'Brien took two sacks (Charles Haley blowing by Alexander on the second) and another savage hit that left him holding his head on the turf.

'O'Brien is going to be a sore young man tomorrow morning, if he isn't already,' said Fouts.

After the game, O'Brien spoke out in support of his line.

'I don't think it's just the offensive line,' he said. 'It's easy to make them the scapegoat. We're all making just too many mistakes. It's pretty miserable when you stop and think we're 1-7.'[14]

The shuffling on the line was the move of a man who was running out of options, and to be fair to Walton, the Jets' cupboard was bare. As O'Brien continued to take a beating, a daring move was made – the Jets picked up Tony Eason off waivers from the Patriots. A small drama then unfolded, as Eason expressed an unwillingness to compete against his best friend, but eventually he joined, and the Jets now had two of the quarterbacks from that famous draft class of 1983. Eason revealed how it

Kenneth Sims sacks O'Brien in week nine, but the Jets prevailed (AP Photo/Mike Kullen)

was a reassuring word from his good friend that convinced him to report to the Jets, having hesitated for a week.

'Kenny had a lot to do with me coming back there,' he said. 'It wouldn't have worked out without talking to him.'[15]

In one of those maddening games that can make a coach wonder why he chose his profession, the team woke up in week nine and amassed 486 yards of offense against the Patriots, winning a 27-26 squeaker. O'Brien was on fire, completing 22 of 29 passes for 386 yards, two scores and a 140.4 quarterback rating. The rating was far from perfect as an indicator of how well someone was playing, but O'Brien's weekly numbers very neatly charted the course of his up-and-down season. Over the first nine games he had posted ratings of 93.6, 43.7, 115.7, 72.2, 55.7, 93.1, 39.4, 83.4 and 140.4.

Two games that saw him throw just one score and five more interceptions resulted in two defeats, and one was especially painful. Against the Dolphins, in week 10, O'Brien appeared to be trotting into the end zone for a touchdown when he was hit by safety Louis Oliver. Replays showed O'Brien was agonisingly close to breaking the plane of the goalline and appeared to ease up just as he was crossing it. Oliver later claimed that O'Brien had anticipated the hit and had wimped out. Either way, Oliver's hit was not especially hard and did not even put O'Brien on the ground, but it was symptomatic of the troubles the Jets quarterback was experiencing. Not even the Dolphins could lift him.

The Jets scratched out a win over Atlanta in week 12, despite O'Brien passing for only 117 yards. Against San Diego, a week later, he passed for just 81 yards before being knocked out of the game after jamming his damaged shoulder into the turf while being sacked. Ryan took over and somehow did worse, amassing just 36 yards from his 11 attempts, but the Jets managed to win. Ryan was named the starter the next week, lasted long enough to throw four passes, and was knocked out again. The one pass Ryan connected on was his last completion as a Jet.

So many careers were coming to an end that the team was becoming unrecognizable. From the heady days of 10-1 in 1986, the Jets had lost Mark Gastineau, Joe Klecko and Lance Mehl on defense, and Marty Lyons was in his last year. They had lost Joe Fields on offense and were in the process of saying goodbye to Mickey Shuler, Wesley Walker, Dan Alexander, Reggie McElroy and Pat Ryan, none of whom would suit up again for the Jets after the 1989 season.

As the team spiralled, talk of surgery on O'Brien's chronically sore shoulder was floated. Despite this, Walton put him into the week 15 game against the Rams (Eason had started) when the Jets were trailing 28-7 and a win meant nothing. O'Brien did throw for a touchdown, but also took three more sacks to raise his season total to 50. As if to comment on the level of punishment he had absorbed, he missed the last game to have shoulder surgery.

The year ended with the Jets at 4-12, the same record with which they had opened the decade back in 1980. The matching records seemed fitting. There was an undeniable sense that this was a team going nowhere.

O'Brien signs autographs at the Jets' 1992 training camp (AP Photo/Mike Albans)

Chapter Eight
The Coslet Years

At the end of October 1989, while the Jets' season was being hooked up to life-support, Dave Anderson penned an article in *The New York Times* that would come to seem prophetic. Anderson wrote that it was time for the team to abandon its quaint operating system and hire a proper general manager.

The Jets liked to do things differently, and that was apparent in the very structure of the team. Instead of one 'football guy' overseeing everything, the Jets employed a three-headed monster. Joe Walton, Mike Hickey (college scouting director) and Jim Royer (pro personnel director) acted as a triumvirate, consulting on all personnel decisions. Above these three stood Steve Gutman, elevated to the role of president the year before.

The dearth of talent on the team was an indictment of that system, and Anderson saw a solution – respected GM Bobby Beathard, taking a year out of football, was rumored to be coming back to head up the Chargers. If Jets owner Leon Hess was motivated, he could surely offer Beathard enough money to reconsider his new destination.

The franchise was at a crossroads at the end of the year. O'Brien was recovering from surgery, Walton was a dead man walking after a campaign that had failed completely, and the team's scouting department was in the doghouse for a string of low- or zero-impact draftees and waiver-wire pick-ups. Less than two months after Anderson's column, the Jets made a move, hiring Dick Steinberg away from his position as player-development director with the Patriots (Beathard had been approached, but was set on staying on the West Coast). Steinberg would be the vice president and general manager and would have absolute power over all personnel decisions – both coaches and players.

Steinberg's first comments as the new GM were telling. He pointed out that although the Jets had some talented older players, and some promising youngsters, there was a void in the middle. There weren't enough of the five-, six- and seven-year veterans who should have been the heart of the team. It was almost certain that Walton would be let go, but what about O'Brien? He had shown himself to be a good quarterback when healthy and given time, but those two stars did not align often enough and he had once more worn down at the end of the season. He was still only 29, but as Indiana Jones once said, it wasn't the years, it was the mileage.

Steinberg could get to work on rebuilding the team starting with the No. 2 overall pick in the college draft, and it was essential to find a top talent. It did not appear to be a good draft for quarterbacks, however, Illinois' Jeff George was a solid prospect but was expected to go to the Falcons with the first selection. After that, the pickings were slim, with names like Andre Ware, Tommy Hodson and Neil O'Donnell attracting interest – none of them looked like a franchise-changer.

An easier decision loomed over the coaches. On Boxing Day, Steinberg dismissed Walton and his entire staff of 10 assistants – the Jets were making a clean break from their recent past. Steinberg had approached former 49ers head coach Bill Walsh, but he was not interested in a return to the coaching ranks and recommended either Mike Holmgren or Bruce Coslet. Other candidates included Michigan

State's George Perles, and for a while it looked like he was the chosen man. Perles flew to New York to sort out the details of his contract, but something went wrong. Perles was denied permission to leave his college post and the Jets had to change course.

That left the two offensive coordinators who were facing off in the Super Bowl. San Francisco's Holmgren was the first choice, but could not be tempted to trade his formidable array of weapons for the Jets' limited arsenal, so it was Coslet, the innovative offensive mind from the Bengals, who got the job. The big question now was how Coslet would work with O'Brien. Would he want a new quarterback to launch his head coaching career?

As Plan B free agency opened, there was speculation the Jets might be in for Bengals guard Max Montoya, who was left unprotected. Instead, he went to the Raiders, where he started 51 games. The Jets brought in Patriots tackle Tom Rehder instead, who did not play a single game for them.

Three more Plan B offensive linemen were brought in. Trevor Matich was reported by *The New York Times* as being a tackle, but they should have known the Jets did not like tackles – he had played his entire career as a center and long snapper and started seven games for the Jets. Former Bear Dave Zawatson was at least a tackle... until he got to the Jets, where he inevitably played as a guard for one season. Far more successful was the addition of Brett Miller. Huge for the era, at 6'7" and 293 pounds, he was undeniably a tackle and had played three seasons for the Jets' new offensive line coach, Larry Beightol, in San Diego. Miller would temporarily solve the Jets problem at right tackle, stepping into the shoes of the departed Reggie McElroy and starting all 16 games in 1990 before sliding into a back-up role for two more seasons.

There was also a talent-filled draft on the horizon and the Jets had plenty of options with the No. 2 pick. The defense would benefit from an imposing lineman like Cortez Kennedy, there was a good-looking running back in Blair Thomas (who could take over from a fading Freeman McNeil), and perhaps the new GM would solidify the other offensive tackle spot. Would Richmond Webb be tempting enough at the second overall pick? Scouting reports mentioned that he was versatile and could also play guard, which would have got the antennae twitching in the old Jets regime.

The Falcons, having insisted it would take a huge trade to prise the top pick from their grasp, gave it up for a shockingly small price, accepting offensive tackle Chris Hinton, receiver Andre Rison, and the Colts' top draft pick *the following year*, to give up the coveted No. 1 spot. Clearly, if the Jets had been motivated enough to get George, they could have put together a better deal, but they stayed put and drafted Thomas. The Penn State running back, coming off major knee surgery, was not a bad player – but as an overall No. 2 pick he was little short of a disaster. Kennedy and Webb, meanwhile, made eight and seven Pro Bowls, respectively.

As the draft unfolded, it became clear that Steinberg was envisioning building around the existing quarterbacks, whether it was O'Brien or Eason who emerged from an open competition. Wide receiver Reggie Rembert was taken in the second round and it wasn't until the fourth that a quarterback prospect was selected, California's Troy Taylor. Two late-round picks were thrown into the offensive line mix, with Dwayne White and Roger Duffy taken in the seventh and eight rounds, respectively. Duffy had played his entire college career at tackle, but in a case of 'déjà vu all over again', he would be moved inside to play guard for the Jets. And then, in the supplemental draft, the Jets cashed in their 1991 first-round pick to take Syracuse receiver Rob Moore. It looked like the Jets' quarterback, whoever he might be, would have one of the tallest receiving corps in the league to aim for in the 6'4" Toon, the 6'5" Rembert and the 6'3" Moore.

Whether that would be O'Brien or Eason was up in the air. O'Brien had not thrown since his shoulder surgery (which had identified inflammation and debris in the joint) and was not expected to start throwing until May. A quarterback competition against his best friend was not what either man wanted, but each was being paid well over a million dollars – they would just have to get on with it. Against such a backdrop, what happened next was unexpected, to say the least. Having failed to play in every game of a season since 1985, the banged-up O'Brien, under serious scrutiny, started every game over the first two years of Coslet's tenure as the Jets' head coach – and he helped his team back into the playoffs.

The first signs that things were looking up came in June 1990, when O'Brien won the Isuzu NFL Quarterback Challenge in Hawaii, beating such names as Warren Moon, John Elway and, yes, Dan Marino. In a range of events to test the necessary attributes for an NFL quarterback, O'Brien led the entire field in both the accuracy and read-and-recognition events, and his arm strength was enough to bring the crowd to its feet several times. There were no pass-rushers at the event, of course, but it appeared to show that O'Brien's arm was getting back up to speed.

As training camp started, Eason was listed as the starter on the initial depth chart, although Coslet insisted that meant nothing. Asked if it was simply a case of alphabetical order, he shook his head, saying, 'It's much more scientific. We flipped a coin... twice.' [1] As if to prove that point, O'Brien started the first preseason game and Eason started the second. O'Brien looked rusty in his start, completing just three of 10 attempts for 28 yards as the Eagle's vaunted defensive front, led by Reggie White, tormented him. Eason replaced him and did much better against the same defenders, completing nine of 12 passes for 100 yards in the second quarter. Colset pointed out that he had changed the blocking scheme by the time Eason came into the game, resulting in a little more breathing room, but it was clear this was going to be a serious competition. Eason also had the general manager pulling for him – at the Patriots, Steinberg had argued against waiving Eason the previous year.

All three of the Jets' California quarterbacks performed well against Kansas City, each throwing touchdown passes in a 20-0 victory. The anticipated receiver trio, however, looked like it was not coming to fruition. Reggie Rembert was offended by the Jets taking Moore in the supplemental draft, and left training camp after just one day. His agent, Gus Sunseri, complained about the lack of faith shown in Rembert and floated the idea that the Jets might be better off trading him. This eventually came to pass, and the decision was justified when Rembert went on to put up miserable career numbers, catching just 36 passes over three nondescript seasons with the Bengals. The Bengals gave up linebacker Joe Kelly (who gave the Jets three decent seasons, starting 24 times) and offensive tackle Scott Jones, who suited up for just three games.

As new names came (Blair Thomas signed his rookie deal on the day the Jets played their third preseason game) more old names departed. Marty Lyons tore a bicep muscle against the Giants and was expected to miss up to 16 weeks. He was soon placed on injured reserve, ruling him out for the entire season. He never played again. Mickey Shuler, meanwhile, expected to be the starting tight end but was waived after the final preseason game. Out too was Roger Vick, the top draft pick just three seasons earlier, who was traded to the Eagles.

Coslet left his decision on who should start at quarterback to the last moment, finally giving O'Brien the nod. His decision was a minor surprise – Eason had outperformed O'Brien in the four preseason games, throwing for 402 yards and a passer rating of 82.8 as opposed to O'Brien's 238 yards and lowly rating of 57.4. Coslet may have fallen back on how he viewed each player from his days with the Bengals. Cincinnati had faced Eason three times and O'Brien four times during Coslet's tenure as offensive coordinator and he would naturally have formed impressions of each man. Whatever the reason, the job of starting quarterback was O'Brien's once more.

Theatrically, the schedule makers had pitted the Jets against Coslet's old team in week one of the 1990 season, and they unveiled a new look on opening day. Black trim had been added to jersey numbers and names, a black facemask had replaced the old white one, and the option of green pants was seen for the first time. It was a look that would last until the 1998 season – by which time the Jets would have burned through three head coaches.

Such dark days had yet to appear over the horizon, however. O'Brien looked good in a loss to the Bengals, after a slow start. Opening with a dark visor, he got rid of it after two unproductive drives but still struggled, completing just three of his first 11 passes, for 18 yards. It was noticeable that Coslet was frequently asking O'Brien to roll out, buying a little more time, and the focus was on short-range passes, with an occasional deep ball. On one of the roll-outs, in the second period, O'Brien still came under heavy pressure, but was able to let a defender run by him, before uncorking a deep ball to a wide-open Al Toon, who jogged in for a 46-yard touchdown.

The new-look Jets offense was showing flashes, with new names like Brad Baxter at fullback, Thomas at halfback and Moore at receiver all contributing in a second quarter that saw them gain 168 yards. O'Brien had 160 yards passing at halftime, but only 10 points had been put on the board. After the Bengals had tied the score at 10-10 on their first drive of the second half, O'Brien responded. Townsell took a pass 18 yards to set the Jets up inside the Bengals' 30, and the announcers commented on how good the Jets quarterback was looking: 'The key to this whole thing is that he has time to throw the football,' said Paul Maguire.

A short connection for nine yards to McNeil prompted Maguire to expand upon that thought: 'You hate to keep harping on the same thing, but the offensive line of the Jets... there's just no penetration by the defensive line. They are really doing a job... they are just keeping the Cincinnati Bengals on the line of scrimmage.'

The drive ended with a nine-yard touchdown to Toon, who made a leaping catch at the back of the end zone. O'Brien's numbers had jumped to 18 of 31 for 211 yards and two scores, and the solid performance of his line was all the more remarkable given that Trevor Matich had been forced into action at right tackle to replace Brett Miller and Dave Zawatson had come in at left guard for Mike Haight.

After a Brian Washington interception gave the Jets the ball at the Bengals 38, they seemed poised to put the game away. The offensive line was bullying Cincinnati's defense, and Coslet switched to a ground attack, churning out yardage and then catching the Bengals with a play-action pass that tight end Mark Boyer almost took into the end zone. From a first-and-goal inside the one, however, the Jets failed to punch the ball in and had to settle for a Pat Leahy field goal at the start of the fourth quarter.

A 10-point lead might still have been enough, but something had switched at the end of the third quarter. The Jets had run two plays and both might have been touchdowns, but O'Brien ignored an open McNeil in the end zone on one play and Cadigan stubbed his toe and fell over while attempting to lead block on the other. Those miscues set the tone for a bizarre period where the game got away from them. After a Bengals touchdown, O'Brien was sacked on three straight passing plays, giving up a safety on the second one. After the Bengals had taken the lead with a field goal, O'Brien threw an incomplete pass on fourth-and-two to set up another three-pointer.

On a desperation drive at the end of the game, O'Brien moved the Jets downfield before suffering his fourth sack and ending the game with an intercepted pass in the end zone. It had been a dizzying turnaround and there was a suspicion that Coslet had been a little too cute. With his offensive line dominating he had called a pass and then a reverse to a slow-footed tight end from inside the Bengals' two-yard line. Then he had gone for it on fourth-and-two, inside Jet territory, with four minutes to play and only trailing by two. O'Brien finished with 300 passing yards in the losing effort, but it would be the only time he cracked the 300-yard mark all season.

The Jets were new... again. Steinberg and Coslet had overseen a dramatic roster overhaul – 20 of the 47 players on the opening day roster had not been on the Jets the previous season, and there were 15 changes out of 22 positions in the starting line-ups, compared to the last game of 1989. There was youth and promise everywhere, and even with the inevitable growing pains of a new regime, it looked like the 1990 Jets were going to be handful. A win over the Browns in week two was followed by the usual drubbing at the hands of Buffalo, but in week four the Jets levelled their record at 2-2 on the back of a strong rushing attack

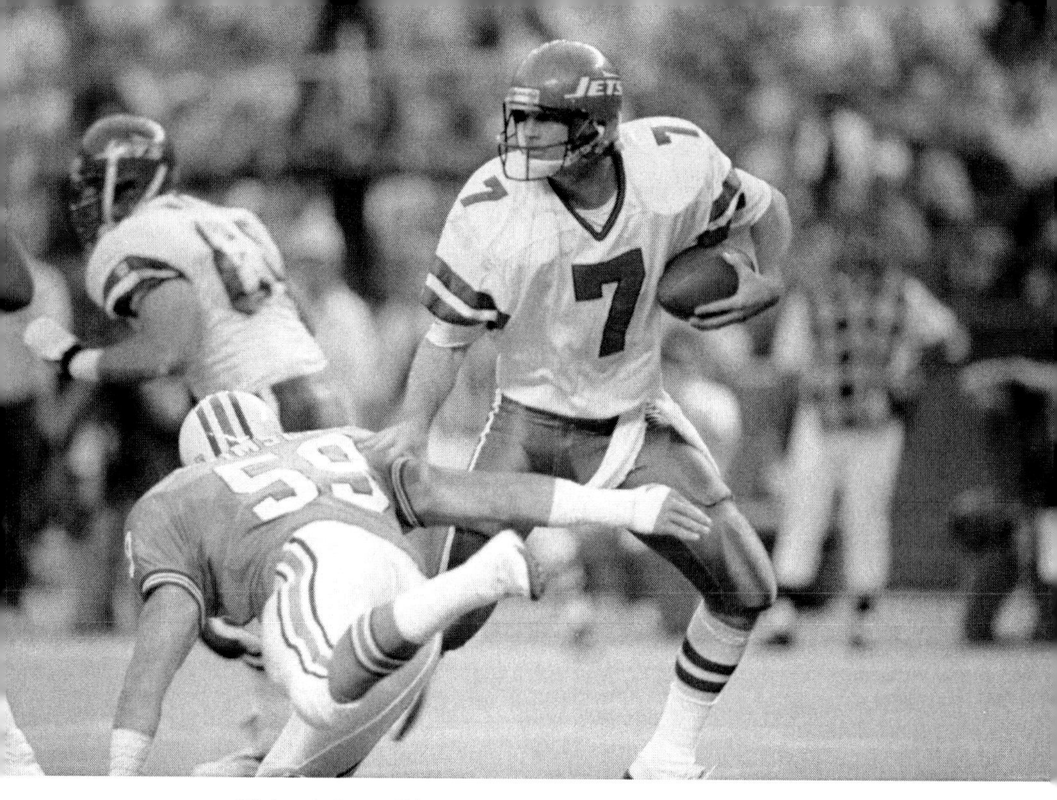

O'Brien eludes an Oilers pass-rusher in a week eight win (AP Photo/Tim Johnson)

and a great day from O'Brien. Two of the young studs on offense – Blair Thomas and Rob Moore – went over 100 yards for the first time in their careers.

Colset had introduced a 'Falcon' formation, where four wide receivers took the field along with Thomas. With the help of this aggressive approach, O'Brien completed 65.8 percent of his passes for 282 yards as the Jets built a 24-6 halftime lead and kept up the pressure in the second half, running out 37-13 winners. The creativity continued, with mixed results. A 'High Five' formation was introduced – featuring four receivers in a diamond formation on one side and a lone wideout on the other – but the players seemed uncomfortable with it and it was only run on three plays.

Although Coslet was eager to emphasise the pass, it was the offensive backfield that was the real strength of the team in the early going. Another successful innovation from Coslet was the 'Road-grader' formation, in which rookie Dwayne White was paired with tackle Brett Miller as lead blockers for a running back. McNeil, Hector, Thomas and

Baxter were all adept at both rushing and receiving and it looked like this, mixed in with the big-play capability of Toon and Moore, was about to usher in a new era for the Jets offense... but the Jets lost eight of their next 10 games, and inconsistency at quarterback was a big reason. Even the two games against Miami, traditional pick-me-ups for the Jets, and O'Brien in particular, failed to work their usual magic, as he threw just one touchdown over both games. To be fair, Marino was not in vintage form either. In the 1989 encounters between the two teams, the two quarterbacks had combined for 1,404 passing yards. In 1990, that number plummeted to just 816.

O'Brien put up some truly terrible games – four for 11 against the Chargers in week six, good for just 56 yards; eight of 23 against the Cowboys in week nine for 87 yards; and then the dismal showing in the second Dolphins game, in week 10, where O'Brien went 12 of 25 for 106 yards and two interceptions. In week 12, he was benched for Eason, after completing nine of 17 attempts in a 24-7 loss.

If those games had been characteristic of his entire year there would have been no doubt the Jets needed to look for a new quarterback, but there were good games as well. He completed 65.5 percent of his passes against the Patriots in that week four win, and he was at least efficient in the first Dolphins game in week five, passing for 256 yards and a rating of 95.0. In a loss to the Colts in week 11 he again topped 65 percent in completions and passed for 272 yards, and then there was the biggest head-scratcher of them all – the second 'perfect' game of his career, in week 16. It was close to being actually perfect, as he connected on 11 of 12 passes for 210 yards against New England, with two touchdowns and no interceptions in a 42-7 romp.

It was tempting to ask the real Ken O'Brien to please stand up, but that was part of the problem. When upright he could still tear a defense apart, but when knocked around his game suffered. The offensive line was coming together when healthy, but was frequently undermined by injury. In the first Dolphins game, the Jets gained 225 yards of offense in the first half, but were then forced to substitute both starting guards –

Haight (dehydration) and Cadigan (bruised knee) – and could manage just 117 yards in the second half as the Dolphins came back to win the game. Cadigan's injury turned out to be worse than feared, and he was ruled out for the rest of the season after ACL surgery.

In contrast to 1989, where it was often the case that the Jets played their best football in the latter stages of games, in 1990 the fourth quarter had become a tarpit. It was week eight before they scored a touchdown in the final quarter of a game, and even then it was a fumble recovery by the defense. It was week 13 before O'Brien threw a fourth-quarter touchdown, and it was to be his only one of the season.

O'Brien passed for just 14 touchdowns all year, but he had lost none of his fire. Against the Cowboys, in week nine, he was speared by defensive end Jim Jeffcoat (who was penalized on the play for roughing the passer) and got up barking at the Cowboys player, prompting an official to jump in to restrain him. He took another heavy hit on the next play, this time from linebacker Jack Del Rio who drove O'Brien to the ground. He landed squarely on his troublesome right elbow but it was his left arm that he was shaking as he got up after the play. After a moment he was back on the turf, as medical staff swarmed around him, and Eason ultimately came on for one play. Merlin Olsen, in the announcer's booth, gave a little insight into why he thought O'Brien was the starting quarterback for the Jets.

'The reason I think, basically, is because Coslet and O'Brien found themselves to be locked in,' said Olsen. 'They really are compatible as personalities.'

O'Brien returned after missing one play to fire a 19-yard pass to Chris Burkett to set up a touchdown run from Baxter, and Olsen touched on another reason why he was still the Jets' quarterback: 'O'Brien showing you the kind of fire that would ignite his teammates, right back on the field after one play and what does he do? Wham! Goes to Burkett down that left-hand sideline... big, big play.'

'Twice has been knocked out of this game,' added Dick Stockton. 'Twice has been roughed by the Dallas Cowboys defense.'

The win over Dallas, the first in franchise history, gave the Jets hope at 4-5, before a five-game losing streak prolonged the suffering of Jets fans. The losses were punctuated by the usual turmoil on the offensive line. Trevor Matich had taken over for the injured Cadigan, but when Matich went down, rookie Dwayne White had to step in. Then Haight was injured yet again, forcing Sweeney to step over to left guard and bringing rookie Roger Duffy in at center against the Steelers in week 12. The two rookies did well, and were among the more successful late-round draft picks made by the Jets during the period. Duffy started 70 games at center and tackle for the Jets over eight seasons, while White (who became known as 'the road-grader' after his appearances in that formation in his early games) started 68 contests over five years. In 1990, though, it was far from ideal to have a rookie tandem at the heart of the line, and the lack of continuity was a major issue. Criswell would be the only offensive lineman to start every game of 1990 at the same position.

Going into the week 16 game against the Patriots (the league had introduced a bye week in 1990, stretching the season to 17 weeks), the Jets were staring down the barrel of another four-win season, but two victories at least ended the year on an uptick. If either of the backups had shown much of anything (Eason passed just 28 times all year, while Taylor had 10 attempts, mostly in garbage time), Coslet would certainly have considered shaking things up. As things stood, help would have to come from the draft, but the Jets had coughed up their first-round pick in the 1991 draft to select Rob Moore. There were no regrets over that decision after he caught 44 passes as a rookie, tying Toon with six touchdown receptions, but it did mean it would be harder to find a franchise quarterback in April. As it happened, the Jets missed getting one by just one pick.

In the aftermath of the 1990 season, Coslet was bullish. He asked reporters how many other first-year coaches could have won six games with the roster he inherited, and he insisted his sense of humor, which was often interpreted as sarcasm, was just a dry wit. He felt he was misunderstood in New York and playfully mused about getting media training. Amid the banter, he made a serious point. He compared O'Brien with his quarterback in Cincinnati, Boomer Esiason, and offered a telling basketball analogy – with Boomer, he could run the fast-break offense. With O'Brien, he had to run the half-court. The implication was that O'Brien needed more of a structure, whereas Boomer was able to cut loose and improvise. The implication was also that O'Brien was not the right quarterback for Coslet, who had so far declined to unveil his no-huddle offense in New York.

Despite his reservations, Coslet had stuck with O'Brien, but as the draft approached it seemed clear that the team was looking to the future. Before draft day, however, there were potential trades and Plan B free agency to consider, and Dick Steinberg soon showed that he wasn't finished addressing the offensive line. Two huge tackles were brought in via trade – Ron Mattes stood 6'6" and weighed 302 pounds, while Irv Eatman was 6'7" and 298. There would be no talk of converting either of these behemoths to guard (Mattes would not play for the Jets, but Eatman started 28 games at right tackle over two seasons with the team).

In a draft lacking star talent, the Jets had Mississippi's Brett Favre as their top-rated quarterback, but he was selected by Atlanta after they traded up in the second round to the spot right before the Jets. Steinberg fell back on Louisville's Browning Nagle. As a second-round pick, there was less pressure to rush him into the starting line-up, so this was still O'Brien's team... for now.

You can get old in a hurry in the NFL. O'Brien would be just 30 years old when the Jets opened their 1991 season against Tampa Bay, but his heir apparent was now waiting in the wings, eager to get his shot. Just eight years after O'Brien had put Richard Todd on notice, Nagle was doing the same to him, and if the Jets' quarterback room was looking crowded (even following the departure of Tony Eason), so too were the offices of agent Leigh Steinberg, who represented all three of O'Brien, Taylor and Nagle. In July, O'Brien moved on from the celebrity agent, although he insisted it had very little to do with the fact that he also represented his rivals for the Jets QB job. The parting of ways was described as amicable by both sides.

Just like O'Brien had been back in 1983, Nagle was installed as the third-string quarterback as O'Brien and Taylor competed for the starting job. When the time came to make a decision, Coslet was not exactly effusive: 'Ken O'Brien is our starter,' the coach said just before the final preseason game. '[There was] nothing that Troy did to lose or win the job. It's just that right now, Ken O'Brien is our best quarterback. I told Troy he better be ready. He's a sprained ankle away from being the starter.'[2]

Coslet's throwaway comment proved prophetic. In week two, with the Jets trying to come back from a 20-6 deficit, Seattle's Rufus Porter sacked O'Brien, twisting his leg awkwardly and forcing him to the sidelines with an ankle injury. Taylor did not do much with his first opportunity, throwing an interception on a desperation fourth-down play. On the Jets' next drive he did better, finding Rob Moore with a perfectly placed 51-yard bomb and then drilling a low pass in from six yards out, again to Moore, for a late consolation score.

O'Brien had opened the season looking shaky. Behind poor protection, he failed to throw a touchdown in the first two games, while tossing up two interceptions. Against Buffalo, in week three, the team seemed determined to get something going. On their first possession, O'Brien heaved a pass that travelled nearly 60 yards through the air and settled in the hands of a streaking Rob Moore... but the pass had drifted too far to the sideline and Moore was out of bounds when he made the catch. O'Brien then looked sharp on a 15-play, 85-yard drive that burned more than eight minutes and ended with Freeman McNeil's 50th (and final) career touchdown.

Moore was on the end of another deep pass from O'Brien on the next drive, but this one came down safely inbounds for a 53-yard gain. With Toon also looking effective at shorter range, and the offensive line opening up holes for the running backs, the offense was beginning to look dangerous. O'Brien completed 11 of his first 15 passes for 143 yards, but as he came to the line of scrimmage after his 11th completion, his body language suggested he was in pain. Just as the camera had panned away following the delivery of the previous pass, he had taken a hard shot from Bills defenders Phil Hansen and Darryl Talley, who had sandwiched him, lifted him into the air, and slammed him into the turf.

Following a handoff to Blair Thomas, Taylor came on and O'Brien could be seen on the sideline having his left shoulder worked on. After coming back in, he went 10 of 20 the rest of the way, for just 94 yards, as the Jets stalled. A chance at a score at the end of the first half came to nothing, as O'Brien took another vicious hit from two Bills (this time Cornelius Bennett and Leon Seals) and then floated a pass into the end zone that was intercepted.

After the break, despite a fumble after a hit from behind, O'Brien stuck at it. It was a gutsy effort by the Jets, who led late in the game after O'Brien found Thomas on a five-yard touchdown pass, but a drive that might have run out the clock was ended when Talley blew through the line unblocked on third down for another sack. Jim Kelly took the ensuing possession and put the Bills ahead on the way to their eighth straight victory over the Jets.

A crisis loomed the following week when the Jets blew a 10-point lead in the fourth quarter against Chicago. Key to the defeat was a fumble by Thomas, but O'Brien was lackluster, completing 16 of 30 passes for just 184 yards. In the first four games, he had just one touchdown pass and 725 passing yards. More importantly, the Jets were 1-3 and in danger of slipping into irrelevancy.

O'Brien then responded with one of the best streaks of his career. Having posted a passer rating over 100 just once in 1990, he proceeded to top that mark five times in the next seven games. The Jets went 5-2 over the streak, catapulting themselves back into contention. As might have been expected, it was a game against the Dolphins that kickstarted the impressive run. O'Brien rediscovered his mojo by completing 75 percent of his passes against his favourite opponent, but equal billing went to a ground attack that piled up 206 yards.

Going into the game, it looked like a barnstormer was out of the question. Marino was in a slump of his own, having failed to throw a touchdown pass in his last two games. With both quarterbacks out of form, the Jets opened up on the ground and Thomas took his first carry for 25 yards, raising hopes that he would put the disappointment of the Bears game behind him. Coslet called the same play again on the second play from scrimmage, but this time O'Brien executed a play-action pass and hit Rob Moore for 22 yards. The two combined again for an easy 17-yard touchdown and O'Brien went on to complete his first seven passes, for 109 yards. But this was not the bomb-hurling O'Brien of old – his longest completion went for 24 yards and the Jets got touchdowns from their special teams and defense on their way to a morale-boosting 41-23 victory.

It was a similar story the following week, in Cleveland, where O'Brien completed over 82 percent of his throws – his highest completion rate in a game where he attempted more than 20 passes. In the first half he was almost unstoppable, throwing with velocity and pinpoint accuracy on his way to 10 completions from 11 attempts. Once more supported by a solid ground attack, and with good blocking from the revamped offensive line, he had settled into more of a game-manager role (although a would-be 45-yard bomb to Moore just failed to connect when Moore dropped the ball on contact with the ground). The Jets were leading the AFC in time of possession, and Coslet was gaining confidence in his quarterback, calling for a pass on fourth-and-five in the second quarter, which O'Brien duly completed to Toon.

'Ken O'Brien is at a point where he is playing with sore shoulders once again,' said Marv Albert, 'but, with the find of protection that he's getting, these are flashbacks to the effectiveness of O'Brien several years ago.'

After a Browns rally, O'Brien hit Toon for completions of 15 and 32 yards to set up Leahy's game-winning field goal in the fourth quarter. The two wins had seen the offensive line protect O'Brien as well as he ever had been. He took no sacks in either game and it was telling that the following week, when the Oilers got to him four times, his completion rate fell to just over 55 percent and the Jets narrowly lost. The defeat was in part due to the failure of the running game, which managed just 43 yards on 21 carries – and a big part of that was the injury suffered by left guard Dave Cadigan after the Jets opened the scoring on a three-yard Brad Baxter run. Cadigan's exit meant a familiar reshuffle on the line, with Sweeney moving to left guard and Roger Duffy coming in at center.

A steady performance against the Colts in week eight was notable for one of Coslet's most daring moves – trotting out reserve lineman and long-snapper Trevor Matich as a tight end, complete with a number switch from 64 to 46. The Jets came out with an unbalanced line during their first possession, with three offensive linemen to the left of the centre, and Matich occupying what looked like the right tackle position. He was actually an eligible receiver and duly broke free upfield, much to the amusement of the announcers, to make an easy catch for a 14-yard gain. On the Jets' second drive, after O'Brien had sat out a play with a twisted ankle following a sack, Colset reached into his bag of tricks again, this time for a flea flicker, and when Hector flipped the ball back to O'Brien, Rob Moore was wide open for the 47-yard score that paved the way for a 17-6 win.

The Jets had followed a 1-3 start with a 3-1 burst to level their record, and a Hail Mary play at the end of the first half against Green Bay the following week led to another long-range score when the ball bounced into Chris Burkett's hands for a 50-yard touchdown. For once, the football gods seemed to be smiling on the Jets, who now had a winning record and were sniffing around the playoff places.

Weeks 10 and 11 of the 1991 season were significant for several reasons. The Jets split the games to push their record to 6-5 and stay in contention for the postseason. The games against the Colts and the Patriots were also the last two where O'Brien would pass for more than 300 yards. It was not enough to get past the Colts, who won a 28-27 squeaker, but against the Patriots, in week 11, he was close to his best.

In his glory days, a three-touchdown performance would have

seen the likes of Toon, Walker and Shuler on the scoresheet. Times had changed, and it was Burkett, Terance Mathis and (believe it or not) Trevor Matich who caught touchdowns. On a field that had just been re-laid the previous Tuesday, O'Brien got to work against the league's 27th-rated pass defense. The Patriots had talked before the game of how well O'Brien would sell a play-action fake, and he repeatedly completed passes after fakes to his running backs, hitting seven of his first 10 attempts into a stiff wind. On a second-down play, O'Brien came under heavy pressure and earned praise from Ahmad Rashad for getting rid of the ball after extending the play as long as possible.

'Ken O'Brien has improved so much in this area of his game,' said Rashad. 'I mean, in the past this would have been a sack, but you see him looking downfield, trying to find a receiver, can't find one... and he's able to at least get rid of the ball. That was a good job by O'Brien of getting rid of the ball and throwing it where noone else could catch it.'

Later in the drive he showed good mobility again, fading left under pressure until Chris Burkett got open in the end zone for an easy touchdown. O'Brien had hit 14 of 20 passes for 154 yards and a score and the Jets had held possession for more than 19 minutes in the first half. His play had confounded the New England defenders.

'The Patriots felt like if they could force him into being a drop-back passer they had a chance to win the game,' commented Rashad as half-time approached. 'That has not been the case. He has been so effective as a drop-back passer today.

'This guy's having maybe his biggest day of this season,' Don Criqui said at halftime.

'And the thing that's been so impressive,' Rashad responded, 'is not only his accuracy, but his mobility. A couple of times he's been under pressure, he's backed out of there, still keeping his head up, looking down the field, trying to find a receiver, and he's come up with a target. He's playing exceptionally well.'

The second half also started well. O'Brien ripped a 28-yard pass to Moore after a play-action fake on the Jets' first offensive play, and then hit Terance Mathis for his first NFL touchdown on a 36-yard strike. O'Brien's play had not been flashy, and the announcers seemed a little surprised when they checked his stats after the drive that put the Jets up 21-0.

'Really some superior numbers here,' said Criqui.

'21 for 29, 250 yards and two touchdowns for Ken O'Brien,' Rashad responded.

It was only then that the announcing team noticed that O'Brien had come to the sideline in obvious pain after the scoring throw. Rookie defensive back Jerome Henderson (who would finish his career with two seasons as a Jet) had come free on a blitz and hit the quarterback late. O'Brien underthrew an open Moore on his next play, missing out on what might have been a 73-yard score, and completed just five of his final 12 passing attempts.

As O'Brien faded (missing on six straight attempts at one point in the second half), the Patriots roared back to tie the game, helped by fumbles on consecutive plays by Brad Baxter. With just over two minutes remaining, O'Brien snapped back into life, completing all five passes on a drive that retook the lead, finishing it with a three-yard toss to Matich. In a dramatic game, the Patriots had a chance to tie things up again, snapping the ball inside the Jets' one-yard line with one second remaining, but the Jets defense held Jon Vaughn to no gain.

This wasn't the same sort of dizzying play O'Brien had served up in his 1986 peak, but he had put together consecutive 300-yard efforts for the first time since that year, and it was not hard to work out why he was playing well. Under Walton, he had taken a sack every 9.5 passing plays. Under Coslet, that had improved to one sack every 14 passing plays. He had played six sackless games over two seasons with Coslet, having enjoyed just three in his previous six seasons (including his nine-attempt relief performance against Miami in 1988). The Jets had won all nine of those games.

Superstitious fans might have noted that the last time O'Brien had thrown for more than 300 yards in consecutive games (against Seattle and Atlanta in 1986) it had been followed shortly afterwards by the five-game slump that almost cost the Jets their playoff place. Cruelly, fate was about to offer Jets fans an unwanted rerun.

The final five games of the 1991 season, the last time O'Brien would be a full-time starter in the league, witnessed a slump very similar to that of the 1986 season. In that year he posted passer ratings of 59.2, 58.1, 37.9, 56.5 and 19.0, while throwing for two touchdowns and 12 interceptions. In 1991, the passer ratings were 68.1, 39.4, 42.9, 61.4 and 57.3, along with a single touchdown and six interceptions. Just as in 1986, there was no single event that triggered the slump, although in both streaks his sack rate went up (he suffered 16 sacks in the 1986 five-game slump, and 14 in 1991). The only feasible explanation appears to be that he just wore down as the seasons progressed.

There was one difference between the slumps, and it was a crucial one. In 1986 the Jets went 0-5 as O'Brien spiralled back to earth. In 1991, they managed to win the first game of the slump, improving the Jets' record to 7-5. Three straight defeats, in which he failed to pass for more than 200 yards in any single game, threw no touchdowns and was intercepted four times, put them in a do-or-die situation in week 17.

The losing streak had been punctuated by some landmark events. O'Brien caught his first NFL pass, a 27-yarder from Al Toon, against Detroit. Toon caught a pass in his 90th consecutive game against the Lions, but was also working on a less welcome streak. He had failed to score a touchdown in 15 straight games. Against the Patriots, Pat Leahy, enduring a difficult year, came into the game nursing a hamstring injury and sciatica in his kicking leg. He missed his last field goal attempt as a Jet, a chip-shot 23-yarder, and was replaced by punter Louie Aguiar, who duly missed a 27-yarder in a game the Jets lost by three points.

It all meant effectively nothing by the time week 17 rolled around. The football gods had thrown the Jets a bone – a win would give them a non-losing record and, more importantly, a wild card berth, while a defeat would leave them on the outside looking in. Their opponents on the critical last weekend of the regular season? The Miami Dolphins. It was perhaps fortunate, because pressure was building to replace O'Brien with the strong-armed Browning Nagle, who had patiently awaited his chance for meaningful playing time. He had thrown just two passes all season. There was always the chance, however, that O'Brien might come to life against the Dolphins, who were his personal version of Popeye's can of spinach. Win or lose, however, the writing was on the wall – O'Brien's time as the Jets' starter was coming to an end. Next year, this would be Nagle's team for as long as he could hold on to the job.

Week 17 of the 1991 season was far from a vintage Jets-Dolphins game. Marino was good, passing for 282 yards and two scores, but O'Brien labored his way to 158 yards on just 13 completions and was sacked four times. The game was heading for a sour defeat, reminiscent of the late-season swoons that had plagued the Jets in the 1980s, but there was one more twist in store. On December 22, the Jets received a visit from two ghosts of Jets teams past. Freeman McNeil and Johnny Hector, the 'Geritol backs', as they playfully called themselves, came to life for one very special game. Blair Thomas carried the ball three times, while Brad Baxter managed just 24 yards. Hector, meanwhile, ran free for 132 yards on just 13 carries, while McNeil added 55 on 11 attempts. It was the second-highest total of Hector's career.

Despite the heroics from their ageing backfield pairing, the Jets appeared ready to bow out when Marino found Ferrell Edmunds for the go-ahead score late in the fourth quarter. The Jets took over at their 30 with just 38 seconds to save their season. O'Brien had less than 100 passing yards up to this point, but threw two big passes on the drive, opening with a 23-yard connection to Moore and then finding Terance Mathis for 14 more. McNeil picked up six yards on a draw play and with just two seconds left, newly signed Raul Allegre trotted onto the field to kick the 44-yard field goal that took the game into overtime.

In the extra period, it was clear how differently each head coach was

Allegre is mobbed after his game-winning kick against Miami (AP Photo/Chuck Burton)

approaching the game. The Dolphins were still Marino's team, and he passed the ball again and again, almost hitting Duper for a long-range score that would have won the game. In contrast, when the Jets' defense held and their offense came back out, it was apparent that Coslet did not trust his quarterback. Hector and McNeil were given the responsibility of moving the ball – and they delivered.

'Johnny Hector having the game of his life,' said Joe Namath in the commentary booth after No. 34 ripped off 17 yards. After he followed up with a six-yard run Namath added, 'Hector is seeing things... every time he carries he seems to be able to find the open hole.'

On a critical third-and-two, Coslet called another draw to McNeil, who picked up five yards to keep the drive alive and move the ball into

Dolphins territory. Coslet then went for the jugular, looking for a deep passing play, but O'Brien was forced to check down to tight end Chris Dressel, who dropped what should have been an easy catch. Hector ripped off another big gain, 12 yards to get to the fringe of field goal range at the 36. He lost a yard on the next play and Coslet, perhaps realizing the Dolphins were selling out to stop the run, called another deep pass. O'Brien dropped a perfect ball into the hands of Moore for a 29-yard gain to the Miami eight-yard line, after which he jogged downfield with his fist raised in triumph. Four plays later Allegre lined up for a 30-yard field goal.

'Does the glass slipper fit Cinderalla?' asked Tom Hammond, and Jets fans got their fairy-tale ending when the kick sailed through. The Jets were in the playoffs and the Dolphins were out. The win made Coslet almost giddy with excitement.

'Don't count us out,' said the second-year head coach. 'I've learned never to count these players out. They don't count me out. That's why we're on our way – maybe not this year where we want to be, but we're on our way to having a hell of a franchise.'[3]

It was one of those statements that rings hollow with the benefit of hindsight. Coslet would be gone after two more years, and the Jets would win just 22 of their next 81 games. For now, though, there was the excitement of a playoff game in Houston. It looked like a mismatch, the Oilers having been to the playoffs for five straight seasons and boasting eight Pro Bowlers, while the Jets had no playoff appearance since 1986 and no Pro Bowlers either. The New Yorkers were nine-point underdogs, but they played the Oilers close and had multiple opportunities in the second half to take the lead or tie the score. There was a little consolation when O'Brien hit Toon for his first touchdown of the year, having been kept out of the end zone for the entire regular season despite making 74 catches for almost 1,000 yards. The touchdown was a beauty, O'Brien looking right, then firing back to the opposite corner of the end zone, where Toon just managed to keep his feet inbounds while completing the catch. It was O'Brien's second and last postseason touchdown pass.

O'Brien then moved the Jets downfield in the closing seconds of the first half to set up a field goal, keeping them in touch at 14-10. After the break, though, the Jets' hopes were swallowed up by mistakes and strong defensive play from the Oilers.

Having driven down to the three-yard line on the first drive of the third quarter, the Jets seemed poised to take the lead. O'Brien had repeatedly found Toon and Moore, while Hector put in another nice cameo performance... but an interception on the 12th play of the drive, on third-and-goal, set the tone for the second half. After Houston added a field goal, O'Brien put together another good drive, hitting Toon and McNeil and then pushing the ball to the 12 with a 31-yard pass to Moore. On a third-and-one inside the Houston five, Brad Baxter was held for no gain – Coslet went for it on fourth down, but McNeil was stopped short. Another promising drive saw the ball turned over on downs again, this time at the Houston 22, and the Jets might have been in the lead if they had simply settled for field goals.

One last chance came with 53 seconds remaining. From his 20, O'Brien found Toon for 21 yards, then Mark Boyer for 12. Houston got away with pinning Boyer to the ground while 10 seconds ticked off the clock, but on the next play the Jets almost forced a tie. A deep pass from O'Brien found a leaping Toon on his way into the end zone, but the ball hit him in the stomach and bounced harmlessly away. To add insult to injury, Toon was called for offensive pass interference on the play. After an incompletion, the clock was down to six seconds and the Jets had 57 yards to travel. A Hail Mary went unanswered, as the pass was picked off for O'Brien's third interception of the game. The 1991 season was over.

The writing had been on the wall for O'Brien for some time. Despite having started all 16 games in both of Colset's first two years in charge, the head coach had made it increasingly clear that he was not able to execute the offense in the way the coach wanted. Browning Nagle would be given his chance to win the starting job in training camp, and steps were taken to tilt the board in his favor. With O'Brien looking for a new contract, the Jets reportedly offered him a deal with a modest raise (10 per cent) on his 1991 salary of $1.4 million. Some saw this as a move designed to prompt a holdout, giving Nagle more time to practice in training camp. O'Brien was on the list of 37 players protected in Plan B free agency, but he was clearly playing the role of insurance policy now.

The year had started well for O'Brien, as he replaced Bernie Kosar in the Pro Bowl. Kosar had already stepped in when Elway and Marino had bowed out through injury, but a trip to Hawaii was still a nice way to end the season, even though he completed just three of nine passes for 12 yards and fumbled the ball to end the game.

As training camp rolled around, the narrative around O'Brien shifted. Now, it appeared, the Jets had only offered him $750,000 for the 1992 season. Such a drastic pay cut was certain to prompt a holdout and it appeared the Jets had wanted him out of the way to give Nagle a clear run at the starting job. It wasn't until August that O'Brien signed two one-year deals, by which time Nagle was installed as QB1. Through training camp, Nagle had enjoyed the undivided attention of Coslet and new quarterback coach Walt Harris, but he had not been able to have a quiet word with the veteran quarterback who would undoubtedly have had some pearls of wisdom to impart. O'Brien threw a pair of touchdowns in the Jets' final preseason game, as if to show he could still get it done even after missing most of the build-up to the 1992 season. For O'Brien, the starter since midway through 1984, the demotion was difficult to come to terms with, especially as it involved a lot of standing on the sideline instead of being in the thick of the action.

'When you have that much time, you start thinking of weird stuff,' he admitted, although he didn't elaborate on exactly how weird his thoughts had become. 'I've always been a little hyper at certain times, but now I have too much time on my hands. I'm trying to get used to that part of it as much as anything else.'[4]

O'Brien's return at least gave Nagle a source of support and information whenever he came to the sideline, and Coslet was quick to point out that O'Brien had embraced this role.

'Kenny had a lot of good suggestions Sunday and I went with some of them,' the coach said after an opening day loss to Atlanta. 'He helped Browning on the sidelines, going over what he'd seen on the field. He's been through it as a quarterback. He's gone through things nobody knows. He's an experienced guy and I'd be nuts not to use him. He has a lot of insight. He's intelligent.'

Nagle had impressed in his professional debut, passing for 366 yards and a score. It was the second-highest passing yardage in a debut since the Elias Sports Bureau started tracking the stat in 1975. He crashed back to earth against the Steelers the following week, completing just nine of 29 passes, but ups and downs were to be expected. Less expected was that O'Brien would look even worse when coming in to relieve Nagle. O'Brien compiled the worst stats of his entire career, throwing three interceptions in just four passes, for a 5.2 passer rating. One of the interceptions was returned 65 yards for a touchdown.

More worrying at the time was the loss of Jeff Lageman, who had worked his way up to be the Jets' best defender. A serious knee injury put him out for the rest of the year and Nagle would miss the next game after bruising the index finger on his right hand against the physical Steelers.

O'Brien's numbers looked good against San Francisco in week three – 23 completions and 263 passing yards, but much of that (and his two touchdown passes) came after the Jets had spotted the Niners a 31-0 lead. The fans at Giants Stadium, quickly watching a season unravel before their eyes, called for backup Jeff Blake to come into the game. A loss against the Rams dropped the Jets to 0-4 and it was beginning to look like they had been drastically misjudged in the preseason, when *Sports Illustrated* guru Paul Zimmerman had dubbed them a 'serious Super Bowl contender'.[5] Dr. Z's prediction had carried a proviso – Nagle needed to come through. He was intercepted twice and fumbled three times in Los Angeles.

He bounced back a week later, tossing two scores as the Jets finally got into the win column against New England, but then he passed for just 102 yards against the Colts as the Jets fell to 1-5. Colset began to suggest that this would be a year to identify the players the team could build around – playoff hopes already seemed fanciful, and whether Nagle could be one of those players was looking increasingly doubtful. After the bye week, things did not become any clearer, as he threw two interceptions against the bogeymen from Buffalo, who had now won 10 games in a row against the Jets. Nagle was banged up again, suffering an injury to his left shoulder and left foot. He was listed as questionable for the next game, against the Dolphins, and the injuries gave O'Brien the chance for one more shining moment as the quarterback of the New York Jets.

Why Miami always brought out the best in O'Brien is open for debate. Whatever the reason, he put up some of his best numbers against the Dolphins. In week nine of the 1992 season, he tore them to pieces. O'Brien completed 21 of 29 attempts for 240 yards, and he had thrown touchdowns of 37 yards to rookie tight end Johnny Mitchell, four yards to Toon and 20 yards to Moore before the Dolphins even made it onto the scoreboard. For his efforts, O'Brien was named the AFC offensive player of the week, and the 26-14 win briefly rekindled hopes that the Jets might bounce back from their miserable start... but the football gods had asked O'Brien to pay for his success with another concussion. Nagle returned to the starting line-up against the Broncos the following week and the losing recommenced.

By the time O'Brien made his last start for the Jets, they were 3-8. His old partner in crime, Al Toon, had been forced to the sidelines with a concussion of his own and would never return to an NFL field. Freeman McNeil had no more carries in him and would make just two more receptions before his storied NFL career ended. Johnny Hector, the hero of the 1991 season finale who had come into the league in the same draft as O'Brien, had just 18 carries left in his tank. Like old soldiers, the last remaining players from the Jets' glory days were fading away.

It did not feel like an ending for O'Brien in the build-up to the game against Kansas City. His previous two starts in 1992 had come because Nagle was banged up. Four days before the Chiefs came to town, Nagle was benched for poor play. O'Brien was the starter once more.

'We'll give Browning a chance to sit back and watch,' said Coslet in explaining his decision. 'He needs to step back from the heat of battle. I feel this will help him in his development.'[6]

The events of O'Brien's last start for the Jets were dominated by the injury suffered by defensive end Dennis Byrd, who collided with teammate Scott Mersereau. The impact left Mersereau stunned and Byrd paralysed, and all other events from the day suddenly, and rightly, seemed insignificant. Just over a week later, Byrd regained movement in his legs and went on to recover enough to walk again. Understandably lost amid the concern for Byrd, O'Brien had thrown his final pass as a Jet. It fell incomplete, as he was hit by a blitzing defender, fracturing his right thumb. He ended the season on injured reserve.

Chapter Nine

Turn Out the Lights...

Coslet had seen enough of both O'Brien and Nagle by now. In the offseason, the Jets traded for the quarterback Coslet had often waxed lyrical about, Boomer Esiason, and handed him the No. 7 jersey before O'Brien had even been released. It was a rather shabby way for the team to say goodbye.

In 10 seasons with the Jets (including his rookie year when he was not active for a single game). O'Brien passed for 24,386 yards and 124 touchdowns on his way to 50 wins. All three stats place him second to franchise legend Joe Namath. His completions (2,039) lead all Jets quarterbacks, as does the painful figure of 338 sacks, which is more than 100 more than the next most-abused passer in team history, Richard Todd. He was credited with 16 game-winning drives – another franchise-leading figure. Wesley Walker had no doubts about how good O'Brien had been at his peak.

'To this day I don't think people knew his ability,' he said when interviewed by Greg Prato, 'the athleticism he brought to the New York Jets. He was just *so* underrated. It makes me angry – I used to train with this guy, and I knew what kind of ability he had. He just needed more of a surrounding cast. I remember him just having this real strong arm, and he could throw with anybody. It was a pleasure not only to know him as a player, but as a friend. He was just a terrific individual.'[1]

'I loved Kenny O'Brien,' he continued. 'If I had to choose a quarterback to play with, I'd take Kenny O'Brien over Dan Marino, John Elway, Joe Namath – he was my guy. If you look at his stats and numbers, he could compare to anybody on the Jets or anybody in the league. Just awesome.'[2]

Walker was also far from happy with the way O'Brien's exit from the Jets was handled. As the team patted itself on the back for bringing in Esiason, O'Brien was picked up by Green Bay, and then by the Eagles.

'It is a business,' Walker conceded. 'And one time, I know you're going to have to leave this game. But they just don't know how to do it properly. This guy was one of the best the Jets ever had, and they didn't do the right thing.'[3]

The title of this chapter is a little premature, though, because although his Jets career was over, O'Brien did throw more passes in the NFL. The Eagles had a place for him on their roster, and he made four starts for them in 1993, throwing four more touchdowns. Perhaps inevitably, his last significant performance was against the Dolphins, who must have been sick of the sight of No. 7. In week 11, he completed more than 62 percent of his passes for 189 yards and two touchdowns.

'What is it about Ken O'Brien against the Miami Dolphins?' asked Chris Collinsworth after O'Brien had thrown his second touchdown of the game to Calvin Williams. 'He just always seems to tear 'em up!'

The scores were not enough to earn a win, and the two touchdowns to Williams would be the final footnote to a career that had now spanned 11 seasons and bumped his career passing total over the 25,000-yard mark. It would take a little time to adjust.

'After you leave football or sports, and it's been your life for so long, what are you going to do?' he asked, rhetorically. 'It's hard to find the kind of commitment, camaraderie, and friendships that you have. There's

Making a cameao appearance on Home Improvement *(Alamy)*

the going out for dinner, going out for beers, going out with the families, going out to compete with each other, and going out to lay it on the line. It's hard to duplicate that and the passion you have for that in any other kind of work. It's really, really difficult.' [4]

He had one more performance in him – a light-hearted appearance on the TV show *Home Improvement*, in an episode titled 'The Eve of Construction', alongside a range of fellow guest stars. Tim Allen introduced them in his inimitable style: 'John Elway from the Denver Broncos... Mile High guy, huh? Good-looking man too, you know? Sean Jones from the Houston Oilers... another mile-high guy. He looks good in cotton, doesn't he? Bill Pickel from the... New York Jets... alright... okay, Ken O'Brien from...?'

'Whoever will take me, Tim', O'Brien replied.

It was a typically self-deprecating comment from a player who had never pointed the finger of blame at anyone but himself, and had always attributed credit to others.

'It was just fun to do,' he remembered about his foray into acting, 'and it's like anything... you learn that other people work hard at their professions as well, and there's a reason they're good, and the best people in it kind of have a passion for it. There's only so much you can do with your physical skills, you have to have a passion for what you do. They were very helpful and very understanding of a couple of big oafs showing up.'[5]

Frank Ramos, the Jets' longtime vice-president of public relations, believed O'Brien had been undervalued: 'I thought that Kenny O'Brien was a much better quarterback than critics would ever say,' he claimed. 'I think the fact is that when people talk about Kenny O'Brien, they will always talk about the fact that the Jets took Ken O'Brien and didn't take Dan Marino. But you can say that for just about every team in the NFL that had an opportunity to move up and take Marino ahead of where the Dolphins did. [O'Brien] was sacked an awful lot – he held onto the ball. But he was one of the most accurate passers to ever play the game. Had very few interceptions, and had a lot of touchdown passes. I think there are a lot of teams that wish they had Ken O'Brien.'[6]

'He really could throw it,' said longtime backup Pat Ryan. 'He had a great touch: he could throw it long, throw it short. He just had a really good knack of passing the football.'[7]

In 2017, there was reminder of just how good O'Brien had been in college – and a further reminder of how modest he was. Informed that he was to be honored by his old school during a game against Southern Utah, O'Brien suggested that the entire Aggies team of 1982 be honored instead. The 35th anniversary of the team that made it all the way to the Division II Championship Game was therefore a team event, including O'Brien's former teammate, Dan Hawkins, a fullback on the 1982 squad and the head coach of the 2017 team.

'Typical Ken O'Brien and typical UC Davis,'[8] Hawkins commented.

When Mike Manico, interviewing O'Brien for his Jets podcast, commented that O'Brien deserved to be in the Jets Ring of Honor, O'Brien's reaction was again what you would expect, but no less admirable for that: 'I haven't given any thought to it,' he replied. 'It would be a tremendous honor, certainly. I think at the end of the day, in terms of football, it's what the people you played with think, they really know what it was all about every day, what they think about you. I thought the world about everybody and I thought everybody was equal and everybody contributed, from the first guy on the team, whoever that is, to the last guy on the team, everyone's a real part of it and when you can get everybody going in the right direction, that chemistry is fully unbeatable, and when I look back we had that going for a while.'[9]

Despite all of this, O'Brien is a controversial figure among Jets fans. Some will bang the table for him as the second-best quarterback in team history, while others will insist that Richard Todd, Chad Pennington or Vinny Testaverde knock him down into third, fourth or fifth place. On a flawed team, O'Brien was sometimes able to produce miracles. When the Jets were healthy, he was the finishing touch to an unstoppable offensive juggernaut, but all too often, in the hurly-burly world of the NFL in the 1980s, with those unforgiving AstroTurf fields, neither the team nor O'Brien could stay healthy. His tenure with the Jets was sometimes a troubled one, but the highs were often dizzying, and there is an undeniable fact, summed up perfectly by Gerald Eskenazi of *The New York Times*: 'There were Sundays when the Jets were pro football's best team.'[10]

A lot of that had to do with the play of Ken O'Brien.

O'Brien drops back to pass against the Seahawks, October 27, 1985 (Kevin Reece: Icon Sportswire via AP)

O'Brien by the Numbers

College passing stats

Year	Team	G	Cmp	Att	%	Yds	TD
1978	SAC	10	65	148	43.9	408	4
1980	UCD	10	143	257	55.6	2,180	13
1981	UCD	10	110	224	49.1	1,481	8
1982	UCD	10	178	291	61.2	2,415	20
TOT		40	496	920	53.9	6,484	45

NFL passing stats

Year	Team	G/S	Cmp	Att	%	Yds	TD	Int	Lng	Y/A	Rtg	Sk
1984	NYJ	10/5	116	203	57.1	1,402	6	7	49	6.9	74.0	22
1985	NYJ	16/16	297	488	60.9	3,888	25	8	96	8.0	96.2	62
1986	NYJ	15/14	300	482	62.2	3,690	25	20	83	7.7	85.8	40
1987	NYJ	12/12	234	393	59.5	2,696	13	8	59	6.9	82.8	50
1988	NYJ	14/12	236	424	55.7	2,567	15	7	50	6.1	78.6	37
1989	NYJ	15/12	288	477	60.4	3,346	12	18	57	7.0	74.3	50
1990	NYJ	16/16	226	411	55.0	2,855	13	10	69	6.9	77.3	34
1991	NYJ	16/16	287	489	58.7	3,300	10	11	53	6.7	76.6	33
1992	NYJ	10/3	55	98	56.1	642	5	6	55	6.6	67.6	10
1993	PHI	5/4	71	137	51.8	708	4	3	41	5.2	67.4	15
TOT		129/110	2,110	3,602	58.6	25,094	128	98	96	7.0	80.4	353

College statistics provided by NCAA.org. NFL statistics provided by Stathead.com/football

Games with passer rating over 100 (by rating)

Date	Opp	Res	Cmp	Att	Yds	TD	Int	Rtg
Nov 2, 1986	@SEA	W 38-7	26	32	431	4	0	158.3
Dec 23, 1990	NE	W 42-7	11	12	210	2	0	158.3
Nov 17, 1985	TAM	W 62-28	23	30	367	5	1	142.6
Sep 7, 1986	@BUF	W 28-24	18	25	318	2	0	140.8
Nov 5, 1989	@NE	W 27-26	22	29	386	2	0	140.4
Nov 27, 1988	MIA	W 38-34	6	9	92	2	0	139.8
Nov 9, 1986	@ATL	W 28-14	26	33	322	3	0	137.6
Sep 18, 1988	HOU	W 45-3	17	26	260	3	0	136.7
Oct 28, 1984	@NE	L 20-30	6	9	81	1	0	132.2
Sep 21, 1986	MIA	W 51-45 (OT)	29	43	479	4	1	126.0
Sep 21, 1987	NE	W 43-24	19	26	313	1	0	126.0
Nov 3, 1985	@IND	W 35-17	16	25	164	3	0	122.3
Oct 26, 1986	NOR	W 28-23	20	32	258	3	0	119.0
Nov 1, 1992	MIA	W 26-14	21	29	240	3	1	117.0
Sep 15, 1985	BUF	W 42-3	16	24	181	2	0	116.8
Sep 29, 1991	MIA	W 41-23	18	24	221	1	0	116.8
Sep 24, 1989	@MIA	W 40-33	27	37	329	3	1	115.7
Dec 18, 1988	NYG	W 27-21	16	26	214	2	0	113.3
Nov 17, 1991	@NE	W 28-21	26	41	309	3	0	110.7
Nov 28, 1985	@DET	L 20-31	23	35	281	2	0	109.3
Nov 9, 1987	SEA	W 30-14	23	30	226	1	0	108.5
Dec 8, 1985	@BUF	W 27-7	25	40	370	3	1	107.3
Nov 10, 1985	@ MIA	L 17-21	26	43	393	2	0	106.1
Oct 21, 1984	KAN	W 28-7	1	1	9	0	0	104.2
Oct 20, 1991	@IND	W 17-6	14	19	205	1	1	104.1
Oct 14, 1985	MIA	W 23-7	18	28	239	1	0	103.1
Nov 10, 1991	IND	L 27-28	23	36	329	1	0	102.7
Sep 29, 1985	IND	W 25-20	20	30	240	1	0	102.1
Nov 24, 1985	NE	W 16-13 (OT)	20	33	311	1	0	102.0
Oct 6, 1991	@CLE	W 17-14	19	23	195	0	0	102.0
Oct 5, 1986	BUF	W 14-13	29	39	288	2	1	101.2

Games with 300+ passing yards (by date)

Date	Opp	Res	Cmp	Att	Yds	TD	Int	Rtg
Dec 2, 1984	NYG	L 10-20	28	41	351	1	1	92.6
Nov 10, 1985	@ MIA	L 17-21	26	43	393	2	0	106.1
Nov 17, 1985	TAM	W 62-28	23	30	367	5	1	142.6
Nov 24, 1985	NE	W 16-13 (OT)	20	33	311	1	0	102.0
Dec 8, 1985	@BUF	W 27-7	25	40	370	3	1	107.3
Sep 7, 1986	@BUF	W 28-24	18	25	318	2	0	140.8
Sep 21, 1986	MIA	W 51-45 (OT)	29	43	479	4	1	126.0
Nov 2, 1986	@SEA	W 38-7	26	32	431	4	0	158.3
Nov 9, 1986	@ATL	W 28-14	26	33	322	3	0	137.6
Sep 21, 1987	NE	W 43-24	19	26	313	1	0	126.0
Dec 20, 1987	PHI	L 27-38	25	49	301	2	0	83.8
Sep 24, 1989	@MIA	W 40-33	27	37	329	3	1	115.7
Oct 9, 1989	RAI	L 7-14	24	48	338	0	2	55.7
Nov 5, 1989	@NE	W 27-26	22	29	386	2	0	140.4
Sep 9, 1990	@CIN	L 20-25	27	49	300	2	1	78.6
Nov 10, 1991	IND	L 27-28	23	36	329	1	0	102.7
Nov 17, 1991	@NE	W 28-21	26	41	309	3	0	110.7

Games with three+ passing touchdowns (by date)

Date	Opp	Res	Cmp	Att	Yds	TD	Int	Rtg
Nov 3, 1985	@IND	W 35-17	16	25	164	3	0	122.3
Nov 17, 1985	TAM	W 62-28	23	30	367	5	1	142.6
Dec 8, 1985	@BUF	W 27-7	25	40	370	3	1	107.3
Sep 21, 1986	MIA	W 51-45 (OT)	29	43	479	4	1	126.0
Oct 26, 1986	NOR	W 28-23	20	32	258	3	0	119.0
Nov 2, 1986	@SEA	W 38-7	26	32	431	4	0	158.3
Nov 9, 1986	@ ATL	W 28-14	26	33	322	3	0	137.6
Nov 16, 1986	IND	W 31-16	20	35	237	3	2	82.7
Sep 18, 1988	HOU	W 45-3	17	26	260	3	0	136.7
Oct 23, 1988	@MIA	W 44-30	18	37	174	3	1	78.0
Sep 24, 1989	@MIA	W 40-33	27	37	329	3	1	115.7
Nov 17, 1991	@NE	W 28-21	26	41	309	3	0	110.7
Nov 1, 1992	MIA	W 26-14	21	29	240	3	1	117.0

Statistics provided by Stathead.com/football

References

Chapter One: The Road to the Draft

1 Mike Manico, Ken O'Brien interview for NYJetsNews.com, 4 Apr. 2016.

2 Greg Prato, *Sack Exchange:The Definitive Oral History of the 1980s New York Jets* (Toronto: ECW Press, 2011), p. 275, Kindle edition.

3 Joe Hamelin, 'Just two NorCal kids', *Press Democrat* (Santa Rosa), 28 Dec. 1985, p. B5.

4 Prato, Sack Exchange, p. 279, Kindle edition.

5 Joe Hamelin, 'Just two NorCal kids', *Press Democrat* (Santa Rosa), 28 Dec. 1985, p. 5B.

6 Scott Whitley, 'Aggies Favored Over Improved Hornets', *California Aggie*, 3 Oct. 1980, p. 8.

7 Scott Whitley, 'Aggie Gridders Take On Pomona Airshow', *California Aggie*, 17 Oct. 1980, p. 6.

8 Scott Whitley, 'Sochor's Aggies In National Playoff Picture', *California Aggie*, 22 Oct. 1980, p. 5.

9 Tom McConnell, 'O'Brien Earns National Spot', *California Aggie*, 19 Nov. 1980, p. 6.

10 Scott Whitley, 'O'Brien Prepares for '81 Football Campaign', *California Aggie*, 28 May 1981, p. 6.

11 Noma Faingold, 'Summer Workouts Prove Beneficial', *California Aggie*, 19 Aug. 1981, p. 6.

12 Scott Whitley, 'Loggers blank Ags in Defensive Duel, 7-0', *California Aggie*, 21 Sep. 1981, p. 10.

13 Noma Faingold, 'Sochor Comments On Frustrating Opener', *California Aggie*, 24 Sep. 1981, p. 8.

14 Noma Faingold, 'Gridders Beat Themselves', *California Aggie*, 28 Sep. 1981, p. 6.

15 *Ibid.*

16 *Ibid.*, p. 9.

17 Tom McConnell, 'Aggies to Let It 'All Hang Out' In SLO', *California Aggie*, 16 Oct. 1981, p. 6.

18 Noma Faingold, 'Ags 'Buzz Sawed' By Cal Poly SLO Runners', *California Aggie*, 19 Oct. 1981, p. 5.

19 Noma Faingold, 'Ag 6-3 Triumph Is Like 'Starting All Over'', *California Aggie*, 26 Oct. 1981, p. 4.

20 Noma Faingold, 'Cal Aggie Pride Is Reborn After Chico Rout', *California Aggie*, 9 Nov. 1981, p. 4.

21 Noma Faingold, 'Aggies Dump Sac En Route To Eleventh Straight FWC Crown', *California Aggie*, 23 Nov. 1981, p. 6.

22 *Ibid.*, p. 7.

23 Ann Walker, 'Sochor Predicts Success', *California Aggie*, 1 Sep. 1982, p. 3.

24 Steve Carter, 'Soccer Team Rounded With Experience' [headline corrected in the next issue to 'Aggies Meet Cal Poly Tomorrow Night'], *California Aggie*, 24 Sep. 1982, p. 4.
25 Steve Carter, 'O'Brien Leads Aggies To Win Over Northridge', *California Aggie*, 4 Oct. 1982, p. 3.
26 Tom McConnell, 'Ags Meet San Luis Obispo Tomorrow Night', *California Aggie*, 8 Oct. 1982, p. 4.
27 Tom McConnell, 'Undefeated Ags Meet Chico Tomorrow', *California Aggie*, 22 Oct. 1982, p. 4.
28 Steve Carter, 'O'Brien, Aggies Dash Chico's Upset Hopes', *California Aggie*, 25 Oct. 1982, p. 6.
29 Tom McConnell, 'The Cal Aggies' Explosive Offense Attack', *California Aggie*, 17 Nov. 1982, p. 3.
30 Tom McConnell, 'Ags Meet Humboldt Tomorrow Night', *California Aggie*, 19 Nov. 1982, p. 4.
31 Peter Kozak, 'Ags Finish Season Undefeated', *California Aggie*, 22 Nov. 1982, p. 3.
32 Tom McConnell, 'A Closer Look at the Aggie Offensive Line', *California Aggie*, 23 Nov. 1982, p. 5.
33 Tom McConnell, 'All-American O'Brien Rewrites Ag Records', *California Aggie*, 2 Dec. 1982, p. 5.
34 *California Aggie*, 3 Dec. 1982, p. 9.
35 Steve Carter, 'Davis Aggies Say: Texas, Here We Come", *California Aggie*, 8 Dec. 1982, p. 5.
36 'SW Texas coach found 'super way to go out", *Press Democrat*, 13 Dec. 1982, p. 37.
37 Ann Walker, 'Bobcats Maul Aggies', *California Aggie*, 5 Jan. 1983, p. 4.
38 Ann Walker, 'Tough First Game For Barry', *California Aggie*, 5 Jan. 1983, p. 4.
39 Tom McConnell, 'O'Brien To Play Last College Game In Japan', *California Aggie*, 20 Jan. 1983, p. 4.

Chapter Two: The Class of '83

1 Tom McConnell, 'NFL Quarterback Draft Ahead For Aggie Football Star Ken O'Brien', *California Aggie*, 19 Apr. 1983, p. 3.
2 Tom McConnell, 'NFL Quarterback Draft', *California Aggie*, 19 Apr. 1983, p. 3.
3 Tom McConnell, 'New York Jets Select O'Brien In First Round Of NFL Draft', *California Aggie*, 27 Apr. 1983, p. 1.
4 Joe Hamelin, 'Just two NorCal kids', *Press Democrat*, 28 Dec. 1985, p. 5B.
5 *Ibid.*
6 McConnell, 'New York Jets Select O'Brien In First Round Of NFL Draft', *California Aggie*, 27 Apr. 1983, p. 1.
7 *California Aggie*, 27 Apr. 1983, p. 3.
8 Tony Hechanova, 'Southern California Students Find Davis Lifestyle Different', *California Aggie*, 2 Dec. 1982, p. 6.
9 *New York Jets 1983 Media Guide*, p. 6.
10 *Ibid.*, p. 5.
11 *Ibid.*, p. 6.
12 'Walton Named Head Coach', *Jet Stream*, Vol. 20, No. 1, Winter 1983, p. 1.
13 'According to Joe Walton…', *Ibid.*, p. 4.
14 *New York Jets 1983 Media Guide*, p. 74.
15 'According to Joe Walton…', *Jet Stream*, Vol. 20, No. 1, Winter 1983, p. 4.
16 'Walton Named Head Coach', *Ibid.*, p. 1.

Chapter Three: First Steps

1 'Kaleidoscope', *San Bernadino Sun*, 23 Aug. 1983, p. 38.
2 Bruce Lowitt, 'Elway not only NFL rookie QB with talent', *Santa Cruz Sentinel*, 28 Aug. 1983, p. 56.
3 Ken Rappoport, 'Jets cut Dwayne Crutchfield', *Franklin News Herald*, 19 Nov. 1983, p. 9.
4 'Jets deal QB Todd to Saints', *Santa Cruz Sentinel*, 19 Feb. 1984, p. 52.
5 'Ex Cal-Davis quarterback may start for Jets in next NFL season', *Press-Tribune (Roseville)*, 21 Feb. 1984, p. 13.
6 Dave Raffo, 'New Jersey Generals: Is team best money can buy in football?', *Ibid.*

7 Mark Andrews, 'The Pub To Become NFL Draft Center On Tuesday', *California Aggie*, 26 Apr. 1984, p. 4.
8 *Auburn Journal*, 31 July 1984, p. 8.
9 Caroline Chadwick, 'O'Brien Named First String QB, *California Aggie*, 1 Aug. 1984, p. 12.
10 Don Seeholzer, *Santa Ana Orange County Register*, 29 Jul. 1984, p. D23.
11 *San Bernadino Sun*, 3 Sep. 1984, p. 20.
12 'Sports Scoreboard', *Press Democrat*, 17 Nov, 1984, p. 16.
13 'Marino ties NFL record', *Santa Cruz Sentinel*, 27 Nov. 1984, p. B1.
14 Gerald Eskenazi, 'Jets Eliminated: Marino Ties Record', *New York Times*, 27 Nov. 1984, p. B9.
15 Dave Anderson, 'Ken O'Brien's Bloodhound', *New York Times*, 28 Nov. 1984, p. B15.
16 'Jets 'go' and fly past hapless Bills', *Santa Cruz Sentinel*, 9 Dec. 1984, p. D6.
17 *Times-Advocate*, 17 Dec. 1984, p. D4.

Chapter Four: Top of the World

1 Scott R. Talan, 'O'Brien ready', *California Aggie*, 19 Apr. 1985, p. 1.
2 *Ibid.*, p. 5.
3 *New York Jets 1985 Media Guide*, p. 5.
4 *Ibid.*, p. 6.
5 *Ibid.*, p. 5.
6 *Ibid.*, p. 73.
7 *Ibid.*, p. 72
8 *Ibid.*, p. 50.
9 *Ibid.*, p. 54.
10 Gerald Eskenazi, 'Walker Injury Puts Jets in Bond', *New York Times*, 2 Sep. 1985, p. 17.
11 'McNeil leads Jets in romp', *San Bernardino Sun*, 16 Sep. 1985, p. C4.
12 'Bengals lose composure, then lose game to Jets, 29-20', *San Bernardino Sun*, 7 Oct. 1985, p. C4.
13 'O'Brien rallies the Jets to first win over Seattle', *San Bernardino Sun*, 28 Oct. 1985, C, p. C4.
14 'Jets, O'Brien toy with Tampa Bay in 62-28 rout', *San Bernardino Sun*, 18 Nov. 1985, p. C4.
15 'Jets set records in 62-38 [sic] triumph', *Oakland Tribune*, 18 Nov. 1985, p. D-3.
16 Dave Anderson, 'O'Brien vs. Marino (Contd.)', *New York Times*, 19 Nov. 1985, p. B14.
17 *New York Jets 1986 Media Guide*, p. 50.
18 'Jets ready to try some tricks on the Bears', *San Bernardino Sun*, 14 Dec. 1985, p. C3.
19 Prato, *Sack Exchange*, p. 333, Kindle edition.
20 Joel Sherman, UPI, 23 Dec. 1985.
21 Joe Hamelin, 'Just two NorCal kids', *Press Democrat* (Santa Rosa), 28 Dec. 1985, p. 5B.
22 'What's up front could count most in AFC wild-card game', *San Bernardino Sun*, 28 Dec. 1985, p. C1 and C4.
23 Chris Jenkins, 'Patriots shoot down Jets in AFC playoffs', *Press-Tribune (Roseville)*, 30 Dec. 1985, p. 13.
24 *New York Jets 1986 Media Guide*, p. 5.
25 *Ibid.*, p. 50.
26 *Ibid.*, p. 49.
27 *Ibid.*, p. 70.
28 *Ibid.*, p. 72.
29 *Ibid.*, p. 68.
30 *Ibid.*, p.66.
31 *Ibid.*, p. 70.
32 John F. Bonfatti, 'Kelly throws for 292 yards, 3 TDs in debut, but Bills fall', *San Bernardino Sun*, 8 Sep. 1986, p. C5.

33 Prato, *Sack Exchange*, pp. 329–330, Kindle edition.
34 'The best is saved for last', *Santa Cruz Sentinel*, 22 Sep. 1986, p. B2.
35 *Ibid.*
36 Gary Mihoces, 'Jets' O'Brien out-guns Dolphins' Marino, 51-45', *San Bernardino Sun*, 22 Sep. 1986, p. C5.
37 Dave Anderson, 'Thank you, Ken O'Brien', *New York Times*, 22 Sep. 1986, p. C1
38 'Jets may succeed where Mets fail', *Salinas Californian*, 21 Oct. 1986, p. 1D.
39 Craig Bennett, 'Streaking Jets rip Seattle, 38-7', *San Bernardino Sun*, 3 Nov. 1986, p. C5.
40 'The Jets fly past Falcons', *Santa Cruz Sentinel*, 10 Nov. 1986, p. B2.
41 Dave Anderson, 'O'Brien's Toughness', *New York Times*, 10 Nov. 1986, p. C3. Gerald Eskenazi, 'The Beat Gets Stronger for Jets (8-1) and Giants 97-2)', *New York Times*, 3 Nov. 1986, p. C1.
42 Eskenazi, 'Living Under Shadow of Doubt', *New York Times*, 23 Nov. 1986, p. 5.1–2.

Chapter Five: The Stall
1 Paul Zimmerman, 'Wake-Up Call for the Jets', *Sports Illustrated*, 5 Jan. 1987.
2 Gregg Patton, 'Jets flame out vs. Rams' defense', *San Bernardino Sun*, 1 Dec. 1986, p. C5.
3 George Vecsey, 'Ram defender's big 14-point play', *Press Democrat* (Santa Rosa), 1 Dec. 1986, p. C1–C2.
4 'Cal will name new coach by Monday', *Auburn Journal*, 3 Dec. 1986, p. B3.
5 'Niners still reeling from Monday's loss', *Petaluma Argus-Courier*, 4 Dec. 1986, p. 6.
6 Dave Albee, '49ers keep Jets on skids, 24-10', *San Bernardino Sun*, 8 Dec. 1986, p. C4.
7 Larry Stone, 'Jets assess damage after crash', *Press Democrat* (Santa Rosa), 8 Dec. 1986, p. C2.
8 Monte Poole, 'O'Brien shows home folks the wrong stuff', *Oakland Tribune*, 8 Dec. 1986, p. D-6.
9 'Jets assess damage after crash', *Press Democrat*, 8 Dec. 1986, p. C2.
10 Bill Varner, 'Needing a victory, Walton shakes up the Jets – again', *Desert Sun* (Palm Springs), 12 Dec. 1986, p. F6.
11 'Jets want to right their nose dive', *Petaluma Argus-Courier*, 24 Dec. 1986, p. 8A.
12 'O'Brien benched; Ryan Jets' starter', *Santa Cruz Sentinel*, 26 Dec. 1986, p. B4.
13 Prato, *Sack Exchange*, p. 337–8, Kindle edition.
14 Angelo Cataldi, 'Ryan brings team back to life once again', *Times-Advocate*, p. C4.
15 Prato, *Sack Exchange*, p. 341, Kindle edition.

Chapter Six: The Strike
1 *New York Jets 1987 Media Guide*, p. 52.
1 'Professionals use videos to teach', *Hanford Sentinel*, 7 July 1987, p. 7-B.
3 Kimberlynn Locklin, 'Famous UCD alumni make it big', *California Aggie*, 12 June 1987, p. 10.
4 Joel Sherman, 'Jets recover from injury-plagued season', *Press-Tribune (Roseville)*, 4 Sep. 1987, p. D-2.
5 Prato, *Sack Exchange*, p. 346, Kindle edition.
6 'NFL's regulars show fill-ins how it's done', *San Bernardino Sun*, 19 Oct. 1987, p. C1.
7 Prato, *Sack Exchange*, p. 347, Kindle edition.
8 'First-place Colts out for fourth straight win', *Santa Cruz Sentinel*, 1 Nov. 1987, p. B-7.
9 'Seahawks: No extra incentive for tonight's game against Jets', *San Bernardino Sun*, 9 Nov. 1987, p. C9.
10 Bill Varner, 'McNeil, Klecko return, lead Jets past K.C., 16-9', *San Bernardino Sun*, 16 Nov. 1987, p. C5.
11 Bill Varner, 'Bills rush past Jets to tie', *San Bernardino Sun*, 23 Nov. 1987, p. C5.
12 *San Bernardino Sun*, 16 Sep. 1988, p. C2.

13 Larry Weisman, 'Bungling Bengals beaten by Jets on return of blocked punt [sic], 27-20', *San Bernardino Sun*, 30 Nov. 1987, p. C5.
14 Joe Klecko, Joe Fields and Greg Logan, *Nose to Nose: Survival in the Trenches of the NFL* (New York: William Morrow & Company, 1989), p. 238.

Chapter Seven: The End of the Walton Era

1 *New York Jets 1988 Media Guide*, p. 5.
2 'Crippled Browns can't ground Jets', *San Bernardino Sun*, 12 Sep. 1988, p. C4.
3 'Hard-hitting Oilers to test Jets offense', *Desert Sun* (Palm Springs), 17 Sep. 1988, p. F7.
4 'Walker's 3 TDs lead Jets', *Press Democrat* (Santa Rosa), 19 Sep. 1988, p. C5.
5 'Jets "Waggle" way to win over hapless Lions', *Oakland Tribune*, 26 Sep. 1988, p. D8.
6 'Bills welcome TV appearance', *Press Democrat* (Santa Rosa), 17 Oct. 1988, p. C4.
7 Zimmerman, 'Wake-Up Call for the Jets', *Sports Illustrated*, 5 Jan. 1987.
8 'Giants lose, then Rams kill their playoff hopes', *Press Democrat* (Santa Rosa), 19 Dec. 1988, p. C3.
9 *New York Jets 1989 Media Guide*, p. 5.
10 'Other NY quarterback ailing', *Press Democrat* (Santa Rosa), 24 May. 1989, p. C8.
11 'Dolphins outscored by Jets again, 40-33', *San Bernardino Sun*, 25 Sep. 1989, p. C4.
12 Barry Wilner, 'Raiders look miserable but still win in Shell's debut', *Oakland Tribune*, 10 Oct. 1989, p. D-5.
13 Tim Keown, '49ers may find a helpless victim in Jets', *Santa Cruz Sentinel*, 26 Oct. 1989, p. B-1.
14 Barry Wilner, 'San Francisco does it again', *Petaluma Argus-Courier*, 30 Oct. 1989, p. 6.
15 'Eason ends stalemate with Jets', *Desert Sun*, 8 Nov. 1989, p. C4.

Chapter Eight: The Coslet Years

1 'Coin flip seals Jets' order', *Desert Sun*, 9 Aug. 1990, p. F1.
2 'O'Brien earns Jets' job', *Oakland Tribune*, 20 Aug. 1991, p. D-3.
3 'Surprise: Jets in playoffs', *Santa Cruz Sentinel*, 23 Dec. 1991, p. B-2.
4 Barry Wilner, 'Jets' O'Brien adjusts to lesser role', *Napa Valley Register*, 12 Sep. 1992, p. 16.
5 Paul Zimmerman, *Sports Illustrated*, 7 Sep. 1992.
6 'Nagle benched', *Press Democrat* (Santa Rosa), 26 Nov. 1992, p. C5.

Chapter Nine: Turn Out the Lights...

1 Prato, *Sack Exchange*, p. 279, Kindle edition.
2 *Ibid.*, p. 312, Kindle edition.
3 *Ibid.*, p. 507, Kindle edition.
4 *Ibid.*, p. 408, Kindle edition.
5 Mike Manico, Ken O'Brien interview.
6 Prato, *Sack Exchange*, p. 312-313, Kindle edition.
7 *Ibid.*, p. 313, Kindle edition.
8 Bob Dunning, 'Looking back on that magical 1982 season', *The Davis Enterprise*, 7 Nov. 2017.
9 Mike Manico, Ken O'Brien interview.
10 Gerald Eskenazi, *Gang Green: An Irreverent Look Behind the Scenes at Thirty-Eight (Well, Thirty-Seven) Seasons of New York Jets Football Futility* (New York: Simon & Schuster, 1988), p. 17.

Bibliography

My primary research material for this book was more than 100 game tapes covering almost the entirety of Ken O'Brien's NFL playing career. In addition to this, the following sources were consulted.

Books

Eskenazi, G., *Gang Green: An Irreverent Look Behind the Scenes at Thirty-Eight (Well, Thirty-Seven) Seasons of New York Jets Football Futility* (New York: Simon & Schuster, 1998)

Klecko, J, Fields, J., and Logan, G., *Nose to Nose: Survival in the Trenches of the NFL* (New York: William Morrow & Company, 1989)

Prato, G., *Sack Exchange: The Definitive Oral History of the 1980s New York Jets* (Toronto: ECW Press, 2011)

Team Publications

New York Jets Media Guides, 1983–1992

Jet Stream

Interviews

Mike Manico interviews with Ken O'Brien, Al Toon, Wesley Walker and JoJo Townsell for NYJetsNews.com.

Greg Prato interviews for *Sack Exchange: The Definitive Oral History of the 1980s New York Jets*

Newspapers and Magazines

Auburn Journal

California Aggie

Desert Sun (Palm Springs)

Franklin News Herald

Hanford Sentinel

Newspapers and Magazines continued
New York Times
Oakland Tribune
Petaluma Argus-Courier
Press Democrat (Santa Rosa)
Press-Tribune (Roseville)
Salinas Californian
Santa Ana Orange County Register
San Bernardino Sun
Santa Cruz Sentinel
Sports Illustrated
Times-Advocate

Annual Publications
Don Heinrich's Pro Preview 1986
NFL ProLog 1985
Ourlad's Guide to the NFL Draft 1983
The Sporting News Pro Football Preview 1988
Street & Smith's Pro Football Yearbook, 1983–93
Street & Smith's College Football Yearbook, 1980–82

Online Reference
pro-football-reference.com
stathead.com/football

Made in United States
North Haven, CT
21 November 2024

60736917R00183